Motherhood in
Mexican Cinema,
1941–1991

Motherhood in Mexican Cinema, 1941–1991

The Transformation of Femininity on Screen

ISABEL ARREDONDO

McFarland & Company, Inc., Publishers
Jefferson, North Carolina

LIBRARY OF CONGRESS CATALOGUING-IN-PUBLICATION DATA

Arredondo, Isabel.
　　Motherhood in Mexican cinema, 1941–1991 : the transformation of femininity on screen / Isabel Arredondo.
　　　　p.　　cm.
　　Includes bibliographical references and index.

　　ISBN 978-0-7864-6804-1
　　softcover : acid free paper ∞

　　1. Mothers in motion pictures.　2. Motion pictures—Mexico—History—20th century.　3. Motherhood in motion pictures. 4. Sex role in motion pictures.　I. Title.
PN1995.9.M63A77　2014
791.43'6522—dc23　　　　　　　　　　　　　　2013039800

BRITISH LIBRARY CATALOGUING DATA ARE AVAILABLE

© 2014 Isabel Arredondo. All rights reserved

No part of this book may be reproduced or transmitted in any form or by any means, electronic or mechanical, including photocopying or recording, or by any information storage and retrieval system, without permission in writing from the publisher.

Front cover: Alma (Evangelina Sosa, left) and Refugio (Lilia Aragón) in *Ángel de fuego*, 1991 (photograph by Daniel Daza, courtesy of Dana Rotberg)

Manufactured in the United States of America

McFarland & Company, Inc., Publishers
　Box 611, Jefferson, North Carolina 28640
　　www.mcfarlandpub.com

To Isabel and Javier

Table of Contents

Acknowledgments ix
Introduction 1

1. Women Filmmakers in Mexico, 1940s–1990s 13
2. The Ideal of Virgin Motherhood 31
3. The Qualities of Classical and Third-Wave Mothers 49
4. Sexuality in Classical and Third-Wave Films 74
5. Reconsidering Mothers' Autonomous Identity 96
6. Looking Back at Classical Idealization 121
7. Maternal Affectivity in Mexican Films 137
8. Making the Private Realm Political 160

Conclusion 184
Chapter Notes 189
Works Cited 204
Index 219

Acknowledgments

I couldn't have written this book without the help of my family, friends, colleagues, filmmakers, journalists, publishers, archivists, my kayak and Lake Champlain. Thanks to those who started my passion for writing about the films made by women, and to those who kept me interested. To Margarita de la Vega, who in 1993, when she was teaching at the University of Michigan at Ann Arbor, inspired me to teach Latin American film. My gratitude to the group of scholars whose intellectual inquiry kept me interested in writing about women filmmaking, those attending the meetings of the Women and the Silent Screen Conference: Kay Armatage, Mark Cooper, Jane Gaines, Jennifer Horne, Christine Gledhill, Rosanna Maule, Selley Stamp and Kim Tomadjoglou.

Thanks to those who accompanied me on this long journey. A very special thanks goes to my friends, Fernando Gaona and Maribel Moheno, with whom I discussed for hours ideas for this book, and to Erin Mitchell, who guided me through challenging readings in psychoanalysis. Elissa Rashkin has been a great companion; her tenacity, determination and knowledge comforted me in the ten long years of writing this book. Thanks also to those who gave me courage; especially to Patricia Vega, who supported me in the decision to argue that the younger generation of filmmakers was feminist. Thanks to Busi Cortés, María Novaro, Dana Rotgerb and Guita Schyfter who allowed me to use their personal archives for my research; to Juan Carlos Vargas at the University of Guadalajara's research center for film, CIEC, for helping me find over five hundred film reviews; and to Antonia Rojas, at the Cineteca de la UNAM, for helping me with the selection of photographs for this book and with additional information that I needed for the notes. Shiloh Whitney motivated me to find a fresh approach with which to look at the works of Mexican women filmmakers. I owe a huge debt to the people who helped with the revisions of the manuscript. Thanks to Susan Rhode's revision of an earlier version, and to Berry Matthews, who patiently and generously spent many hours helping me to go chapter by chapter. The thorough editing of Juan Carlos Vargas for the Spanish part was also very much appreciated.

Thanks also to my students at SUNY Plattsburgh, whose interest kept me motivated in teaching film.

Several institutions allowed me to carry on my project. The Center of Sponsored Research at the State University of New York at Plattsburgh, and especially its director in 1998, Sue Spissinger, guided me to successfully apply for a Drescher Award. With this fellowship, granted by the teachers' union, United University Profession, I was able to work on my manuscript a whole year at full pay. With the help of Kathy Lavoie, Dean of Arts and Sciences at SUNY Plattsburgh, I was able to arrange my schedule so that I could attend classes for my MA in film studies and work full time at SUNY Plattsburgh. Thanks to my teachers at the Mell Hoppenheim school of Cinema at Concordia University; to my thesis adviser, Rosanna Maule; and to the thesis committee: Maule, Catherine Russell, Tom Waugh and Norma Iglesias for their insightful comments. I am grateful to McGill University's Center for Research and Teaching on Women, now the Institute for Gender, Sexuality and Feminist Studies. My thanks go especially to the center's director in 2001, Shree Mulay, who helped me to find a reliable caregiver, Anne Caines, for my newborn daughter, and who provided me with a place to grow intellectually, work comfortably, and have delicious lunches during my sabbatical. She also hosted me afterwards for many years, while pursuing my MA in film studies part time at Concordia University. Thanks also to Mulay's mother, Vijaya Mulay, whose dedication and passion for the study of film was an example to follow. Many friends in Montreal contributed to this book, including Ingrid Birker, who provided me with a copy of *Perfect Madness: Motherhood in the Age of Anxiety*.

The help of my family has been indispensable during the different stages of the manuscript. Thanks to my husband Doug Yu, who during my stay at McGill University had to separate from our new-born daughter, and thanks for all the support he gave me so that I could study at Concordia University and work full time. Thanks to my children, Javier and Isabel Yu, who had to live with one or the other parent during my extended stays in Mexico and Montreal. Thanks also to my mother, María Isabel Díaz, who understood that writing was my passion and respected the long hours I spent at my computer.

Introduction

Motherhood in Mexican Cinema, 1941–1991 examines how femininity and motherhood are understood in Mexican film from the 1940s to the early 1990s. Film analysis, interviews with filmmakers, academic articles, and film reviews from newspapers are used to trace the changes the representation of mothers goes through. The films of Busi Cortés, María Novaro, Dana Rotberg, and Marisa Sistach, whom this book refers to as third-wave filmmakers, are central to this transformation.[1] The book sets a contrast between third-wave films and films from two time periods, Mexican classical films (1935–1950) and Mexican films from the 1970s to the early 1990s. Mothers in the third-wave films *Elvira Luz Cruz, pena máxima (Elvira Luz Cruz, Maximum Punishment,* 1984), *Lola* (1989), *Los pasos de Ana (Ana's Footsteps,* 1989), *El secreto de Romelia (Romelia's Secret,* 1988), *Ángel de fuego (Angel of Fire,* 1991) and *Danzón* (1991)[2] are compared to mothers in the classical films *Salón México* (1949), *Una familia de tantas (An Ordinary Family,* 1948), *Cuando los hijos se van (When the Children Leave,* 1941) and *María Candelaria* (1943). And, the mothers in third-wave films are also compared to those in *Mecánica nacional (National Mechanics,* 1971) and *Los motivos de Luz (Luz's Reasons,* 1985).

Third-Wave Films in Conversation with Classical Films

A comparison is established between third-wave films and other Mexican films for several reasons. Third-wave filmmakers explained that their films were a response to Mexican cinema. Marisa Sistach (*Conozco a las tres,* 1983; *Los pasos de Ana*) said that for her, it "all started with watching Mexican films [from the classical period]" (Millán 1999, 160). She situated her filmmaking in relation to Golden Age melodramas by saying that her films respond to classical films' reduction of women to the roles of "good mother" or "prostitute."[3] In her response, she created "a kind of woman who exists in the Mexican reality, but who has not been represented on the screen before."[4] *Conozco a las tres*, a film in which mothers are single or divorced, responds to the nuclear families of classical melodramas. In *Los pasos de Ana*, the reference to Golden Age cinema is more explicit. Carlos, a friend of the protagonist, literally compares the protagonist, film graduate Ana, to a famous classical actress, Sara García.

Third-wave filmmaker María Novaro (*Lola*, *Danzón*) declared in press conferences and newspapers that her films were a response to the melodramas of the Golden Age. In particular, she emphasized that classical Mexican films were very important as she grew up. Novaro remembers: "I would watch the movies of suffering mothers or redeemed prostitutes to the tune of my mother's critique, who would say how those women were idiots. Mother was a feminist in the making, and so I looked at female characters from a somewhat critical perspective. Nevertheless, I was fascinated by the beautiful women of Mexican films since childhood — above all, María Felix" (Arredondo 2013, 161).[5] Novaro considers classical melodramas central for third-wave filmmakers' emotional education, which explains why classical films play such a significant role in her rethinking of motherhood and womanhood. In *Danzón*, she stated, "The scenes were constructed very much in the style of the Mexican cinema of the Golden Age, but we came up with totally different [scenes], and I hope surprising, resolutions" (157). *Danzón*, then, was a response to the filmmaker's immersion in classical films as she was growing up. However, in the late 1980s, when third-wave filmmakers were making their first features, Golden Age films were not exclusively a thing of the past.

Melodramas of the classical period, such as *Salón México*, *María Candelaria* and *Doña Bárbara* (1943), were frequently seen on television. Mexican film scholar Susan Dever claims that in the late 1980s and early 1990s classical films had a special role in the political reality of Mexico. The North Atlantic Free Trade Agreement (NAFTA) brought about a process of globalization that caused anxiety for Mexicans; they were afraid of the opening of the Mexican borders to U.S. commerce. The anxiety about NAFTA was very similar to the anxiety created during the modernization of the 1940s, which is reflected in films of the Golden Age. In a chapter entitled "Re-Birth of a Nation: On Mexican Movies, Museums and María Felix," Dever (2003) affirms that during the 1990s, the state revamped the melodramas of the classical period as a way to ease national anxiety about NAFTA. A case in point is the homage paid to María Felix, the actress who played the leading role in El Indio Fernández's *Río Escondido* (*Hidden River*, 1947). In the film, Felix, a teacher sent from Mexico City, plays a mediating role between the small community of Río Escondido and the Federal Government. In the summer of 1990, the Tijuana Cultural Center organized a retrospective of Felix's work

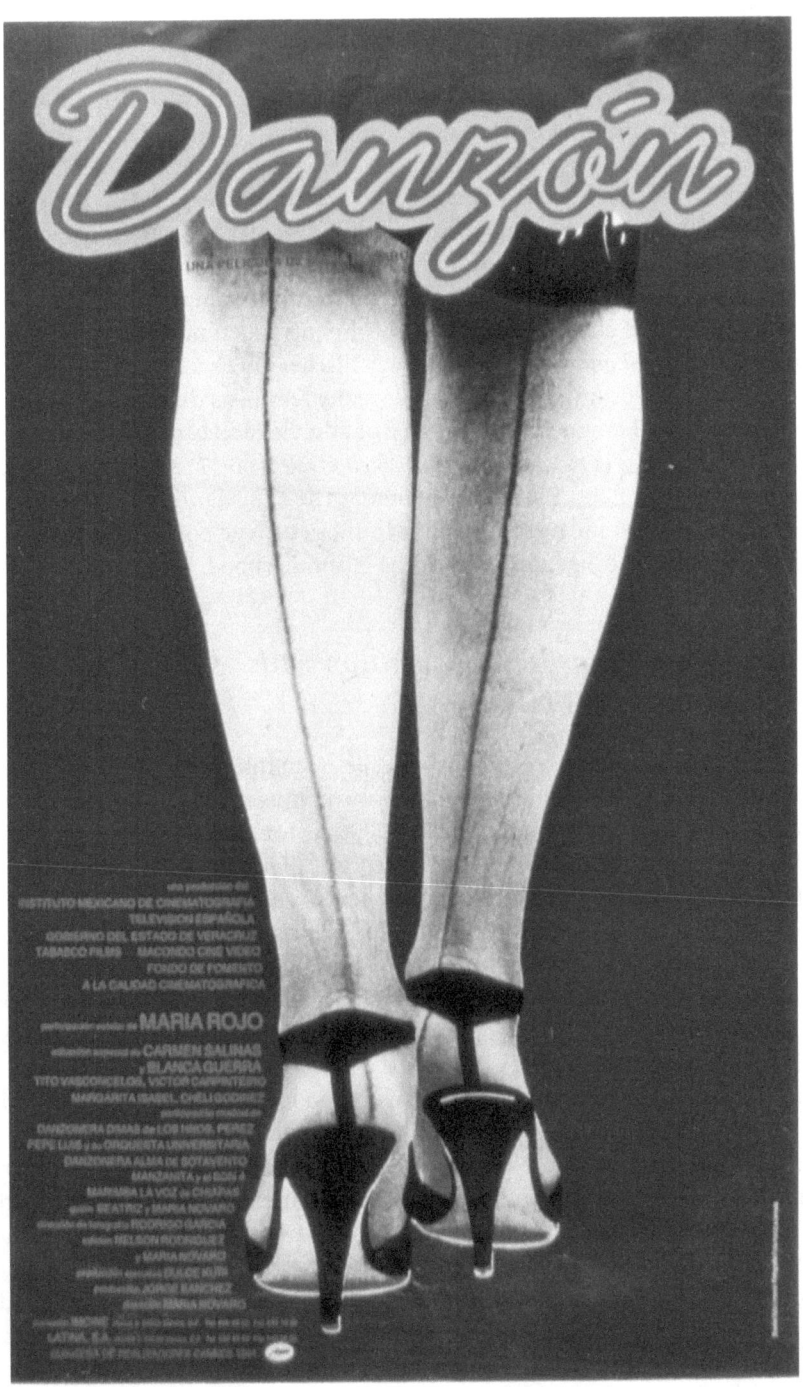

Poster of *Danzón* (Cineteca de la UNAM).

and invited her to attend. According to Dever, Felix repeated her mediating role between the marginalized groups and the state at Tijuana (49); she mediated between the Salinas' government, which was opening Mexico's borders to U.S. commerce, and the Mexican people, who feared they would lose their jobs because of the disappearance of protectionist measures for national products.

Comparing classical and third-wave films also makes sense from a theoretical perspective. Feminist film criticism scrutinized motherhood by looking at Hollywood classical narratives. In the introduction to *Cinematernity: Film, Motherhood and Genre* (1996), Lucy Fischer (1996, 12–14) explains that from the late 1970s until the early 1990s many feminists discussed the representation of motherhood in three texts from the classical canon: Michael Curtiz's *Mildred Pierce* (1945), King Vidor's *Stella Dallas* (1937) and Douglas Sirk's *Imitation of Life* (1959).[6] *Motherhood in Mexican Cinema, 1945–1991* reexamines classical films for reasons similar to those of North American feminist film critics: to examine normative ideas of motherhood.

Third-Wave Films in Conversation with 1970s and 1980s Films

This book sets up a second dialogue, between third-wave films and Mexican films of the 1970s and 1980s. Third-wave films respond to the attack on mother love that was common in the 1970s, as for example in the mocking of Sara García in *Mecánica nacional* (Alcoriza). The conversation with films of the 1970s and 1980s also includes responses to third-wave films. Male filmmaker Felipe Cazals responded to the representation of the mother in Dana Rotberg's *Elvira Luz Cruz* by making his own film, *Los motivos de Luz*, in which he reinterprets the associations established by Rotberg. Cazals' reaction elicits the question: What problems did Cazals see in Rotberg's film to cause him to respond as he did?

In the early 1990s, third-wave films generated responses on two fronts. Novaro explained the reception for *Lola* by saying: "A certain sector of feminist critique disagrees with the way *Lola* ends and thinks it should be different. It seems strange to me that this feminist criticism is in agreement with a segment of the male audience that is bothered when Lola starts to cry and can't control herself" (Arredondo 2013, 153). Novaro's comment shows that both males and feminists had problems with her portrayal of motherhood. Some feminists reacted negatively to third-wave films. According to Sistach, at a feminist conference in Tijuana in 1990 the audience attacked her film, *Los pasos de Ana,* because they considered it to be sexist.[7] By 1995 all the third-wave filmmakers included in this study had declared to the press that their films were not feminist.⁸ Despite the dialogue between third-wave filmmakers and feminist filmmakers alluded to by Novaro and Sistach, third-wave films are not compared to second-wave films. Second-wave films are not included because their main issue is not motherhood. Although there are mothers in second-wave films, these films avoid associating womanhood with motherhood.

Second-wave feminists in Canada, United States and Mexico eluded the issue of motherhood because they perceived it as complicit with patriarchy. Maureen Turim (1991), for instance, underscored the difficulty early feminists had with motherhood by saying that they "implicitly or explicitly attacked motherhood as a by-product of the attack on marriage as an institution" (24). In the same vein, Andrea O'Reilly (2005) believes that 1970s feminist theorists avoided discussing motherhood "because women's reproductive capacity historically had been used to define and confine them, motherhood was rightly seen as the paramount source of oppression" (*Motherhood: Power and Oppression* (2).⁹ According to O'Reilly, after the 1970s, motherhood began to be associated with creativity and power.¹⁰ For example, influenced by Adrienne Rich's *Of Woman Born* (1976), O'Reilly advocated for differentiating between motherhood and mothering, a distinction that in her opinion leaves space for mothers to transgress social limits.¹¹

Second-wave Mexican filmmakers also avoided the subject of motherhood. Their feminist goal was to reject equating womanhood and motherhood. Matilde Landeta, who directed films during the Golden Age era, explains, "In the Judeo-Christian tradition, woman's only mission was to get married and procreate. The Catholic Church thinks of women as a womb only" (Arredondo 2002, 201).¹² To avoid making women synonymous with mothers, the classical filmmaker highlights her heroines' deeds and diminishes the importance of the woman's role as mother in her films.

Lola Casanova (1948), Landeta's first feature, portrays an energetic, vivacious and confident white woman of European descent (Lola Cassanova, played by Meche Barba), who stops the war between the Seri group from Sonora and the Mexican government by negotiating a treaty. Through her marriage to a member of the Seri community, Casanova becomes "the legitimate mother of the mestizo race" (Rashkin 2001, 49). Her primary role is to be a negotiator, not a mother.

In *La negra Angustias* (1949), Landeta created another heroic woman, Angustias, a colonel in the Mexican Revolution and a woman with a clear aversion to marriage and motherhood. Angustias' repugnance for motherhood begins at an early age. As a child, in 1903, she watched as a huge billy goat mounted her favorite goat, resulting in her goat's pregnancy and ultimately death due to complications with the birth. Watching the goat die and then hearing how her own mother had died as a consequence of giving birth to her, traumatized Angustias. Her abhorrence of motherhood is used to explain why the heroine refuses El Coyote's marriage proposal; she does not want the fate of her goat.[13] Landeta's third feature, *Trotacalles* (*Streetwalker*, 1951), de-idealizes middle class marital arrangements, showing them as financial transactions to secure money. Landeta's three narratives from the classical period feature heroines or transgressors who avoid motherhood or have occupations outside of it.[14] Thus, while Landeta's characters took a feminist position, they avoided motherhood rather than transform it.

In the 1970s, another second-wave filmmaker, Marcela Fernández-Violante, made a similar choice. She focused on reinterpreting Mexican history, in particular the Cristero Wars, not on the issue of motherhood. According to Fernández-Violante, *De todos modos Juan te llamas* (*Whatever You Do, It Is No Good*, 1975) demystifies the Mexican Revolution, arguing that "contrary to conventional wisdom, the Revolution was not won. At the point of 'consolidation' between 1917 and 1926, it was lost" (Burton 1986, 199). Fernández-Violante challenged the interpretation of history provided by Mexico's main political party, Partido Revolucionario Institucional (PRI), which for seventy years, claimed that the revolution had been won. Her position gained her the support of the film union membership, who backed her bold reinterpretation of the Mexican Revolution. In *Cananea* (1977) history is examined in the broader context of a mine strike in northern Mexico, using the views of both the North American owner and the miners. Fernández-Violante wanted to "confront two different ideologies, two ways of looking at the world: what it means to be a white, Anglo-Saxon Protestant; and what it means to be a brown-skinned, Catholic Mexican. Protestantism teaches that the rich get rich through God's help. Catholicism teaches that the rich do not get to heaven" (199). The director's political approach to U.S.–Mexico relations is thought-provoking, but the topic is not related to motherhood, perhaps intentionally so. For Fernández-Violante, being a feminist filmmaker is not about making claims about gender, it is about questioning the prevalent interpretation of history.[15]

The present work relates the work of third-wave filmmakers to feminism. Some scholars do not consider the filmmakers studied in this book to be feminist. After the filmmakers publically announced that their films were not feminist, Mexican film scholars referred to third-wave films as "films made by and for women" and "feminine" films. In order to establish the relationship between third-wave films and feminism, the question is asked and answered: What makes the specific representation of mothers in third-wave films feminist?

Previous Studies

The dialogues established in *Motherhood in Mexican Cinema, 1941–1991* bring a new approach to the study of Mexican film. Classical cinema and third-wave films have been studied together before but not in the same way and consequently with different results. Some scholars argue that patriarchy dominates classical film and view third-wave films as an effort to portray a nonpatriarchal society. Julianne Burton-Carvajal views classical film in relation to patriarchy in "Mexican Melodramas of Patriarchy: Specificity of a Transcultural Form" (1997). The author argues that many classical films can be considered melodramas of patriarchy, that is, melodramas that establish patriarchy. Burton-Carvajal distinguishes between what she calls "patriarchal melodramas," those melodramas whose theme is the inflexibility of the father, and "melodramas of patriarchy," films that present the patriarchal authority as the locus of order. Burton-Carvajal examines Emilio Fernández's *Flor Silvestre* (1943), a film in which the father dies at the hand of Mexican revolutionaries. She points out that despite his death "Don Francisco's portrait, [is] still intact in its place of honor on the wall" (188). His portrait is a reminder that patriarchy is the established order. Thus, despite Don Francisco's death "the power of the father, [is] even more potent and pervasive in death than in life" (190). As Don Francisco dies at the beginning of the film and the narrative continues, so does patriarchy. "The arrogant and inflexible patriarch, earliest justly denounced by his wife and equally justly defied by his son, manages in death to annul the autonomy of both" (188). According to Burton-Carvajal's interpretation, patriarchy is pervasive in classical melodramas.

Scholars have argued that third-wave films counter the patriarchy established in classical films. In *Identidades maternacionales en el cine de María Novaro* ("Maternational Identities in Maria Novaro's Films," 2005) Oscar Robles argues that Novaro's films overcome patriarchy on three levels. *Lola* leaves behind the patriarchal values that dominate the Golden Age film at the local level, *Danzón* (1991) within the regional context, and *El jardín del edén* (1994) in the international arena. Thus, for Robles, Novaro's nonpatriarchal films show that Mexico has left patriarchal values behind during the Salinas' *sexenio*.

The approach to motherhood in this book differs from that of Robles. It follows Judith Butler's critique of the feminist search for a nonpatriarchal state seen as utopian in *Gender Trouble* (1990) and avoids the idea of patriarchy. Also, the way in which the relationship with classical cinema is established differs. Robles examines the evolution from classical films to third-wave films. This study revisits classical films from a 1990s perspective. The central question in *Motherhood in Mexican Cinema, 1941–1991* is: What problems must third-wave filmmakers have seen in the representations of mothers in classical cinema that caused them to respond as they did? That is, if third-wave filmmakers see a problem in the representation of mothers in classical films, what is this problem? And how do third-wave films respond to this problem?

How mothers are represented is a complex question when seen within the broader context of Mexican film studies. From the 1960s to the 1990s, Mexican film scholars (Ayala Blanco, Ramírez Berg, López, Torres San Martín) have argued that the representation of mothers in classical cinema is problematic because women are given only two alternatives: to be a "good mother" or a "whore." These alternatives, film scholars argue, set limits on mothers' sexuality and morality and are contradictory, because mothers are asked to be chaste and sexual at the same time. For example, Ana María López's article "Tears and Desire in Mexican Classical Cinema" (1994) studies norms of sexuality by looking at the roles in which Mexico's most prominent actresses are cast. She relates the actresses' roles to the spaces they occupy in the film. In López's topography, the center is inhabited by those female characters who respect norms of female sexuality, while at the margins one finds those women characters who transgress these norms: the further away from the center, the more a character transgresses. The center is, thus, inhabited by the "good wife," represented by actress Sara García (153–154). Women who become prostitutes because of economic hardship live one step away from the center (156); beyond them live *rumberas* (women who dance in cabarets), often portrayed by Ninón Sevilla (158). Rumba dancers live in spaces that are the furthest away from the center because they openly display their bodies while dancing rumba, a strong prohibition at the time. Interestingly, in López's topography, "malas mujeres" (bad women), typically played by actress María Felix, share the same central space as the good mothers, because neither of them transgresses sexual norms (153–154). However, isn't it a contradiction that the "bad woman" and the "good mother" inhabit the same space?[16] If good and bad occupy the same space, then they cancel each other.

This book considers alternative possibilities. What if strict sexual norms are not the most important problem in the representation of mothers in classical cinema? What if the representation of mothers is problematic for other reasons? Third-wave films allow us to consider the possibility that other issues in the representation of mothers are problematic. If, as the filmmakers themselves claim, third-wave films are a response to classical cinema, then what are third-wave films responding to in classical films?

Since third-wave films do not create mothers who transgress sexual norms, we must conclude that third-wave filmmakers do not see strict sexual norms as the most important problem in classical films. Instead, mothers' obligation to be submissive, their denial of agency and an autonomous identity, and the idealization of the maternal are issues that third-wave filmmakers found problematic in representation of mothers in Golden Age films. *Motherhood in Mexican Cinema, 1941–1991* asks the questions: How would López's topography look if it is organized not around sexuality, but around the issues of agency and an autonomous identity? Would the "good mothers" and "malas mujeres" occupy the same space?

This book adds to scholarly dialogue by addressing the relationship between third-wave films and Latin American filmmaking. Many feminist films are studied only as films by women. An important question raised here is: What are the reasons for studying films by women in a separate category? What can we learn about third-wave films by comparing them to other 1970s and 1980s films?

Description of Chapters

Chapter 1 provides a history of third-wave filmmakers that includes their education in films schools, the exclusion of third-wave filmmakers and other film graduates from the Mexican film industry during the mid–1980s, and the factors that allowed third-wave filmmakers to enter the industry at the end of the decade. It also provides an introduction to feminist filmmaking in Mexico and explains the differences in the position of second-wave and third-wave filmmakers with regard to the issue of motherhood.

Chapter 2, "The Ideal of Virgin Motherhood," examines the role the Virgin played in defining patterns of motherhood in the Mexican films from the Golden Age to the 1960s. Inspired by Marina Warner's and Julia Kristeva's analysis of the construct of the Virgin Mary, the chapter introduces the term Ideal of Virgin Motherhood to describe the type of motherhood that dominates classical films. The "Ideal of Virgin Motherhood" conflates motherhood and womanhood and demands that women act like the Virgin by adopting a self-effacing personality whose core identity is that of a caretaker. The chapter explains the benefits of using the notion of the ideal to approach classical cinema and not the idea of stereotype. The chapter contends that taking a historical approach to the construction of motherhood changes the way we understand motherhood. Influenced by Rebecca Jo Plant's (2010) use of soldiers' letters to document changes within the history of motherhood in *Mom: The Transformation of Motherhood in Modern America*, chapter 2 sees parallels between the construction of the Virgin Mary and Sara García, a star from classical cinema known for her role as mother. The Virgin and the actress, the chapter argues, are expressions of the maternal.

Chapter 3, "The Qualities of Classical and Third-Wave Mothers," is the first chapter that compares classical and third-wave films. It examines the moral qualities exalted in classical melodramas and in third-wave films. Some scholars assume that the moral qualities of a mother in classical films are an exact copy of Catholic morals. This chapter demonstrates that classical films only exalt some Catholic qualities, those that promote mothers' self-effacement. Consequently, one cannot say that classical films are based on Catholic values and that third-wave films are not. Rather, the film analysis of *Una familia de tantas* (Galindo) shows that classical films exalt humility, whereas third-wave films exalt self-asserting Catholic qualities, such as hope, fortitude and justice. Self-assertion, as seen in the character of Alma, in Rotberg's *Ángel de fuego* (the Bible's Angel of Justice, 1991) is part of Christian thought, but is uncommon in the representation of mothers in Mexican film.

Chapter 4, "Sexuality in Classical and Third-Wave Films," examines the norms of sexuality. Third-wave films do not create mothers who have an overt and liberated sexuality. Rather, they promote an understanding for the conservative sexualities of the 1940s, like Romelia in Busi Cortés' *El secreto de Romelia*. The main issue third-wave films respond to is agency. The chapter examines the Golden Age melodrama *Señora tentación* (*The Temptress*, Díaz Morales, 1947), a film that includes three women who transgress sexual norms in different degrees and who have different degrees of agency. The film analysis reveals that the woman whom the film condemns is not the rumba dancer, whose half-naked body is overtly displayed, but the one who searches for a professional identity. Agency is what makes the temptress a bad woman in the film. Her ability to act without the supervision of men is considered the most dangerous behavior women can exhibit in classical films.

Chapter 5, "Reconsidering Mothers' Autonomous Identity," is the third chapter dedicated to contrasting classical and third-wave films. It addresses the Ideal of Virgin Motherhood's prohibition against mothers who create an identity for themselves other than that for caretakers of family members. In negative examples of the Ideal of Virgin Motherhood, such as *Doña Bárbara* (1943), the protagonist is disciplined for creating an identity as a powerful landowner. Unlike classical films, third-wave films encourage mothers and women to establish autonomous identities that coexist with their identities as caretakers. In Novaro's *Una isla rodeada de agua* (*An Island Surrounded by Water*, 1985), a teenager's identity is associated with seeing the world in extravagant colors. Yet, the establishment of women's and mothers' separate identities is not always a peaceful and rewarding process, as in Cortés' shorts, where women engage in violent acts to de-colonize their private spaces.

Chapter 6, "Looking Back at Classical Idealization" from the 1980s, is the fourth and final chapter that contrasts classical and third-wave films. The chapter examines the way in which classical and third-wave films idealize mothers. Inspired by Kaja Silverman's study of idealization in *The Threshold of the Visible World*, the chapter questions the extent to which mothers in classical films must demonstrate a degree of goodness that is impossible to achieve. The chapter uses Silverman's understanding of idealization to examine *María Candelaria* (1943). The chapter concludes that in classical narratives the imperative to achieve the Ideal of Virgin Motherhood proves deadly; María Candelaria, the film protagonist, has to die in order to become as good as the Virgin. Third-wave narratives respond to classical idealization by staying at a critical distance from classical idealization. In *Lola*, for example, Novaro uses humor to portray a mothers' unsuccessful attempts to be perfect in a positive light. Unlike classical films, whose narratives encourage women in the audience to aim for perfection, in third-wave films the narrative leads the audience to maintain a distance from the desire to be ideal mothers.

Chapter 7, "Maternal Affectivity in Mexican Film," is the first chapter that puts third-wave films in dialogue with contemporary films. It compares the motherly roles that actress Sara García played in *Cuando los hijos se van*, *Mecánica nacional* and the third-wave film *Los pasos de Ana*. Feminist narratives of the 1980s rejuvenate rather than reject maternal affect. Reclaiming mother love after it was assaulted during the 1970s in films like *Mecánica nacional*, and after film scholars attacked it in the 1980s, is possible because motherhood has been dramatically transformed. In classical films like *Cuando los hijos se van*, mothers are happily loved by omnipresent fathers. In third-wave narratives like Sistach's *Los pasos de Ana* or *Lola* romantic ideals have failed, fathers are absent, and children and their games are the emotional sustenance of depressed mothers. The idea that mothers' love for children helps them live in a world deprived of affect makes mother love compatible with feminist ideals.

Chapter 8, "Making the Private Realm Political," focuses on mothers' mental pain. It establishes a dialogue with films and audiences of the 1980s. The chapter approaches the representation of pain with ideas from the feminist psychoanalysis of 1990s. Classical psychoanalysis, Freudian analysis of the 1910s and 1920s, interprets mother's depression in relation to her biology and her family. After the 1990s, however, influenced by cultural studies, feminism and postcolonial studies, feminist psychoanalytic scholars analyze mothers' depression in relation to the society in which they live. The same is true of the representation of mothers' sufferings in third-wave film; in these films, a mother's depression is an accusation to the social, judicial, political and economic structures in which they live. By making mothers' mental pain a social problem, third-wave films make motherhood, previously considered a private issue, political. Third-wave interpretations of mothers' depression caused turmoil among audiences when the films were exhibited. The chapter studies the specific case of *Los motivos de Luz*, by Felipe Cazals, a popular Mexican filmmaker. Cazals approached the same court case that third-wave filmmaker Dana Rotberg had selected the year before for her *Elvira Luz Cruz, pena máxima*. Cazals, however, depoliticized motherhood by situating the mother's mental pain in relation to her biology and beliefs, not her environment.

By situating third-wave films in conversation with classical and contemporary Mexican films, this book presents third-wave filmmakers as part of both a feminist tradition and a Latin American film tradition. *Motherhood in Mexican Cinema, 1941–1991* claims that third-wave filmmakers are an essential component of the second phase of the New Latin American cinema. By turning toward interiority, the feminist filmmakers of the third-wave make motherhood political, their contribution to Latin American cinema.

1

Women Filmmakers in Mexico, 1940s–1990s

Chapter 1 provides background information about filmmaking in Mexico from the 1940s to the early 1990s in order to situate feminist filmmaking within this country's film industry. The chapter gives an overview of feminism filmmaking by describing the diverse interests and professional experiences of three generations of feminist filmmakers. This information is important to understand who the feminist filmmakers were who transformed motherhood, and what the specific professional and cultural conditions were in which they made their films.

Third-Wave Filmmakers

During the Echeverría administration the national film schools were expanded to ensure the production of Mexican films. In 1971, the Centro de Capacitación Cinematográfica (CCC; Center to Train Specialists to Work in the Film Industry), was created to train professionals in the field.

As a significant part of the film industry was nationalized at this time, the state created the CCC within its own studio, Estudios Churubusco. In 1975, the unions allowed the CCC to train producers, directors and scriptwriters who would work in state cinema productions.[1] The second film school in Mexico City, the Centro Universitario de Estudios Cinematográficos (CUEC), was founded in 1963 within the Universidad Autónoma de México (UNAM; Autonomous University of Mexico), Mexico's public university system. It began as a place for study film analysis and film appreciation, what is today called film studies. Later, when the unions "opened up," CUEC introduced courses in film production as well.[2] Third-wave filmmakers learned their trade at film schools. Several third-wave Mexican women filmmakers attended

Busi Cortés as a student at CCC (courtesy Olga Cáceres).

CCC, including Busi Cortés, Dana Rotberg and Marisa Sistach; others, including María Novaro, attended CUEC. Cortés said at her 1997 presentation at the Latin American Studies Association meeting in Guadalajara: "I would like to end by repeating that in my case, as in those of my women colleagues, without the film schools we wouldn't have been able to do much. The experience that the film schools gave us has been fundamental in enabling us to break into the film industry" (Arredondo 2013, 60). Film schools were essential for the younger filmmakers; they received an education that prepared them for an active role in the film industry.

Filmmaking in the 1980s

The working conditions for film graduates from Mexico City's public film schools, like Cortés and Novaro, were limited during the early 1980s. Film directors who did not belong to a film union were not allowed to show their films in commercial theaters; strict union regulations forbade the commercial exhibition of films made without union workers. Graduating filmmakers were able to make movies in 35 mm using nonunion members, but they could not exhibit these films in commercial theaters. Without commercial exhibition, nonunion directors could not recoup their investment, and therefore few graduates made 35 mm films.[3] Instead, nonunion directors, like Cortés and Novaro, made money by working for public television, by working as assistant directors for film directors who belonged to the unions, or by teaching. In addition, they did nonremunerated activities such as making 8 mm or 16 mm films for noncommercial exhibition. María Novaro summarizes the conditions of production and distribution during the mid and late 1980s by saying: "A lot of people of my generation began to make films— political films, militant films, documentaries.... I belonged to a women's film group once — we made films any way we could and showed them wherever we could."[4] Novaro is describing a time before Salinas was president, when filmmakers produced and exhibited their 16 mm films "wherever they could"; that is, in film clubs and at universities, not in commercial theaters.

The history of Mexican cinema is often studied by *sexenio*, or six-year presidential terms, because Mexico's different governments have taken different approaches to the film industry. A government's approach could facilitate the interests of private producers or could view cinema as an artistic form that was supported by the state, what is known as state cinema. The Salinas administration (1988–1994) favored state cinema; it created an arts council, the Consejo Nacional para la Cultura y las Artes (CONACULTA), within the Education Department, and put IMCINE, el Instituto Mexicano de Cinematografía, under its auspices. The change, long sought by the film community, symbolically represented a new emphasis on the cultural mission of state cinema, which was different from the interest of private producers.

The Salinas sexenio brought a sudden change to the working conditions of filmmakers; the Mexican film industry went through a process of privatization that provided capital for making films and forced film unions to loosen their hold on the industry.[5] Ignacio Durán, director of public television (Unidad de Televisión Educativa y Cultural [UTEC]) was chosen as director of IMCINE.[6] Durán was able to negotiate with the unions the use of nonunion directors in state productions. However, unlike during Echeverría's sexenio (1970–1976), when the state was wholly responsible for all the costs, during Salina's time, IMCINE established coproductions in which the government provided half the cost of production; the rest of the cost was borne by coproducers or the filmmakers themselves.[7] The change in state policy toward cinema had a direct effect on women filmmakers. In 1988 and 1989 three women directors made their first commercial films: Cortés' *El secreto de Romelia*, Novaro's *Lola*, and Rotberg's *Intimidad* (*Intimacy* 1989). Sistach's *Los pasos de Ana* was made in 16 mm and blown up to 35 mm later. These filmmakers were able to make key films about motherhood as a result of the change to state cinema brought by the Salinas administration.

New films by women filmmakers were a surprise for everyone, including the directors themselves. In 1987, critics and filmmakers from Mexico, Latin America and the Caribbean gathered in Mexico City for the Primera Muestra del Cine y Video Realizado por Mujeres Latinas y Caribeñas (First Film and Video Screening by Latino and Caribbean Women) and a televised roundtable discussion called Cocina de Imágenes (Kitchen of Images), organized by documentary filmmaker Ángeles Necoechea.[8] Director Busi Cortés was chosen to be part of Cocina de Imágenes, together with María Novaro and María del Carmen de Lara. Cortés was surprised: "María Novaro astonished me when she said that she would love to make 35 mm films for the movie theaters and with the unions. My mouth hung open in surprise and I said, 'Look at her. Boy, is she brave!'" (Arredondo 2013, 90). Despite believing it was impossible, two years after Cocina de Imágenes Cortés directed her own 35 mm film, *El secreto de Romelia*. The change in state cinema policy suddenly opened up possibilities for nonunion directors. They were able to become part of the film industry.

The release of films made by women attracted the attention of Mexican journalists, who wondered if there had been other women filmmakers in Mexico. In 1989, a review of María Novaro's *Lola* was entitled "The Fourth Female Director Is Born" (Feliciano 1989).[9] The title shows that in the national imagination of 1989, women filmmakers were a novelty and that early women filmmakers were unknown at this time. In 1990, Novaro was listed as number twelve on a list of directors made by Patricia Vega, a feminist journalist. Filmmakers from the silent and early sound period, such as Mimí Derba, Cándida Beltrán, Adela Sequeyro and Eva Liminaña, were part of list. This started the acknowledgment of women filmmaking in Mexico, a history that went back to 1917.[10] As awareness of women's filmmaking (both past and present) increased, film critics and scholars began to write histories of women filmmakers that covered a seventy-year period. These studies have much in common, in as much as they focus on auteur cinema,[11] use Mexico as a frame to situate the group of women filmmakers,[12] and see contemporary filmmakers as part of a long tradition of women filmmakers in Mexico.[13]

The Encuentro de Mujeres Cineastas y Videoastas Latinas

Vega presented the list of Mexican women directors at conference that took place in Tijuana, an event that deserves attention. In 1990, El Colegio de la Frontera Norte sponsored the Encuentro de Mujeres Cineastas y Videoastas Latinas (Gathering of Latina Women Filmmakers and Videomakers) as part of a series of events that involved people on both sides of the border.[14] Three different generations of Mexican women filmmakers attended the event: Matilde Landeta, who had directed films in the 1940s; Marcela Fernández-Violante, who made films in the 1970s; and Marisa Sistach and María Novaro, who had finished their first feature film the previous year. Women filmmakers who had made their films independently in 16 mm as part of the feminist collective, Cine-Mujer, such as Mari Carmen de Lara, participated. Filmmakers of Mexican origin who lived in the United States, like Rosalinda Fregoso, attended, as well as women filmmakers of Hispanic origin, like Puerto Rican Frances Negrón-Muntaner. Academics and journalists who would write the history of women filmmaking in Mexico in future years were present: from the United States, Ruby Rich and Joanne Hersfield, and from Mexico, Márgara Millán and Patricia Vega.

Norma Iglesias and Rosalinda Fregoso, the conference organizers, published the preceedings of the conference, *Miradas de mujer: Encuentro de mujeres videoastas y cineastas chicanas y mexicanas* (1998). Their book contains roundtable discussions, panel presentations, interventions by the audience, and a list of films shown at the conference, as well as a detailed biography of the directors and academics who attended the conference. *Miradas de mujer* reflects the preocupations of Mexican feminist filmmakers at the turn of the 1980s and is thus an invaluable source for the creation of a history of women filmmaking in Mexico.

In the presentations and discussions described in *Miradas de mujer*, the end of this decade appears as a moment of change for feminism. To give one example, each of the three generations of Mexican women filmmakers who attended the conference proposed different ways to solve the gender inequality within the Mexican film industry. One of the films shown at the conference, Marisa Sistach's *Los pasos de Ana,* is a self-reflection about the experience of a graduate from film school working in Mexico in the 1980s. Sistach creates gender inequality between director Vidal and assistant director Ana. At their first meeting, Vidal asks Ana if she has a family and if she could commit to working in a medium that does not have regular scheduled hours. In an interview, Sistach explained, "The position Vidal takes in examining the familial obligations of the person who will be his assistant is a very sexist position, but it also has its logic. Film is a career that consumes your life. You get involved in a movie and you are in the movie virtually twenty-four hours a day, no matter what you do" (Arredondo 2013, 133). Sistach, who makes her character a single mom with two children, commented on the difficulties of mothers who want to pursue careers in filmmaking by saying: "It's a job that is particularly difficult for a person who is a mother and has other sorts of responsibilities. It's not the same for men, because they do have other people who take care of these responsibilities for them, nor for women with no children, because they can devote all the time they want to their work" (Arredondo 2013, 138).

The three generations of women attending the conference had different proposals on how to resolve problems of discrimination in this male-dominated industry. While Matilde Landeta and Marcela Fernández Violante suggested bringing gender equality to the film unions, the younger generation, represented by Sistach and Novaro, preferred to avoid unions altogether. An examination of the experience of these filmmakers explains the solutions they favored.

To Belong to the Union or Not

Despite having worked in the industry at different times, Matilde Landeta and Marcela Fernández held the same position. Landeta made her films in the 1940s within a privatized film industry; she had to rely on private producers for the production, distribution and exhibition of her films. In contrast, Fernández-Violante began making films during the sexenio of Luis Echeverría, a time in which the state subsidized most production and took almost complete financial responsibility for films, which had secure distribution and exhibition through the nationalized state circuit.[15] The experience of having made their films within the film unions united Landeta and Fernández Violante.

Landeta learned her trade by going up the three grades of the union: script-girl or continuity person, assistant director, and then director.[16] Many members of the Sindicato de Trabajadores de la Producción Cinematográfica (STPC), especially women, remained in the same grade because in the 1940s promotion was determined by the grade above.[17] Landeta, for example, had to ask permission to advance to the grade of assistant director and found resistance from those above her. Learning within the hierarchically organized film union was difficult. Landeta worked for thirteen years within the film union STPC, before she asked to be promoted to assistant director. The assistant directors within the union denied Landeta's promotion arguing that she couldn't do the job because she was a woman. She had to bring her case to a STPC general assembly, where her promotion was granted. Fernández Violante also had the experience of having worked as a union director.[18]

At the meeting in Tijuana, Fernández Violante asked the younger generation of directors to become part of the union and to help reform the organization from within: "Things are going to change, they have to change, but for that we have to infiltrate to the unions.... Why isn't Maria Novaro a union member? Why isn't Dana Rotberg? Why isn't Busi Cortés? Why don't they belong to the union as we do? ... Why don't they help us to change, from within, how tasks are assigned according to gender roles?" (Iglesias and Fregoso 1998, 33).[19] Fernández Violante takes a feminist position; aware of gender discrimination, she wants to change how tasks in a film production are assigned. She expects to change the discriminating institution, not to get rid of it. Third-wave filmmakers, who had not had the experience of working their way up the hierarchy of the film unions, had a negative view of unions. According to Novaro, who preferred small film crews with fellow graduates, "The unions have been holding us back for a long time" (27).[20] During the conference, Novaro stated that she encountered a lot of prejudice and hostility when she worked with union members doing *Azul celeste* (1987; 27–28). In addition, Novaro liked to work with women in the crew, as she had done when she made her 16 mm films at CUEC. This was not possible with union crews, as there were very few electricians, directors of photography and sound technicians who were women (27). In general, third-wave filmmakers had gained their professional experience by attending film schools, and they did not want to work under the discrimination of the unions.[21]

Third-Wave Filmmakers and Film Schools

Film schools provided a less discriminating environment to learn how to make films than unions did. While the unions were structured hierarchically, film schools organized horizontally. "From the first year," third-wave director and CCC student Eva López Sánchez explained, "the director is a student; the films are by the students. In the first exercise, the people studying to be cinematographers are in charge of their filming, and the ones studying to be directors have to direct classmates" (Arredondo 2013, 230). Students changed jobs: "In contrast to our own exercises, when we worked on those of our other classmates, we would rotate" (230). Film school gave women equal standing to men, providing them with the same opportunities as those of male students.

Film schools provided another advantage: female students could support each other. In *Matilde Landeta (My Filmmaking, My Life* 1992), a documentary film about the Mexican pioneer Matilde Landeta, made by CCC graduate, Patricia Martínez de Velasco, the director interviews Landeta, Novaro and Fernández Violante. Novaro explains that in the 1980s "there was a lot of solidarity and a lot of collective thought and support" and adds, directing her words at Landeta who is seated across from her, "a lot more than you must have had." In the 1940s Landeta had to fight by herself; there were no other women to fight with her. In the 1980s, by contrast, a whole generation of women filmmakers was studying at film schools.

In 1989 negotiations began to allow film school graduates to direct their own films. These filmmakers hired small crews that included many of their old classmates. These small crews were more flexible. They allowed for the needs of young mothers; they could bring their children to their film productions. In contrast, it would had been unthinkable for a director to bring a child to one of the union film productions in which Landeta or Fernández Violante had been directors. Sistach and Novaro explain in the biographies, included in *Miradas de mujer,* that they arranged the production of their films around their children's schedules. Novaro explained:

> My children have always taken part in the shooting of films. I did it with the older ones and now with Lucero. It is crazy! Because suddenly I lost my mind. Lucero is hungry, cries and requires my attention. All of this drains me, and I finish more tired at night. But I have taken the decision that it is important that they do not feel relegated because of my work, that they have a clear idea of what

Busi Cortés directing *Los afanes* at CCC with actress Lillian Liberman at left (courtesy Olga Cáceres).

I do, and that they take part of what is going on as they want and be at the shooting. Lucero, for example, appears in a scene in the film [*Danzón*]. She became a fan of María Rojo [the main actress in the film].... She went to the rehearsals with María Rojo, copying her. However, we did not lose any time, because I am the first one who thinks that time is money [Iglesias and Fregoso 260].[22]

Novaro clearly enjoyed having her four-year-old daughter, Lucero, at the shooting of *Danzón*. Working with a smaller crew allowed her to join family and work. She felt that her contribution to feminism was to change the conditions at the work place: she brought her children with her so that she could enjoy having them with her while she was working. All three generations wanted to establish equal opportunities for women, though their goals were different.

Mexican Feminist Filmmaking as of the 1990s

The turn of the decade was a time for change, not only for the Mexican film industry, but also for Mexican feminist filmmaking. At Tijuana in 1990, it was understood that the condition for all women was the same, and the conference was organized accordingly. The underlying principle shared by all the panels was the idea that all women had a similar life experience and being a woman was defined by opposition to male experience. This underlying belief manifested in the use of the word "woman," used in the singular in the names of the sessions' titles, such as "Woman's Film," "Woman's Film Today," "Popular Culture and Woman's Film," "Film and Video, The Feminine Experience," "The Quotidian Life and Woman's Film."[23] Viewing women as sharing a similar experience allowed the participants in the event to contemplate the possibility that there could be a "feminine aesthetic,"[24] shared by all women. The ideas expressed in naming the panels and in discussing the possibility of a feminist aesthetic suggest that in 1990 feminism was seen as a movement with a unified goal. However, the proceedings of the conference at Tijuana, published eight years after the conference took place, show signs of change. The title of the book, *Miradas de mujer*, can be translated literally as "Looks of woman." The title implies that there are many looks (*miradas*) but that all come from a female perspective. Although the female perspective is seen as unified, the use of the plural in the word "looks" is a change from to the panels, where the words were all singular: Woman's Film.

Clashes Among the Generations at Tijuana

At the Tijuana conference there were already signs that feminism was evolving. Conference participants disagreed about which films were feminist or not. Specifically, people considered whether or not Sistach's *Los pasos de Ana* was feminist. Sistach explained, "At the conference in Tijuana about a half-dozen people stood up and said that the movie [*Los pasos de Ana*] was sexist and machista. And the worst of it was that they were filmmakers!" (Arredondo 2013, 132). Sistach thought that Ana's romanticism was negatively received: "It is something the American feminist audience finds strange, almost disgusting. It is something, we might say, that is somewhat hard for them to 'swallow'" (Arredondo 2013, 131). Another issue for debate was Ana's close friendship to a gay man, not a woman. And, significantly, conference participants debated whether motherhood should be considered a political issue worthy of analysis.

Fernández Violante told a joke about a mother filmmaker who had to divide herself between the sewing machine and the shooting of a film. Her child ended up going to the Christmas play as a devil instead as an angel because, in the mother's absence, the father made the child's costume for the play.[25] In her view, feminists needed to consider the social constrains that reduce women to mothers, leaving them without any possibility for self-development as professionals.[26] To counter this reduction, she proposed to give women's professional life first place: "A woman professionally trained inside and outside the university has to show that she can do everything, and that family is second, because a woman is first a creator and then the rest" (Iglesias and Fregoso 1998, 34).[27] Thus, the older generations, represented by Landeta and Fernández Violante, held the position that women are filmmakers first and mothers second.

In contrast, the younger generation had a different life experience; they did not have to choose between a sewing machine and the shooting of a film. Sistach mentioned the birth of her son Valdiri in her biography in *Miradas de mujer* where she weaved together her student and professional identity with her identity as a mother (Iglesias and Fregoso 1998, 267–268). Smaller production crews, like those used in *Danzón*, and independent cinema structures, like the one in *Los pasos de Ana*, were more flexible and allowed mothers to integrate caring for the children into their working life.

The younger generation at the conference felt that their view of feminism had been rejected. Sistach was upset when feminists in the audience criticized her film, made as a contribution to the feminist movement. Being rebuked, she concluded, "If *Los pasos de Ana* is sexist and machista, then I don't want anything to do with feminism any more" (Arredondo 2013, 132). Other third-wave filmmakers studied in this book declared to the press that their films were not feminist.[28] Because the filmmakers separated themselves from the movement, journalists and academics have been ambivalent about using the term "feminist" to refer to the younger generation (including Hersfield, Millán, Vega, Rashkin, and my previous works).

The filmmakers' rejection of the word "feminist" to describe their work is a sign that the younger generation had new goals, and this is the reason why they are called third-wave filmmakers. The name implies that they are a different type of feminist than their predecessors, Landeta and Fernández Violante, whom I call second-wave filmmakers. I am using the word "feminist" to mean that these films take a gender perspective with the intention of achieving equality. However, the word "feminist" had a different meaning in 1990 and in 2002. In the 1980s, feminist filmmaking conveyed a political alignment with the left, something that third-wave films do not do. An example, in her welcoming speech Patricia Torres San Martín (2004) clarified that films made by women were not to necessarily feminist films (11–12). Probably, her comment pointed out that the films to be exhibited at Guadalajara were different from the militant films of Cine-Mujer.

Feminist Filmmaking in 2002

In the years following the Tijuana meeting, new perspectives on feminism and women's film and video-making emerged. This evolution in thought was clearly revealed twelve years later at the conference, 'Encuentro de Mujeres y Cine en América Latina' (Gathering of Women and Latin American Cinema) held in 2002 in Guadalajara, Mexico. The conference organizer, Torres San Martín, published the proceedings, entitled *Mujeres y cine en América Latina* (2004). Looking side by side at the proceedings from Tijuana (1990) and Guadalajara (2002) it is clear that these conferences shared the goal of building a common front among women filmmakers. However, the comparison also illustrates a shift in feminist thought; in 1990, the emphasis was on building a common front, while in 2002 the emphasis was on accepting differences among women.[29]

By 2002, the idea of "woman's film" and the possibility of a feminine aesthetic had lost ground as theoretical concepts. Historian Julia Tuñon asked the audience on several occasions to elaborate on what constituted a feminine aesthetic, but the audience did not respond.[30] Parallel to changes taking place in North American feminism, and possibly related to the establishment of feminism as a theoretical framework within academia, the emphasis in Guadalajara was on acknowledging diversity among women. At Guadalajara, women's experiences were not contrasted to men's experiences any longer; rather, the focus was on women themselves, who were seen as having a variety of individual perspectives. In her welcoming speech, for example, the organizer explained that the meeting was planned around the idea of inclusion and plurality of positions.[31] The panels were given names that refer to plurality; for example, the title "Ruptures, Encounters and Diversity in Languages and

Narratives" assumes that there are multiple ways in which women can propose political and ideological changes. The Guadalajara conference was organized around the notion of women, not woman. The use of the plural, the emphasis on diversity, and the silence that followed Tuñon's question about the possibility of a feminist aesthetic show that a change has taken place in Mexican feminist film. The meeting also had the goal of inclusion, which was achieved through the idea of common practice; by organizing the sessions around documentary, fiction and experimental cinema, the Guadalajara meeting gathered together women who shared similar practices, such as making documentaries.[32]

Different Ways to Enter the Industry

The last section of this chapter is a history of the conditions under which third-wave filmmakers made their films. It shows the paths that these filmmakers took after graduation, making films at the margin of the industry from the early to the mid–1980s. It also includes the strategies they used to become nonunion directors.

WORK IN PUBLIC TELEVISION

Public television, where most of third-wave filmmakers learned their trade, plays an important role in this history. The most popular option within public television was to work for the Unidad de Televisión Educativa y Cultural (UTEC), part of the Department of Public Education. UTEC's programs were aired in the evening, around 8 P.M. on channels 11 and 13, the cultural channels.[33] In the early 1980s, when Ignacio Durán Loera was the general director of UTEC's teaching division, UTEC took a leading role in the production of cultural media.[34] From 1983 through 1985, Durán supervised a total of 2,000 programs in series that could have between 52 and 104 programs each. Durán's view of what constituted Mexican culture included old and new concepts of culture. Some of the series were dedicated to what we could consider high art, for example, *Los libros tienen la palabra*, a series about writers of the nineteenth and twentieth century, or *Los que hicieron nuestro cine* (*The People Who Made Our Cinema*) about filmmakers of the past. Series such as *Los barrios*, about Mexico City's neighborhoods, and *Grandes maestros del arte popular*, about Mexico's art and craft artists, viewed culture as folklore — as the habits, traditions and material culture of the folk (or pueblo). Other series held a contemporary view of culture, such as gender and ethnicity. *De la vida de las mujeres*, for example, explored contemporary women's lives in Mexico, and *Mexico plural* looked at Mexico's ethnic groups from the perspective of cultural anthropology.[35]

UTEC was the training ground for several third-wave filmmakers. Between 1983 and 1984, Busi Cortés worked at UTEC with Marisa Sistach, Olga Cáceres, Consuelo Garrido and Dora Guerra in the series called *De la vida de las mujeres* (*On Women's Lives*, 1984). They did thirty half-hour programs that dealt with the different developmental stages of women, including sexual relations, birth control, abortion, widowhood and retirement. They used a variety of genres, from melodrama to comedy to tragedy. Making programs for UTEC prepared Cortés for making 35 mm films; she used what she had learned in the series *La mujer de Nicolás* (*Nicolas' Wife*) and *Las costureras de Aguascalientes* (*The Seamstress of Aguascalientes*) to create Doña Romelia in her first feature film, *El secreto de Romelia*, and she based Romelia's grandchildren on children from the series *Las rumberitas* (*The Rumba Dancer Girls*) (Arredondo 2013, 99).

Similarly, Marisa Sistach relied on her experience at UTEC in the mid–1980s when she made her full-length feature film at the end of the 1980s. In 1983 and 1984 Sistach worked on the series *De la vida de las mujeres* and on another UTEC series about contemporary Mexican writers entitled *Los libros tienen la palabra* (*Books Have Their Say*). In 1985 Sistach was involved in the series called *Gilberto Owen, el recuerdo olvidado* (*Gilberto Owen: The Forgotten Memory*). References to this program are made in Sistach's film, *Los pasos de Ana*. Other third-wave directors, like Guita Schyfter, also worked at UTEC.[36] Working within television had limitations, but it helped third-wave filmmakers to practice their trade.[37]

Work as Assistant Directors for a Union Director

During the 1980s, most third-wave filmmakers worked with a director in union productions. The director could pay a loss of wages fee to the union and the graduates could work as script supervisor or assistant directors.[38] For five years, Dana Rotberg assisted Felipe Cazals in the making of *Los motivos de Luz*, *Las inocentes* (1986–1988), *El tres de copas* (1986) and *La furia de un dios* (1987). Rotberg describes her job as a cross between an assistant director and an assistant producer. She made the work schedule, took care of the shooting, prepared the actors and organized the postproduction (De la Vega Alfaro 1991, 12). She felt that she was underpaid and worked as hard as a slave.[39] Other graduates also worked with union directors. Marisa Sistach, a graduate from CCC, worked as script coordinator with Cazals in five 35 mm films for the union STPC and as assistant director to Jorge Fons in a film about the life and work of Mexican painter Diego Rivera, entitled *Diego Rivera, vida y obra* (UTEC, 1986). The conditions under which graduates worked, especially female graduates, are depicted in Sistach's *Los pasos de Ana*. Sistach's first feature film portrays the life of a graduate from the CCC who, like Sistach, has to earn her living as an assistant director on a television show because she can't work as a film director.[40] Some of the graduates of film schools became teachers in film studies programs.[41]

FILMS IN 8 OR 16 MM

Often, graduates worked both for profit and for pleasure doing their independent work. In *Los pasos de Ana*, Ana makes a video about her children while working as an assistant director. Making feature-length films in 16 mm or video allowed graduates to explore their craft using cinematic structures or topics that interested them. Independent filmmaking created its own channels to produce, distribute and exhibit films at the margins of the industry. Cooperatives, with nonunion workers, made cheaply produced films that were distributed by alternative companies, such as Zafra and UNAM. These films were then exhibited in video clubs and cultural centers, where young audiences discussed them.

In the mid-1980s, third-wave filmmakers also made independent films, such as Marisa Sistach's independently produced *Conozco a las tres* (*I Know All Three*, 1983). The director used Zafra, an alternative distributor, which showed her 16 mm film at cultural centers and universities where forum were organized to discuss films. In the late 1980s, however, the independent 16 mm cine-club circuit disappeared. By the end of the 1980s, the industry had changed and new options opened up for third-wave filmmakers.

The Mid to Late 1980s

During 1976–1988, the two sexenios that followed Echeverría's, the state's interest in film production declined; most production reverted to the private sector. In November of 1987, at the end of the sexenio of President Miguel De la Madrid, the creation of two institutions were key to the state's involvement in cinema: the Instituto Mexicano de Cinematografía (IMCINE) and the Fondo para la Producción Cinematográfica de Calidad (FOPROCINE). Starting in 1988, state support for film production increased and lasted for the next six years. Salinas's sexenio (1988–1994) invested in state cinema.

It is not coincidental that Busi Cortés, who was in charge of directing programs for *De la vida de las mujeres*, produced her first films with IMCINE as a coproducer. Cortés was able to make her film because with the establishment of state cinema institutions like IMCINE, money became available for making films. The Salinas sexenio saw the emergence of many young directors, among them third-wave filmmakers. With production costs rising, producers sought to secure their investments by choosing graduates trained in new technologies rather than experienced union directors.[42] A private institution to finance film production was the first of the big changes that brought life back to the state film sector. The FOPROCINE allowed filmmakers to borrow seed money and acted as a coproducer in the making of quality films.[43]

Access to seed money was coupled with easier labor conditions. Given the difficulties the film industry faced, specifically in the area of the production, film unions were now willing to negotiate with IMCINE, and gradually nonunion directors were allowed to direct films. The opening of the unions created animosity in the union ranks; union directors and assistant directors resented the fact that an outside director who had not gone through the ranks was brought in to direct, narrowing their opportunities. Resentment was particularly strong against women directors, whom some male union members considered to be incapable of directing.

Due to the economic stability during the sexenio, a large number of state-sponsored films was produced. The most important films that took a new perspective on motherhood, Cortés' *El secreto de Romelia*, Novaro's *Lola* and Rotberg's *Ángel de fuego*, were made soon after unions loosen up. Most of them were made with IMCINE as a coproducer. In the early 1990s, Mexico became known for its women filmmakers; representatives of international film festivals came to the Muestra de Cine Mexicano in Guadalajara with the specific mission of selecting films made by women.

Production Paths

The state's role in film production during Salinas's sexenio has been described as that of a broker who shares financial responsibility with other investors or partners.[44] To produce their films in Salinas's sexenio, third-wave filmmakers took different production paths. One option available to the third generation of filmmakers was to use private producers. Dana Rotberg made *Intimidad* with a nontraditional private producer (a term used in Mexico in the late 1980s to refer to private producers interested in investing in art films). León Constantiner, owner of Producciones Metrópolis, wanted to produce a high-quality film that would entertain the upper middle class and at the same time be of interest to people who did not like to read subtitles.[45] So, rather than investing $1,000,000 in cheap labor as traditional private producers did, Constantiner spent $450,000 on hiring highly qualified personnel and purchasing film rights to a script that had already enjoyed great theatrical success: *Intimidad*, written by the well-known writer Hugo Hiriart.

He paid a fee to the union to compensate for using Rotberg, a non union director; hired Leonardo García Tsao, a teacher and film critic from the CCC, to adapt the screenplay; and then employed Carlos Marcovich, a creative and highly trained cinematographer. Rotberg found that working for a private producer had advantages; she was able to direct without having to raise funds for the film. It also had its limitations: she had no impact as director after she finished the first cut (Vega, 1990b). *Intimidad* foreshadows problems that came with the privatization of culture in the 2000s. Working with a private producer, directors lost decision-making power.

Another option for women filmmakers was to produce a film outside of the film industry and then find a way to use it as an introduction into the industry after it was made. Sistach preferred to remain within the film-club circuit. She founded a cooperative with friends and shot *Los pasos de Ana* in 16 mm with few resources and with nonprofessional actors. However, the film eventually appeared in commercial theaters via the following sequence of events. Peter Schumann, one of the organizers of the 1991 Berlin Film Festival, wanted to bring the film to a retrospective on young Mexican cinema to be held at the festival. However, since there were no 35mm copies available in 1990, Schumann negotiated with IMCINE to finance the transfer to 35 mm; in exchange the film institute became a coproducer in the film. Sistach was able to finish editing her film by selling the exhibit rights to Mexico, Germany, and the Netherlands.[46] However, it was not until 1993 that *Los pasos de Ana* was shown in Mexico.[47] Sistach's experience shows the limits imposed by industrial filmmaking. While making her film, Sistach was able to make decisions based on what she wanted to say, but with the collapse of the film-club circuit and her entrance into the industry, issues such as audience sophistication and commercial success had to be considered in her decisions.

The third production option for women filmmakers was to have a film school as sponsor. For her first film, Cortés was able to finish her script with a soft loan from the FOPROCINE but she did not have the funds to begin shooting. Then, in 1988, as a teacher at the CCC, she came up with the idea of having the film school as coproducer. The status of the CCC as an institution under Estudios Churubusco, the state studios, made this easier. She asked individuals and institutions to donate what they could to the production. Actor Pedro Armendariz worked almost for free. Cortés also made use of school discounts for film stock and other film material and used students as workers. When shooting her film, Cortés combined paid workers from Section 49 of the film union Sindicato de Trabajadores de la Industria Cinematográfica (STIC) with CCC second-year students, who worked for free. This considerably reduced the production cost. After the success of Cortés' experiment, the film school established a contest for opera primas; the student who won the contest would be able to direct his or her first feature film within the school. With the school's support, Cortés had discovered a legal loophole by which students could produce low-budget high-quality films.

A fourth production path women filmmakers used was to create a cooperative and participate in an international coproduction. In making her opera prima *Lola*, Novaro looked for a way to produce her film that would allow her the freedom to address women's issues. She was able to film in 35 mm without large union crews by joining a cooperative. Novaro and her working team, mainly a small group of CUEC graduates, jointed the Cooperative José Revueltas. Since cooperatives are labor associations similar to unions, the producers were able to legally make the film without using union members. The small crew made production expenses affordable, given that the budget of the film, $300,000, was rather small. Novaro's ability to control the decision-making in *Lola* was predicated on the way she secured the funding. She received $150,000 from Televisión Española through Quinto Centenario, a program in support of Latin American cinema in celebration of Columbus's arrival in the Americas. In exchange for the funding, Television Española held a portion of the distribution rights. In an interview with Conchita Perales, Novaro explained that $150,000 allowed her to begin *Lola*: "In all truth, the production funds from Spanish Television were not extra money. The money allowed me to begin making the film.... The film was ready, but up until then, nobody had shown any support, not even with a 'maybe,' nothing" (Perales 1991, 39).[48] Novaro felt comfortable with this international coproduction, which in her view did not interfere with her decision-making power: "Unlike a normal co-production, in which the co-producers are involved in making decisions about the film, [in the case of *Lola* and *Danzón*] we in Mexico were able to manage the money Televisión Española gave us, very freely, through the private company Macondo. Because they weren't done as formal co-productions, both productions were under my control, within what the money permitted" (Arredondo 2013, 155). Because of the support from Televisión Española, IMCINE, through CONACITE II, became coproducer after the film was made (Perales 1991, 37). The third investor was a nontraditional producer, Jorge Sánchez, who worked with Novaro as part of her team. She was in charge of making the film, while he negotiated its funding, distribution, and exhibition. This production scheme worked well for Novaro, who was able to explore themes that interested her with a small crew in a pleasant environment.

In the late 1980s and early 1990s, the mix of private, or semiprivate, capital with state funding worked well for women interested in raising gender issues in film. In general, gender issues were not as censored as heavily political issues. However, as IMCINE's role as a funding institution diminished during the early 2000s, support of the arts became more privatized, and there was a shift toward profit-making as the primary concern, making it more difficult for women directors to raise issues of gender. From the perspective of the 2000s, state funding is key to the creation of feminist films, and small productions are an ideal way to shoot these films.

Conclusion

Motherhood in Mexican Cinema, 1941–1991 studies Mexican women filmmakers in two groups, second- and third-wave filmmakers. The personal experiences of the filmmakers within the film industry, the changes within feminism and the changes within Latin American cinema are key factors in understanding why motherhood is not a political or feminist issue for second-wave filmmakers, while it is for third-wavers.

2

The Ideal of Virgin Motherhood

Chapter 2 describes the approach *Motherhood in Mexican Cinema, 1941–1991* takes in examining the maternal in classical Mexican films and the reasons behind it. This analysis of Golden Age melodramas departs from previous scholarly approaches: the Virgin Mary, not the Virgin of Guadalupe, is used as a model for motherhood. The chapter uses the perspective of cultural studies to examine the maternal in the Golden Age era. This includes cultural manifestations, like the cult of the Virgin Mary; practices, like Mother's Day; and the creation of cultural artifacts, like Sara García's films. Finally, the chapter introduces a concept, that of the Ideal of Virgin Motherhood, which will be used throughout the book when discussing the maternal in classical films.

Scholarly Approaches to Classical Cinema

The study of women characters in Mexican films began in the 1960s. In *La aventura del cine mexicano* (1968), a study that went through seven editions between 1968 and 1993, Jorge Ayala Blanco (1993) distinguishes between two types of characters: mothers, studied as part of "La familia," and prostitutes, studied as part of "La prostituta" (108–127).[1] In the 1980s and 1990s, film scholars based in the United States added an association to the stereotype of the "good mother." Carl Mora (1985), Charles Ramírez-Berg (1992), and Joanne Hershfield (1996) drew a connection between the stereotype of the good mother and the Virgin of Guadalupe. Their studies relate the good mother of classical cinema to the Virgin of Guadalupe, as described in Octavio Paz's *The Labyrinth of Solitude* (1961).[2] In his book, which went through over sixty editions, Paz uses two archetypes for women, the whore and the mother. Taking a Jungian perspective, Paz traces the archetype of the mother back to the Conquest. After the Spaniards dismantled the Indian pantheon, the Indians needed a figure that expressed the protection they were searching for.

This need for safety resulted in the cult to the Virgin of Guadalupe, which Paz describes as a return to the nurturance and protection of the womb [85]. For the Mexican writer, the Virgin of Guadalupe is someone who "consoles, dries tears and calms passions" (85). Love and nurturance are at the core of Paz's archetype of the mother. However, the Virgin of Guadalupe is not the model of femininity and motherhood in Mexican cinema.

The Virgin as the Patroness of Mexico and as a Model for Motherhood

In their examination of Mexican cinema Mora, Ramírez-Berg and Hershfield made a notable effort to bring cultural specificity to their studies by incorporating, via Paz, the Virgin of Guadalupe. However, these studies do not take into account the transnational nature of Catholic culture. The fact that Catholicism is a transnational culture explains why Mexicans can, at the same time, venerate a national virgin, Guadalupe, and educate their children following an international model, Mary. Middle- and upper-class Mexican girls, attending private Catholic schools, and other family members, attending Sunday mass, participate in the cult of Mary. At the same time, they celebrate the Virgin of Guadalupe's birthday on December 12, as one of the most important days of the year. December 12 is arguably even more important than Independence Day or the celebration of the Mexican Revolution. The point is not that the cult of Mary is more important than the cult of Guadalupe, but that Mexicans participate in both.

Historically, the transnational dimension of Catholicism has been problematic for Mexican sovereignty. Mexico positioned itself as anticlerical after its independence in 1821; the constitutions of 1857 and 1917 have articles that restrict the power of Catholicism. President Calles's implementation of the antireligious articles of the Constitution of 1917 led to the Cristero Wars (1926–1929). Calles's position on Catholicism was based, in part, on a conflict about sovereignty. The priests who lived in Mexico received orders from the Vatican, an institution outside Mexico's borders. Priest and, by extension, Catholics who followed them, had two nations: the Vatican and the country in which they lived. Mexican Catholics played an important role at the transnational level. The petitions of Catholics, many of whom were Mexican, led to the Vatican changing dogma surrounding the Virgin Mary, as will be explained later.

Tepeyac

There is another reason why Mary is used instead of Guadalupe. Although the Virgin of Guadalupe is a mother, "the mother of Mexicans," her primary function is not to model femininity and motherhood, but to intercede and be a patroness. This function of the Virgin is clear in Paz, who describes the Virgin as someone who consoles and protects. The first Mexican film to feature the Virgin of Guadalupe, *Tepeyac* (José Manuel Ramos, 1917), does not relate Mexico's most revered Virgin to preoccupations of femininity or mothering.

The silent film *Tepeyac* is structured as a story within a story. The film begins with a scene in which the protagonist, Guadalupe Flores (Pilar Cota), reads the story of the Virgin of Guadalupe. After receiving news that the boat in which her fiancé is traveling has capsized, Guadalupe reads to calm her anxiety. Soon, she is transported, as if in a daydream, to the settings of the story she is reading and she "sees" an apparition of the Virgin in Tepeyac.

When the story of the apparition has been told, the film returns to Guadalupe, who awakens from her reverie to receive the good news that her fiancé is alive. After he returns home, they go to the basilica of Tepeyac, in Mexico City, to pay homage to the Virgin of Guadalupe. The film includes

The Virgin of Guadalupe appears to San Diego in *Tepeyac* (Cineteca de la UNAM).

documentary footage of the cult of the Virgin of Guadalupe in the early 1910s.

Tepeyac associates the Virgin of Guadalupe with protection not motherhood. In Ramos's film, Guadalupe Flores does not learn how to be a mother from the Virgin of Guadalupe; instead, the patroness of Mexico intercedes on her behalf to bring Guadalupe's fiancé home safely.[3] In addition, *Tepeyac* asserts Mexico's national identity contextually. By creating a film about a national symbol, the amateur director and actors of *Tepeyac* wanted to counter the dominant role played by foreign films in the Mexican theaters of the 1910s. Thus, we can conclude that in *Tepeyac* the Virgin of Guadalupe fulfills two functions: within the narrative she is associated with intercession; outside of the narrative, within a film market dominated by foreign films, she is a symbol of the nation, of Mexicaness.

Marina Warner's (1976) two-thousand-year historical study of the Virgin, *Alone of All Her Sex: The Myth and the Cult of the Virgin Mary*, shows that intercession, national identity, gender identity and maternity are interrelated but different ideas. Warner's study leaves no doubt that the Virgin has fulfilled many functions from before the first century to the present; although, several aspects of Mary may overlap, and an aspect of Mary might be developed over several periods.[4] Initially, the similarity between the Virgin and Jesus was emphasized; later on, during the Middles Ages, the idea that the Virgin was a queen was highlighted. Later still, the Franciscans made the Virgin into a more human figure, linked to motherhood (172). Warner proposes that, in chronological order, Mary was seen as virgin, queen, bride, mother, and then intercessor.

Looking through the lens of Warner's detailed study gives the scholarly approaches used to study Mexican classical film a different perspective. Mora (1985) argued that "The Mexican cinema created an ideal of motherhood unmistakably inspired by the cult of the Virgin of Guadalupe" (229) but his assertion seems unlikely seen from the perspective of *Alone of All Her Sex*. In Aztec dances performed at her basilica in Mexico City, as well as in the art of Chicanas in the United States, Mexico's most revered virgin is a symbol of protection toward the Mexican nation.[5]

The Virgin Mary, by contrast, is the unstated but ever present symbol of femininity and motherhood in classical cinema. To study different aspects of the maternal in Mexican melodramas, *Motherhood in Mexican Cinema, 1941–1991* draws from several chapters in which Warner examines Mary as mother. The chapter "Let It Be" focuses on the cult of Mary at the crib and the development of the culture of domestic idealism, "Mater Dolorosa" examines the Virgin as mourning mother, and "The Immaculate Conception" analyzes the Virgin as the only human without original sin.[6]

THE VIRGIN AS A CONSTRUCT

This book also differs from previous literature in the way it understands how Mary came to be. Based on Warner's study, *Motherhood in Mexican Cinema, 1941–1991* emphasizes the idea that Catholics created the construct of Mary. Warner compiled literary and apocryphal works on the Virgin in order to prove that the story of the Virgin, as it appears in the Catholic cult of Mary, is not referenced in the Bible. The New Testament does not give details of the Virgin's birth, childhood, or death. There is only a marginal reference to Mary as the mother of Jesus in Paul, probably written in AD 57. More importantly, the Bible does not mention fundamental concepts of the cult of Mary, such as the Assumption or even the Immaculate Conception. For the most part, the belief in Mary's ascension to the skies without dying or in Mary's birth without an original sin are ideas created and discussed outside the orthodoxy of the Catholic Church (that is, outside the Vatican). The Catholic Church only accepted them as dogma many years or centuries later. Some theological points were debated well into the twentieth century.

The Immaculate Conception, for example, illustrates the constructed nature of the Virgin. "Nothing in the New Testament refers to the absence of sin in the Virgin" says Warner (1976, 238) in the chapter dedicated to this issue. Yet, since the twelfth century the Immaculate Conception had been an issue "stormily discussed" (236) in popular belief and within ecclesiastical circles, including the Council of Trent (1545–1563). At Trent, following St. Agustine, the Virgin was declared exempt from universal sin (245). Jesuits, funded in 1534 by a Spaniard, "applied themselves with the fierce militancy of their order to spread the belief in Mary's Immaculate Conception" (247). Mary's absence of sin was especially important for colonial Latin America, where Jesuits had a strong presence. Moreover, the Jesuit's defense of Mary's birth without sin had very clear transnational implications; it separated Catholics from other Christians, who were opposed to this idea. The idea of the Immaculate Conception was "one of the special Catholic ideas that roused the Reformers' tempers, and therefore proclaimed Rome's defiance and fearlessness" (247). By accepting the Immaculate Conception as dogma in 1854, Catholics expanded the differences between themselves and other Christians.

Another scholar who also studies Mary as a construct is Julia Kristeva. In "Stabat Mater," published in 1977, a year after Warner's study, Kristeva emphasizes Warner's point even further; she quotes the brief (no longer than three lines), marginal references to Mary in the Bible (Kristeva 1986, 164). Kristeva explains, "Starting from this programmatic material [citations in the Bible], rather skimpy nevertheless, a compelling imaginary construct proliferated in essentially three directions," the parallel between Mother and Son, giving Mary "patents of nobility" (164) and making Mary "the prototype of love relationships" (165). Kristeva proposes that these biblical citations led to a creative process through which ideas about the maternal emerged.

Warner and Kristeva are not interested in the historical Mary but in what Warner refers to as the "myth of Mary." By myth, the historian does not refer to an unfounded or false notion, but rather to a traditional story of ostensibly historical events that expresses the world view of a people or to explain a practice, belief, or natural phenomenon (*Merriam-Webster Dictionary* 2011). Warner's emphasizes that the myth of Mary explains the values of the people who created it, which is in line with the dictionary's definition of the term. When she writes: "A myth of such dimension is not simply a story, or a collection of stories, but a magic mirror like the Lady of Shalott's, reflecting a people and the beliefs they produce, recount, hold" (Warner 1976, xxiii) she stresses that the construct of the Virgin tells us about the people who created the myth. The myth of Mary is not imposed by an outside force, but is made by the society who believes in it; it's origin is within society. The idea that the Virgin is a construct contradicts important aspects of previous studies of Mexican classical film.

From Stereotypes to Ideals

Previous literature on Mexican cinema, Mora, Ramírez-Berg and Hersfield's articles and books, assume a passive relationship between the female characters and the models of femininity prevalent in the society depicted in the films.[7] In these studies, women have a passive role: it is understood that society creates stereotypes that are imposed on women. As a consequence of this imposition female characters have two options: to be a whore or a good mother. The concept of stereotype conveys a governing function; the stereotype of the good mother, for example, is used to regulate women's behavior. In this way, the Virgin controls the conduct of Catholic women.

It would be a contradiction to think that the Virgin is a construct and then to agree that the behavior of women is regulated through the use of stereotypes; the idea of construct implies an active participation in the making of ideas, while the concept of stereotype does not. Thus, if we agree with Warner and Kristeva that the Virgin is a collectively constructed myth, we have to accept that society creates rather than is burdened with ideas that regulate women's behavior. In other words, if the Virgin is a collectively constructed model of femininity, the models of motherhood and femininity that derive from this idea must be collectively constructed as well. If society creates the ideas that regulate femininity, then the concept of stereotype, which refers to the imposition of precepts, to passive receivers, is inappropriate in studying the representation of women and mothers in classical Mexican cinema.

The concept of ideal is important for Warner and Kristeva's interpretation of Mary. In the *Threshold of the Visible World* (1996), Kaja Silverman defines idealization as "the increase in an object's value which occurs when it is elevated to the level of the impossible non-object of desire" (40) and explains that some objects are so widely represented as being worthy of idealization that they assume the status of normative ideals. Silverman relates ideals to what she calls the cultural screen, which can be described as an imagined screen that constantly takes in and projects images through which a particular society expresses its views (18).[8] In a chapter entitled "Screen" (195–227), Silverman proposes that the cultural screen is not a mirror, a direct reflection of society, but rather a social creation. She situates the cultural screen at the intersection of the individual (the look) and the social (the gaze); individuals are the creators of the cultural screen, yet at the same time they are subject to it. If we understand the mothers of Mexican melodramas through Silverman's notion of the cultural screen, then these women are not an oversimplification of real women (a stereotype), but an ideal, a cultural construction that reflects society's creative process. Silverman's understanding of the notions of ideal and screen and Warner's interpretation of history establish both a passive and an active relationship between society and its cultural products: a particular society is *governed by* and *subject to* ideas about the maternal.

Film, Mother's Day and the Virgin

Using the notion of ideal to theorize motherhood opens up the maternal to a number of issues not taken into account before. Viewing Mary as a social construction, we can also inquire into other social constructions that also relate to the maternal, like celebrations and actresses that play maternal roles. These can be studied along with the construct of the Virgin. In this way, Catholic dogma regarding the Virgin, the creation of Mother's Day in México, and the professional career of actress Sara García, known for her motherly roles, can be studied as manifestations of the maternal. Since Mexico participates in the transnational culture of Catholicism, then García's star persona can be studied in conjunction with the Catholic construction of Mary.

The creation of Mary's role as mother was particularly active in the second half of the twentieth century, at the time when García gained popularity. The Assumption became Catholic dogma in 1950 by a Vatican fiat (Kristeva 1986, 169). This meant that after 1950 (toward the end of the Golden Age of

Mexican cinema), all Catholics had to believe that Mary ascended to heaven and did not die as part of their faith. The possibility that Mary ascended had been discussed for a long time, but it is in 1950 that idea became dogma. More changes followed; Pius XII officially proclaimed Mary a queen in 1954, and the Virgin was made the "Mother of the Church" in 1964 (170).

García's popularity rose in the years that preceded the declaration of Mary's Assumption. From 1933 to 1937, García made ten films in which she played the good mother and good wife. Reflecting on her films in a 1976 interview, García remembers that after the premiere of *Malditas sean las mujeres* (*Damned Be Women*) in 1936, people began calling her "The Mother of Mexican Cinema."[9] In García's view, she was given this name because she had always played the role of mother, especially during the late 1930s and 1940s in films such as *No basta ser madre* (*It Is Not Enough to Be a Mother*, 1937), *Mi madrecita* (*My Little Mother*, 1940), *La gallina clueca* (*The Old Hen*, 1941), *Mama Inés* (1945), and *Madre adorada* (*Beloved Mother*, 1948). Two years later, the Assumption became dogma. Other Mexican practices during these years add to the story of the construction of motherhood in Mexico.

Mother's Day in Mexico and Sara García's Rise to Stardom

Mother's Day in Mexico was created in 1922, and in the 1940s, its celebration on May 10 was an important national holiday everywhere. Schools created their own traditions, from poetry recitals to discourses honoring mothers. Newspapers, especially the *Excélsior*, organized drawing and writing contests and included crossword puzzles with maternal themes (*Excélsior*, May 10, 1942), columns that described the particular characteristics of Mexican mothers (*Excélsior*, May 10, 1942), and descriptions of events honoring mothers, such as President Franklin Roosevelt's, at elegant theaters (*Excélsior*, May 10, 1942).

Mother's Day also had a clear economic dimension: newspapers ran advertisements with suggestions for presents, and shopping was encouraged as a patriotic act, since it would help the national economy (*Excélsior*, May 10, 1937). With the development of sound films about ten years later, it became a tradition to show films portraying long-suffering mothers on May 10.

Often times theaters screened García films in one of her motherly roles.[10] As García repeated her role of sacrificing mother over the years (she acted in 150 films), her films were almost mandatory for screenings on Mother's Day.

2. The Ideal of Virgin Motherhood 39

Announcement of Sara García's film on Mother's Day (courtesy *Excélsior*).

For example, in 1942, El Palacio Chino played *La abuelita* (*Excélsior* May 10, 1942), and in 1943, *Resurrección* (*Excélsior* May 10, 1943).

The advertisements in the paper, which included full-size photographs of García with her name in big letters, demonstrate that García played a central role in Mother's Day celebrations. In the 1950s, she was expected to play the same role in melodramas and comedies, to continue to be the "official mother."[11]

Sara García's motherly roles had little to do with her real life. García (1895–1980), who was born in Orizaba, Veracruz, lost her father at age nine and her mother at ten. Having no family to rely on during her adolescence and early adulthood, García lived with the nuns she had studied with, and she taught within their school.[12] As a young woman she had to take care of herself, and having an aptitude for acting, she made her living for eighteen years as a theatrical actress (Mora 1985, 230). Working conditions were hard: she had to learn parts for plays that changed every week and act in more than one theater on a single day for low pay.

With the advent of "the talkies" in the mid-1930s and the growth of the Mexican film industry, some theater actresses crossed over into film. Despite the expanded job opportunities, actresses like García, who were not particularly beautiful, had a difficult time getting parts. The story that García had fourteen teeth extracted in order to more realistically play the role of an elderly mother has been used to argue that she had an innate penchant for suffering.[13] While this might be the case, it is important to remember that at that time, García was desperately trying to sustain herself. Since jobs for women of her age were very competitive, she took her chances and had her teeth removed in the hope that she would get the role of grandmother. Interestingly, when she got to be a more mature woman, she was substituted by a younger actress in the remake of *Cuando los hijos se van* (1968), unlike the actor who played her husband.

García's motherly roles were also in sharp contrast with her life as a single mother. García never belonged to a family, except, of course, in film. She married actor Fernando Ibáñez, and they had a child, Fernanda, but soon after their marriage, they separated. This is a sharp contrast to her role as Doña Lupe in *Cuando los hijos se van*, where she plays an elderly mother who always stays at home. Her biographers describe her as an emancipated modern woman, driving her own car to get to film sets and taking care of Fernanda simultaneously (Muñoz 1998, 25–30). Unfortunately, García's daughter died at age twenty, the year before her mother played Lupe in *Cuando los hijos se van*. Thus, García's melodramatic acting in Bustillo Oro's film can be seen as part of a real mourning process, representing a grief that encompassed a lifetime of tragic losses.

Cuando los hijos se van (1968) (Colección Filmoteca de la UNAM).

It is not clear whether García took advantage of the conservative notions of motherhood in order to make a living or whether she created an ideal world for herself, perhaps both. García's star persona is created from the desires and values of Mexican society from the 1930s through the 1960s. Comments such as "Sara García's glorious masochism ... [is] representative of 'little white heads' and of Mother's Day, the nation's Oedipus complex day" (Ayala Blanco 1993, 43) might lead us to think that García herself played a role in creating Mother's Day in Mexico. But the celebration of Mother's Day originated at least a decade before García began playing the roles that made her famous. It began as a reaction against liberal measures by the governor of Yucatán, who, in the early 1920s, proposed laws for divorce and sexual education for women (Muñoz 1998, 34). On April 13, 1922, in response to this "criminal campaign against motherhood," the director of the newspaper *Excélsior* wrote a column proposing the establishment of a day to recognize the sacrifices mothers make for their families, following the lead of a woman from Philadelphia who had made this suggestion in 1908.[14] And so, Mother's Day was born in Mexico. A decade later, García played her first motherly roles.

Virginal Representations of Mothers in Mothers' Day

In the same newspaper that ran advertisements on García's films on Mother's Day, mothers were associated with the Virgin. In 1937, *Excélsior* held a drawing contest for Mother's Day. The drawings show that a majority of children in Mexico associated motherhood with the Virgin. When asked to draw a mother, some children directly drew the Virgin at the cross and her ascension into heaven; others associated motherhood with the Virgin as mother. One drawing shows a mother in the room of a contemporary house leaning over the bed of a child. The mother's posture resembles many paintings of the Virgin with Jesus in the manger and thus establishes a parallel between the mother and the Virgin Mary. These drawings "speak" about the connection Mexican children establish between motherhood and the Virgin by using the symbol of the crown. Children drew contemporary mothers with virginal attributes; for example, a mother of four was shown wearing a crown. The drawings anticipate the importance that Mary as mother will play across Catholic countries in the second half of the twentieth century. In the Mexican culture of the 1930s, motherhood was associated with the Virgin, and the Virgin was represented through her crown. So, in the *Excélsior*'s Mother's Day contest of 1937 children drew their mothers with crowns to express the connection between the Virgin and the maternal.

Three decades after the contest, the Virgin and the actress who represented the maternal in Mexico also received crowns. During the 1940s and 1950s the importance of Mary as queen grew, culminating in 1954, when the Vatican gave the Virgin Mary the title "Queen of the Church." In 1968, jour-

Mother and Crown, Excelsior, May 10th, 1937 (courtesy *Excelsior*).

nalists of the magazine *Reseña de Acapulco* nominated García as their queen (Muñoz 1998, 66), and in 1969, journalists writing for *Guía Cinematográfica* made her the "Queen of National Cinema" (66). Interestingly, the Virgin has undergone a similar process to that of the famous actress. Thus, García was crowned as "Queen of National Cinema" a decade after the Virgin officially received her title as "Queen of the Church." The process of giving crowns is represented as a parody in *Mecánica nacional* where Sara García dies on screen and the mourners make her a tin-foil crown (see chapter 7). Alcoriza's film directly addresses the association between mothers and the Virgin, and between motherhood and Sara García, by including the crown as a prop. In the film the crown is a prop used to give visibility to the maternal.

The Language of the Franciscans and of Melodrama

Golden Age films had several points in common with the Franciscan idea of motherhood. Melodramas use blood and tears to express the maternal, a symbolism used before by the Catholic Church. Warner explains that the cult of Jesus' blood and Mary's tears was constructed by the Franciscans in the twelfth and thirteen centuries. This religious order wanted to reach people who did not read Latin. Warner (1976) sees the cult of blood and tears carrying a strong nonverbal weight and emphasizing images and emotions (211). Like the Franciscans, Bustillo Oro's films wanted to address large audiences, and used an emphasis on emotions and images to convey their message. People in the audience such as Fernando Muñoz, appreciated García's portrayal of motherly love. He suggests that in *Cuando los hijos se van* García was able to "personify and give life to the Mexican mothers of that time [1940s]," something that in his view "gave her a place among popular sensibilities" (Muñoz 1998, 40). For him, García was "an innocent and tender mother able to cry in one of the more convincing weeps of the films of that time" (40).[15] The Franciscan symbols for the maternal, blood and tears, are also present in the melodramas of the 1940s.

The Ideal of Virgin Motherhood

Motherhood in Mexican Cinema, 1941–1991 uses the concept of the ideal, rather than stereotype, to talk about the socially constructed norms that regulate women's behavior in the Golden Age of Mexican cinema. In particular, the term "Ideal of Virgin Motherhood" is used throughout the book to underscore that female characters follow the Virgin Mary as a model of femininity and motherhood.

The words "Virgin Motherhood" refer to the assumption, prevalent in Mexican melodramas, that womanhood and motherhood are one and the same. For example, in *Una familia de tantas* (1948), Don Rodrigo, Maru's father, gives a speech at Maru's fifteenth birthday party. The quinceañera party represents Maru's coming of age and is explicitly linked to motherhood. After the party, Don Rodrigo tells his wife Doña Gracia: "Your daughter is all woman now; she should be a good mother." In Freudian psychoanalysis as well as in Don Rodrigo's understanding of motherhood, a woman's identity is based on mothering, and since mothering is the same for mothers and daughters, Maru is essentially the same as Doña Gracia. Don Rodrigo's conflation of women with mothers is represented by the hyphen. The Ideal of Virgin Motherhood conflates motherhood and womanhood and prescribes that all female characters follow this construct.

In classical cinema women are encouraged to mimic the Virgin, not only by acting virginally (that is, by showing that they are sexually pure), but also by acting Virginally (by imitating the Virgin's role as a sacrificing, self-effacing and mediator woman-mother). The emphasis on performance, and the allusion to a model of woman who is sexually pure and acts like the Virgin is influenced by Charles Ramírez Berg's ideas. In examining the ideological dynamics regarding women during the classical period of Mexican film, he proposed that roles for women were rigid and there were few options. Naming the options women could have, he calls one section: "Women as virgin/Virgin/whore/wife/mother." Later on, he clarifies the differences between "virgin" and "Virgin" by saying: "Women are expected to be not only virginal, but Virginlike, emulating the Virgin de Guadalupe, the spiritual patroness of Mexico" (Ramírez Berg 1992, 23). Ramírez Berg suggests that characters approach normative ideals by imitating the Virgin. Emilio Fernández's 1943 canonical film is a good example of the imperative to mimic the Virgin.

María Candelaria, A Lesson in Acting Virgin-like

The narrative of *María Candelaria* is structured as a learning process in which the protagonist learns to act like the Virgin. At the beginning of the film, María Candelaria (Dolores del Río) acts chastely, gazing down in the presence of strangers. Her model is the Virgin, as displayed in a portrait in her house. Yet, as the daughter of a prostitute, she has not been taught Virginity. In the middle of the film, she walks into the church (a patriarchal space par excellence in Mexico) and learns to emulate the Virgin. As the film ends, this campesino woman from Xochimilco, through dying and sacrifice, becomes the Virgin herself.

María Candelaria suggests the parallel between the protagonist and the Virgin in its title, which literally means "Virgin, Virgin." "María" alludes to the Queen of Virgins, Mary; "Candelaria" refers to a much respected Virgin: la Virgen de la Candelaria, a dark-skinned Virgin who carries baby Jesus in one hand and a candle (therefore the name of the Virgin, Virgen de la Candelaria) in the other.[16] María Candelaria's emulation of the Virgin is best represented in a sequence inside the church of Nuestra Señora de los Dolores.[17] Before this sequence takes place, María and her fiancé, Lorenzo Rafael (Pedro Armendariz), are walking toward the church to get married. As the priest meets them, the police arrest Lorenzo, who has been accused of stealing a wedding dress from the overseer's shop. After the police take Lorenzo away, the priest asks María into the church.

The lesson on Virginity begins as María Candelaria walks into the church to ask the Virgin to intercede for Lorenzo, in the belief that the Virgin will mediate between the Christian community and God. The film uses a high-angle shot which represents the point of view of the priest and thus of the symbolic order. As María lies on the church floor, she sobs loudly, showing that she is not in control of her emotions or her body. The priest recommends that she offer her pain to the Virgin. Instead, María angrily complains about the lack of justice for the poor, thus showing her initial unwillingness to be guided by the priest and ultimately the Virgin.

This scene emphasizes that María Candelaria does not know how to act like the Virgin because she cannot control her anger. María's words to God inside the church ("Why don't you listen to me? Your eyes don't notice us down here.") sound like a legitimate social complaint. The campesino woman believes that the authorities have unfairly taken Lorenzo to jail. Previously, the audience has seen the overseer (who had made advances to María) deny Lorenzo's request for an early payment of his salary. Thus, when María explains to the priest that she and her fiancé have tried to pay for the dress, the audience considers her claim to be truthful. It is understood that the dress is a necessary item to legitimize her relationship to Lorenzo before God and society. For a moment, the film suggests that God plays favorites and gives help only to the rich. But it becomes clear that María's accusations against the legal and religious authorities pose a threat that needs to be controlled.

In response to María's protest, the priest reprimands her and reminds her that she is hurting the Virgin. As the priest says that her anger is like a knife in Mary's heart, the camera pans to the left, simulating the movement of María's eyes as they discover a statue of La Virgen de los Dolores (Our Lady of Sorrows) that she hadn't noticed. A medium shot of a Virgin with a knife stabbed in her heart adds a literal dimension to the priest's words; it is as if María's anger had literally stuck a knife in Mary's heart.

When the camera pivots to show this Mater Dolorosa, María's behavior "pivots" as well. She enters a transitional period in which she progressively learns to act like the Virgin. As the series of parallel shots comes to an end, a new element is introduced: the Virgin's tears. A close-up of the Virgin's face, emphasizing her tears, is paired with a similar shot that shows María's tears. This series of shots anticipates an idea that is developed at the end of the film: that María gains social status by sublimating her pain, like La Virgen de los Dolores. Yet, before her total transformation takes place, she has to accept the Church's power structure. In the final shot of the sequence, on her knees, María says: "There are so many of us asking you for things at all times! It is still not my time to be helped." When we contrast this scene to the one in which María complains that God is favoring the rich, it is clear that her mimicking the Virgin also involves relinquishing her ability to analyze and make social claims.[18] Instead, she has to accept that others, God in this case, make these decisions. The ability to think independently, we can conclude, is the price to pay for becoming the Virgin in the final scenes.[19] In *María Candelaria*, the protagonist learns to act Virgin-like: rather than complain, she accepts with humility that someone else, above her, knows better. That her acceptance is part of learning to act according to the Ideal of Virgin Motherhood brings up the question: What does María Candelaria, and the women characters who imitate Mary, gain from acting like the Virgin?

Women Imitate the Virgin to Gain a Place in Society

By imitating the Virgin, María Candelaria gains, according to Kristeva's interpretation of the Virgin, a place in society. For women, Kristeva argues, the Virgin plays a different role than for men. Following Freud's postulates, she assumes that women undergo a different psychological development in relation to the maternal figure. While men have to completely separate from their mothers, women do not have to separate so much, because usually they will also be mothers.[20] Starting with this difference, Kristeva postulates that for women, Mary is a model of motherhood; women become good mothers by imitating the Virgin.

Countering scholars who have viewed the figure of the Virgin exclusively as a vehicle to exercise social control over women, Kristeva argues that the construct of the Virgin helps to counter the abjection of women, giving women a position within the symbolic realm, or the Law of the Father. Kristeva maintains that patriarchal societies abject the female body on the grounds that it is unclean; women's bodies, with their presumed lack of order, cannot be accepted in the Catholic Church.[21] Abjection is the (recurring) state of attempting, but yet not being fully successful, in separating oneself from waste, polluting bodily fluids/excrescences/corpses, etc. Such separation is also from the maternal, and the maternal body becomes "the abject" object of revulsion which is neither self nor fully other. However, in the case of the Virgin, the association with abjection does not apply. The Virgin, especially in her aspect of Jesus' mother, is a construct that belongs to the Symbolic; Jesus is King and Mary is the Queen because she is his bride.[22]

Kristeva maintains that the feminine gains new, more positive meaning through Mary's entrance into the Symbolic. For example, breast milk and tears—bodily fluids associated with the semiotic, a pre-symbolic state, and abjected — are resemanticized in the cases of the Mater Dolorosa and the Virgin of Milk. The Virgin's tears and milk are associated with nurturance; in symbolically nurturing the Catholic Church, such fluids lose their threatening aspects. The Virgin facilitates the entrance of the female body into the Symbolic; although, as Kristeva admits, it does not completely get rid of the association of the semiotic with the abject.[23] By imitating the Virgin, as the case of María Candelaria illustrates, women can enter the Symbolic. However, the identification with Mary imposes clear limitations on women; María Candelaria is made to comply with the status quo. Thus, the Virgin is an ambivalent sign: it facilitates access to the Symbolic in exchange for submission to social control.

Conclusion

Chapter 2 calls for a reconsideration of the use of the concept of stereotype to study the representation of women in classical films. The chapter argues that the assumption that women are presented in a stereotypical way implies that films deform reality, creating a distorted cinematic world, and also that such distortion is imposed upon the audience rather than created by the society the audience belongs to. *Motherhood in Mexican Cinema, 1941–1991* moves away from binary oppositions used in previous scholarly studies such as "good mother" versus "bad mother" and instead uses the notion of ideal. The concept of a normative ideal is preferable in studying film because it implies that society actively revokes its ideals about how to be a woman; it assumes that individuals within a society create cultural projects, such as films, that manifest societal ideals.

The analysis of *Tepeyac,* in which the Virgin of Guadalupe is associated with intercession and wish fulfillment and not with how to be a mother or a woman, demonstrates that the Virgin of Guadalupe is not a paradigm of motherhood in the film. In contrast, a historical examination of the Virgin Mary across two thousand years reveals that Mary has been associated with motherhood, especially after the 1400s. Thus, the examination concludes that the Virgin Mary and not the Virgin of Guadalupe is the model of motherhood in Mexican cinema of the Golden Age.

Based on Warner and Kristeva's studies on the Virgin, Mary is understood as a construct. A constructed Mary can be studied with other cultural manifestations of the maternal. The advertisements and the drawing contest in the newspaper *Excélsior* on May 10 reveal that Mexicans connect the Virgin to mothers, and mothers to Sara García, through the symbol of the crown. In the chapters to follow, *Motherhood in Mexican Cinema, 1941–1991* treats the acceptance of the Immaculate Conception as dogma, the establishment of Mothers' Day, and the making of Sara García into an icon of motherhood as interrelated expressions of the maternal.

As *María Candelaria* illustrates, the Ideal of Virgin Motherhood consists in emulating the Virgin Mary; in the melodramas of the Golden Age, to be a woman and a mother is to act Virgin-like. The chapters that follow are dedicated to specific aspects of acting like the Virgin, such as adopting self-effacing personalities and acting as mediator. Each chapter contains at least one example from classical melodramas on how to act Virgin-like and the response third-wave filmmakers give to this particular issue of the ideal. Looking back from a third-wave perspective to films of the Golden Age opens up classical films, laying bare other prohibitions. Chapter 3 approaches the changes made to the mothers' moral attributes; chapter 4 examines the restrictions posed on mothers' agency; chapter 5 exposes the limitations mothers who want to have an autonomous identity have. Chapter 6 brings up third-wave responses to the perils of classical idealization in which mothers are held to a standard of goodness that is impossible to achieve.

3

The Qualities of Classical and Third-Wave Mothers

Chapter 3 examines the characteristics a "good mother" has to have in classical and third-wave films. The moral qualities of Doña Gracia, the mother in *Una familia de tantas*, are compared to those of a third-wave mother, Alma in *Ángel de fuego* (1991). The chapter focuses on a particular characteristic, humility, which is a core trait of the Ideal of Virgin Motherhood. To examine humility in relation to the maternal requires both tracing a history of how humility has been connected to femininity within Catholicism and how third-wave filmmakers have challenged humility. Also, given that the Ideal of Virgin Motherhood is based on the Virgin and that the Virgin is not a model for mothers in third-wave films, can we say that the characteristics of classical mothers are based on Christian values, while the attributes of third-wave mothers are not?

The second part of the chapter examines who benefits from classical and third-wave moralities. Do these moralities benefit children, mothers or both? After Judith Warner's critique of attachment theory, we can ask the question: how do classical and third-wave films balance the interests of children and mothers? To answer this question, chapter 3 compares the classical film *Salón México* (Fernández 1949) and the third-wave narrative *Danzón* (Novaro 1991).

A History of Humility

The Ideal of Virgin Motherhood is based on a particular idea about the Virgin: Mary as a humble mother. Up until the thirteenth century, the Virgin was thought of as a queen, not as a woman; that is the reason why she appeared at the side of a grown-up Jesus. Starting in the thirteenth and early fourteenth centuries, however, she was transformed into a humble mother. Fundamental to this lowering of status from queen to humble servant was the doctrine of Francis of Assisi (1181–1226), founder of the Franciscans. This radical brand of Christianity, which emphasized poverty and humility, eventually removed her regalia and transformed her into a mother and housewife (Warner 1976, 177–191).

Although the prejudice against women, Warner (1976) maintains, is present in Greek and Jewish thought (177–80), the emphasis on women's humility is particularly strong in the Late Middle Ages. With the transition from feudalism to a bourgeoisie society, the incipient thirteenth-century bourgeoisie needed a new ideal for women. In the new society, based on commerce, middle-class women were able to stay at home instead of working outside in the fields. Europe's newborn bourgeoisie class used Assisi's ideas to serve their needs: "The cult of humility, understood as female submissiveness to the head of the house set the seal on the Virgin's eclipse as a matriarchal symbol" (Warner 188). Saint Francis of Assisi's ideas about humility and obedience were used after the fourteenth century to make women's submissiveness seem logical and natural.

The Characteristics of Classical Mothers in *Una familia de tantas*

In classical films, it is important that women and mothers are humble and submissive. In *Una familia de tantas*, the most important characteristics of housewife and mother Doña Gracia (Eugenia Galindo) are purity, self-sacrifice, and submissiveness. Her name, Ms. Grace, alludes to a state of grace, and thus to purity, innocence and a state of kindness and favor toward others. Chapter 4 examines Doña Gracia's purity, the first characteristic of the Ideal of Virgin Motherhood. This chapter is dedicated to Doña Gracia's humbleness and modesty as a mother, the second characteristic of the Ideal of Virgin Motherhood.

Like a post–thirteenth-century painting of Mary, Doña Gracia keeps her head lowered. For example, Doña Gracia spends most of the time at the kitchen working during her second daughter's coming-of-age party.

Even though, as the mother, she is an important member of the family, in *Una familia de tantas* her humbleness is not presented as degrading. The mother's self-effacement is such that it is as if she prefers to be in the kitchen; her modesty is presented as something natural. Doña Gracia does not resemble a Pantocrator Virgin, who stands erect by the side of her son (or daughter in this case), but rather humble Mary, who lowers her head at the sight of Jesus. At her daughter's celebration Doña Gracia "lowers her head," like Mary,

3. The Qualities of Classical and Third-Wave Mothers 51

Una familia de tantas, daughter's party (Colección Filmoteca de la UNAM).

by staying behind in the kitchen. Audiences in the 1940s viewed Doña Gracia as a morally superior being for this kind of self-effacement.

Doña Gracia also has submission, the third characteristic of the Ideal of Virgin Motherhood. In Mexican melodramas, submissiveness is portrayed as a positive trait because of its association with mediation. Obedient wives such as Doña Gracia play the same role that the Virgin plays within the Christian community at large: they intercede for the community before God, making sure that the community obeys his law. The role of the mother in *Una familia de tantas* (as well as in many other maternal melodramas) is to act as a mediator between the strict, old-fashioned, intransigent father and his modern, dynamic children. Father and children are portrayed as two groups that stand apart from each other. As mediators, mothers have a twofold task: they intercede for the children, but at the same time they subject them, and themselves, to the patriarch.

Doña Gracia, for example, intercedes for their daughter Lupita in a scene in which the father has punished her by ordering her to go to school without breakfast. The mother does not contradict the father in front of him, but once the father is gone, she doesn't stop Guadalupe, the maid, from sneaking some breakfast to Lupita. It is assumed that despite his good intentions, the patriarch is too harsh with his children, and it is up to the mother to function as intercessor, lessening the punishment, so that the connection between father and children remains. We can say of Doña Gracia what was said of fourteenth-century housewives: "The woman, sweet and submissive to her husband, could be honored at the cradle, kitchen, and in medieval times, the spinning wheel" (Warner 1976, 188). Like a medieval wife, Doña Gracia would not assert her ideas against those of Don Rodrigo.

THE SELF-ASSERTING ATTRIBUTES OF THIRD-WAVE MOTHERS: *ÁNGEL DE FUEGO*

Unlike classical mothers, third-wave mothers, like Alma in Dana Rotberg's *Ángel de fuego*, have self-affirming characteristics. This film, made by

Alma as an innocent thirteen-year-old (photograph by Daniel Daza, courtesy Dana Rotberg).

a Jewish filmmaker, questions the role of religious leaders and the association between self-effacement and motherhood. As the title hints, Rotberg links the actions of the thirteen-year-old mother to the Bible's Exterminating Angel. At the beginning of the film, Alma, a circus performer, has a number that is called the Angel of fire; at the end of the film, the protagonist becomes the Angel of Fire. Rotberg's *Ángel de fuego* examines, confronts, and at times reaffirms the religious thought in the Bible.

Confrontation versus Submission

In *Ángel de fuego*, trapeze artist Alma (Evangelina Sosa) has incestuous relations with her father, the clown Renato (Alejandro Parodi). The clown dies near the beginning of the movie, and Alma, pregnant by her father, insists on having the baby, and because of this she must leave the circus. She joins a group of puppeteers who enact passages from the Bible and whose leader is the priestess Refugio (Lilia Aragón). Horrified by Alma's incestuous relations, Refugio promises to "cleanse" her through sacrifice and fasting. Alma's desire to having her child clashes with the philosophy of the evangelical group at many levels. The first indication of this conflict takes place at a performance of the story of Abraham. Refugio's voice introduces the story by saying that Sarah and Abraham were very old, and thus had lost hope of having a child, but that God was good to them and gave them a son, Isaac. At this point, the voice of God is played in a tape recorder, telling Abraham: "Take your son to the mountain and offer him to me. Kill him with your own hands."[1] The scene cuts to a medium shot of anguished Alma and then to a counter shot of Noé (Noé Montealegre), a child puppeteer, gesturing to Alma to calm down and recite her part of the dialogue: "Don't do it Abraham. By showing your willingness to sacrifice your son you have proven your respect for God. Sacrifice a lamb, God will have it instead of your son."[2] After the puppet show is over, Alma questions the logic of the Old Testament. She asks Noe: "Why did God ask Abraham to kill his son?"[3] Noe answers: "He was only testing him."[4] Alma responds, "Yes, but he was going to kill him."[5] Alma's reservations about the cruelty of the Old Testament are expressed in her conclusion that "Abraham loved God more than his child."[6] Although Alma is only a naïve thirteen year old, her words challenge the thought in the Bible. Because of her defiance, the audience watching *Ángel de fuego* is pointed in the direction of thinking that the religious thought in the Old Testament is cruel. From this, the audience may infer that religious thought hinders Alma's development as a human being. Rather than accepting religious thought, as classical films do, third-wave films like *Ángel de fuego* question its rationale.

Ángel de fuego also questions the institutions and people who deliver religious thought. In the film, sinners seeking forgiveness need to repent and, in many cases, go through penance and sacrifice. This idea is introduced through a book, *El libro del perdón* (*The Book of Pardon*), that the priestess Refugio carries with her to all her religious puppet shows. After each performance, she brings out the book, and people in the audience can inscribe their names in it and be pardoned. It is assumed that the people writing their names have repented. Yet, in some cases, repentance is not enough. When Alma gets in line to have her name written in *El libro del perdón*, Refugio, denies her pardon.

Refugio argues that Alma is not yet "clean." Horrified by her incestuous relation, the priestess insists that Alma go through penance and fasting. Refugio's refusal to pardon Alma for her incest is questioned by the film's narrative: if Alma is a victim of poverty and a dysfunctional family, why should Refugio deny her pardon? Alma's willingness to follow the religious leader's request and honest desire to cleanse her sin of incest leads the audience to consider whether she should have to prove her faith by fasting.

The *libro del perdón* scene reiterates the idea that the cruelty in the Bible reappears in the religious leader herself. The suspicion about priestess Refugio turns to anger once the audience learns that she is a corrupt leader who uses

Alma waiting to be pardoned (photograph by Daniel Daza, courtesy Dana Rotberg).

religion for her own benefit. She is willing to sacrifice Alma's unborn child to advance the future of her son, Sacramento (Roberto Sosa). A scene of Refugio talking to God and asking for a sign that God has chosen Sacramento as a leader is followed by another scene in which Alma loses her child.

Afterward, Refugio thanks God for having answered her prayer. In the context of the story of Abraham, the conversation of the priestess with God underscores Refugio's hypocrisy: she offers a gift to God as a proof that she loves him. However, she does not offer her own son, but someone else's. *Ángel de fuego* exposes Refugio's double standards: while requesting sacrifice and fasting from a sinner, she sins herself by using Alma's unborn child to help advance the career of her son. Refugio's actions are used in *Ángel de fuego* to show that leaders can be corrupt and use religion for their own benefit.

From Submission to Rebellion

The characteristics of the mother in *Ángel de fuego* evolve as a response to the dubious religious context in which Alma finds herself. At first, "blind"

Alma's defiant look at Refugio (photograph by Daniel Daza, courtesy Dana Rotberg).

Alma is submissive, and innocently follows the religious leader's directives. She tells Refugio: "With the penance that you gave me I feel cleaner. I think that now my baby is going to be beautiful."[7] But Refugio quashes Alma's hopes by responding, "God spoke to me and told me that your sin was very big." At this point Alma protests: "You told me that with obedience and faith it would be pardoned."[8]

Alma follows the directives given to her, despite her suspicions that Refugio has personal reasons for insisting that she fast. She is aware that the penance puts the life of her unborn child in jeopardy. She believes that fasting is the only way in which her son will not become a monster, and so she surrenders to the path indicated by the religious leader out of maternal love. Since the audience knows that Refugio is using Alma's unborn child to advance the career of her son, Alma appears innocent and unprotected.

Alma's rebellious reaction is accentuated by her change of clothing. Until the fasting scene Alma has been wearing the red dress she uses for her Ángel de fuego performance. In the fasting scene, however, she is shown wearing a tunic and kneeling in a circle of stones with her arms extended as if she were Jesus. As she dreaded, fasting causes a miscarriage. She is shown bleeding profusely with her legs closed tightly, saying: "Don't come out. Don't come out." By trying to abide by Refugio's rules and secure a place within the religious community, Alma loses what is more dear to her, her baby.

Alma's reaction to the death of her unborn child is a shock. If she would have been a mother in a classical film, Alma would have been obedient and accepted God's decision; she would have sobbed and cried for her lost child. Instead, Alma reacts with anger, becoming the Bible's Angel of Fire. Like the Fourth Angel, who "poured out his bowl on the sun, causing it to scorch everyone with its fire (Rev. 16:9, New International Version, 1984), the thirteen-year-old mother turns to fire. She returns to the circus to bring justice to those who did not support her through her pregnancy. After freeing the circus animals, she burns the circus' high top with herself inside. It is a long scene in which the fire destroys the circus piece by piece; the scorching of the big top at night lasts four minutes. The length of the scene is essential to connect Alma to the Angel of Fire. At the beginning of the film the protagonist dresses in red and has a trapeze act as the Angel of Fire, by the end she has become the Fourth Angel.

Alma brings justice to the evangelical group too, figuratively blazing them. Angered at the priestess, whom the protagonist blames for the loss of her child, Alma punishes her. In a scene before Alma's miscarriage, *Ángel de fuego* had hinted that Sacramento sexually desired Alma and also that he had not acted on his desire because Refugio had imposed a strict celibacy rule. If he wanted to be a prophet, he had to maintain sexual purity. While Refugio

Alma makes love to Sacramento ((photograph by Daniel Daza, courtesy Dana Rotberg).

is absent, Alma makes love to Sacramento, and once the prophet to be has lost his virginity, he commits suicide. Thus, through Alma's seduction, Refugio loses what is most precious to her.

The death of Sacramento, like the burning of the circus, is presented as biblical justice. On the way back from visiting Sacramento, Alma meets with Refugio in the street. As they look at each other, Alma tells the religious leader: "An eye for an eye." Refugio's long and deep wail indicates that she understands the meaning of the biblical sentence: "A son for a son. You killed my son, I killed yours." This scene raises the question: is Rotberg reasserting religious values or is she being ironic?

The substitution of self-effacing qualities for self-affirming ones in the characterization of her mother seems to indicate that *Ángel de fuego* has moved away from religious values. Yet, Rotberg uses biblical ideas, like the existence of an Angel of Fire, and biblical wisdom, like "an eye for an eye," to point in the opposite direction. We can conclude that what *Ángel de fuego* leaves behind is the prejudice against women that was prevalent in Greek thought and Judaism and became part of the Bible.

Mary and the Theological and Cardinal Virtues

The construct of Mary only emphasizes some virtues of the Catholic ethic (Warner 1976, 184–186). In analyzing a fourteenth-century enamel plaque that portrays the Virgin and the child at the center of a tree in which the virtues are perched, Warner notes:

> Of the theological virtues only charity is present (faith and hope omitted); of the cardinal, only prudence (not fortitude, justice or temperance). Humility, patience, obedience, compassion, purity, truth, praise, all take their place around Mary [185].

Examining the virtues represented in the plaque, Warner concludes that Mary's qualities are only selectively Christian. Self-affirming virtues like fortitude, justice or temperance are omitted, while self-effacing virtues are emphasized. The omission of self-affirming virtues in the construction of Mary, Warner remarks, points to the misogyny prevalent in Christian thought. The ideal of the humble housewife and mother is used to make women comply with humility, patience, obedience, compassion, purity, truth, and praise. Just like the Virgin, mothers like Doña Gracia do not need to have fortitude or bring justice in order to be considered "good."

JUSTICE, FORTITUDE AND TEMPERANCE

Ángel de fuego responds to classical films by giving its young mother some of the virtues that classical mothers lack. If we look at *Una familia de tantas* from the biblical perspective set by the story of Abraham and the Fourth Angel, Doña Gracia lacks justice, fortitude and temperance. Despite living with domineering Don Rodrigo, who is presented as extremely inflexible and authoritarian, Doña Gracia does not show courage to oppose his inflexibility. She acts meekly by letting Lupita have breakfast once the father is gone. Doña Gracia lacks fortitude and her actions do not bring justice. For justice to occur, the dominant father would be made more flexible. Doña Gracia doesn't exhibit temperance either. When she clasps her hand as if praying and covers her face with her hands but says nothing, she exhibits self-restraint, but her action is closer to cowardice than temperance.

In contrast, Alma's actions as the Fourth Angel do exhibit fortitude, temperance and justice. Alma acts with the same justice that the Angel of Fire acts when he marked the doors of those who had to be killed: the circus community and Refugio had acted unfairly and Alma brings them to justice. In conducting these actions, Alma acts with self-restraint, determination and resolution; at no time is she shown losing control, doubting or whimpering.

When she becomes the Fourth Angel, she exhibits resilience, strength, and determination. *Ángel de fuego* redefines the qualities of mothers, bringing self-assertive values to an otherwise psychological make-up of self-effacement.

Rotberg's Third-Wave Mother: A Challenge to Film Critics

How did Mexican audiences respond to Rotberg's challenge of the Ideal of Virgin Motherhood? Most of the reviews written about *Ángel de fuego* do not directly address the change from self-effacement to self-assertion, however there is an indirect response in the film critics' position with regards to incest.

Incest plays an important role in defining Alma in *Ángel de fuego*. Rebellious Alma is not ashamed of having had an incestuous relationship with her father. This idea is conveyed through a large photograph of clown Renato that Alma wears around her neck after her father dies at the beginning of the film.

Despite Josefina and Refugio's accusations that incest is a very big sin,

Alma with Renato's photograph (photograph by Daniel Daza, courtesy Dana Rotberg).

Alma does not feel guilt or shame. Her response is purely practical: out of motherly care for her child she submits to penance and fasts so she can save the child from becoming a monster. Her violent response after she losses her child is also without remorse; she commits suicide not because she feels "dirty" for having had a sexual relationship with her father, but because she has lost what she loved the most.

The representation of incest in *Ángel de fuego* challenged audiences in Mexico. The film that opened the Quinzaine des Realizateurs at the Cannes Film Festival in 1991 was nominated for fourteen Ariels, the Mexican equivalent of the Academy Awards. In spite of all these nominations, the film did not win any awards in Mexico (Ramos Navas 1993). The reasons why *Ángel de fuego* was not awarded any Ariels can be found by looking at the reviews written by Mexican film critics.

In general, the press reacted not against incest itself, but against the film's ability to show incest from Alma's perspective: from the meager economic and emotional conditions in which she lives. Using Kaja Silverman's concept of assimilation, film critics' reactions to the film can be divided into three categories: those who assimilated Alma, those who assimilated some aspects of Alma but not all of them, and those who respected the distance that separated them from Alma.[9] The critics in the first group viewed Alma's insistence on having her father's child as odd and sickening, and surely as something that did not happen in Mexico. At times, love is intertwined with pity for the deidealized motherhood that in their view Alma represents. For instance, in the review "Ángel de fuego," Julia Elena Melche (1992) refers to Alma as "small" and "defenseless."[10] Melche's wish to protect defenseless Alma is an emotion that implies assimilation; it is a love that wants to protect but in doing so, disregards Alma's point of view. Gabriela Bautista also wants to protect Alma, but rather than showing pity, she makes the father, whom she refers to as "an incestuous and decrepit father," a scapegoat.[11] Bautista reacts with self-righteousness, not wanting to accept Alma's situation as she perceives it or her need to love the only person who cared for her.[12] Like Bautista, male critic Naief Yehya (1993) also feels that Alma needs protection, but unlike Bautista he expresses this using sarcasm. He writes: "Alma, trapeze actor, throws fire from the Fantasía Circus. She is a girl who is in love with her father, who would also be the father of his grandchild if he would not die of being so 'hot.'"[13] Yehya defends Alma by accusing Renato of being "hot," sexually aroused by his own daughter. His accusation, however, implies a rejection of the reasons that Alma had to sexually love her father, and consequently his protectiveness implies assimilation of Alma's point of view to his. Despite their good intentions, these critics identify with Alma in a cannibalistic way by disregarding Alma's otherness, her desire to have her child.

The second group of critics partially respected Alma's desire to have her child. For Susana López Aranda (1993), Alma's incest is a "desperate act of love,"[14] and for Jesús Ortega Mendoza (1993) "a reality that is incomprehensible for her [Alma]. She has in her womb the product of an incestuous love that she has had with her father clown Renato (Alejandro Parodi), a man of bad health that dies when she most needs him."[15] While these critics accept the film's tenet that incest took place in a loving situation, their views express aversion to such an act; incest is associated with desperation and presented as something incomprehensible. These critics came halfway toward respecting Alma's desire to have her child; while they acknowledge Alma's perspective, they do not respect it — instead assimilating it to their own point of view.

The third group of critics takes a critical distance from Alma's wish to have her child. For example, Ysabel Gracida (1993) approaches *Ángel de fuego* by trying to understand the situation. In her review she mentions that "*Ángel de fuego*'s incest contradicts the tabloid press" because it "is an incest that is born not from violence, but that takes place almost as a natural behavior in a hostile medium where the traditional idea of a family has lost all its conventions." Given the emotional and economic poverty in which Alma lives, incest, according to Gracida, is the trapeze artist's way of getting affection. Gracida writes:

> Underworld?, circus of poverty, redundant if it could be, the context in which Alma (Evangelina Sosa) has grown up takes her, in an almost natural way to the arms of her aging and sick father, the only affective tie that the trapeze artist wants to perpetuate.[16]

By searching for Alma's unique perspective in the social conditions that surround her, Gracida is able to understand Alma's motivation and thus move away from assimilation. The respectful love that Gracida shows for Alma contrasts with the protective love shown by the critics from the first group, Melche and Bautista. Gracida (1993) loves Alma in spite of her love for Renato. When she writes that Alma's incest is "a natural behavior in a hostile medium where the traditional idea of a family has lost all its conventions," she is accepting the conditions from which Alma has come. Thus, unlike Bautista, Gracida does not assimilate Alma's otherness into her own. What is more, Gracida's description of Alma leads to an identification with her condition of being other. Rather than considering Alma's incest an aberration, Gracida's explanation illuminates Alma's life by calling attention, with love, to the conditions in which Alma lives: extreme emotional and economic poverty.

Tomás Pérez Turrent, who wrote five reviews about *Ángel de fuego*, shares Gracida's understanding. In "*Ángel de fuego* y otros asuntos" Pérez Turrent (1992) mentions that "Dana Rotberg does not have a self-righteous look, she has a look of surprise towards a world that she can't grasp because of its complexity and that attracts her for its unforeseen possibilities."[17] For Pérez Turrent, Rotberg replaces a self-righteous look, one that knows what is right and wrong, with a look of surprise, a look that is open to understanding a world that is hard to grasp. In other words, Pérez Turrent makes a distinction between being condescending, knowing what is good or bad for the other, and being open to the differences of the other, what he calls "a look of surprise."

Ángel de fuego received mixed reviews. Some critics accept Alma's way of being a mother, given the conditions in which she lives; others reject her actions. The fact that the film did not receive any Ariels together with the reaction of the critics, shows that Rotberg's mother challenged prevailing views of motherhood in Mexico.

Psychoanalysis and Incest

The interpretation of incest and monstrosity in Barbara Almond's *The Monster Within: The Hidden Side of Motherhood* (2010) gives us another way to examine incest in *Ángel de fuego* and the responses from film critics. A psychoanalyst, Almond examines real cases and literary accounts of women who are afraid of having a monstrous child. "My interest in maternal ambivalence began when I was treating a patient who feared any baby she had would be a 'monster,'" Almond explains (51). "Thinking about other women with similar worries, I realized that maternal aggression is frequently handled by being experienced as residing in a demanding and insatiable child, often described as a monster" (51). Almond relates the mothers' fear of monstrosity to several psychological concerns (51), most importantly to incestuous feelings. She proposes that mothers' shame at having had incestuous feelings surfaces in the fantasy of having a monstrous child; such is the case of one of her patients which in the book she calls Amanda (65, 67).

The psychoanalyst's interpretation of monstrosity when analyzing her patients is in sharp contrast to *Ángel de fuego*. In Roterg's film the fears of monstrosity belong not to the mother, but to the society the mother belongs to. For example, at the beginning of *Ángel de fuego* Alma is not afraid that her child is going to be a monster. This fear is introduced by Alma's surrogate mother, Josefina (Merche Pascual), who tells Alma that her sin of incest is so evil that her baby will be born a monster. Priestess Refugio is another person who instills the fear of monstrosity into the thirteen-year-old mother; she tells Alma that her sin of incest was very bad.

Rotberg and Almond relate the feelings of monstrosity to very different sources. Provocatively, in Rotberg's film external agents (Refugio and Josefina) create the sense of guilt and shame in the mother. In contrast, in Almond's interpretations the fear of monstrosity is within the mothers psyche and related to the mothers relations to family members. This idea is implied in the title of Almond's book *The Monster Within: The Hidden Side of Motherhood*. The title suggests that the shame of mothers at having had incestuous feelings resurfaces in the fear that they have a monster lurking inside them that will come out in the form of a baby. *Ángel de fuego* proposes a completely different understanding of monstrosity and incest. Not only does Alma not feel shame for having had an incestuous relation, she is also not afraid of having a monster lurking inside her. In Rotberg's film the monster is not within the mother, it is outside, in the society in which the mother lives. The positioning of monstrosity indicates the internalization of shame: in Almond's examples the mothers have internalized shame. In contrast, in the third-wave film Alma has not internalized shame. What are the implications of creating a mother who is not ashamed of incest and reacts with anger to the loss of her child?

From Shame to Healthy Anger

In *The Colonization of Psychic Space*, Kelly Oliver (2004) suggests that anger is a healthier way to react than shame. Oliver dedicates a section entitled "Shame and Depressive Identity" (112–120) to an examination of the underpinnings of shame and anger as they relate to the subject's ability to act. She refers to a study by Helen Block Lewis (1978) in which Lewis compares the way in which male and female undergraduates explain why things did not work in their lives. The study shows that female undergraduates were more likely to blame their character than male undergraduates, who tended to blame their behavior. From Lewis's distinction between being and behaving, Oliver (2004) concludes that women tend to react with shame, while males tend to react with guilt (112). She considers both feelings oppressive but points out that "Shame is more deeply seated in subjectivity than guilt" (112). Looking at the implications of Lewis's study for society at large, Oliver writes: "Those excluded or abjected by dominant values are made to feel ashamed, not about something they have done, but about who they are" (114). She then proposes that alienated people are the depository for the shame of the dominant culture (117). In other words, the dominant culture uses shame to make the marginalization of certain groups, including women, seem logical.

Oliver's study of shame puts *Ángel de fuego*'s mother into perspective. Unlike the female undergraduates in Lewis's study Alma does not feel shame. The photograph that Alma wears around her neck expresses the young mother's defiant love for her father and her desire to see her pregnancy to term. What is more important, in defying shame, she moves away from the position allotted to women in the dominant culture. If, as Oliver claims, shame is used to make alienation seem logical, by creating a character who does not feel shame Rotberg moves away from society's alienation.

In the same study, Oliver (2004) explains that the negative images that society projects on women can be treated by women in two ways. If they internalize them, they feel shame: "The subject experiences itself as a damaged, defective or flawed being who deserves to be ostracized" (114). If women reject the negative images, they will feel anger. Oliver argues that rage provides a much healthier response than shame, since the feeling of being flawed leads to inaction and thus to depression. Her explanation of the consequences of internalizing shame further corroborates the idea that Alma's reaction to the death of her unborn child is a healthier way to react. By reacting with anger, Alma avoids alienation.

The externalization of shame and the surfacing of anger were noticed by two Mexican film critics who wrote reviews about *Ángel de fuego*. Tomás Pérez Turrent (1993) titled his review "Ángel exterminador" ("Exterminating Angel") in order to highlight a dramatic emotional change in Alma: at the beginning of the film, Alma is a thirteen-year-old trapeze artist dressed as an angel of fire, but by the end of the film, Alma incarnates the Bible's cruel Exterminating Angel.[18] Another critic, Jesús Ortega Mendoza (1993), suggested that the sect that Alma joins transforms her into a vengeful angel (*angel de venganza*). Is it revenge, as Mendoza suggests, or is it justice, like Pérez Turrent hints?

Clearly, Rotberg does not create a heroic character, but a tragic one. Alma is wronged by the community, but by acting against the community and making Sacramento commit suicide, she loses her innocence. Pérez Turrent and Ortega Mendoza's reviews illustrate two possible interpretations of Alma's anger and of moral virtue. Ortega Mendoza's emphasis on revenge suggests reprisal and retaliation, and links Alma's actions to immorality and blame. In contrast, Pérez Turrent's association to the Fourth Angel and justice suggests fairness, impartiality and rightness, and relates Alma's actions to virtue, morality, and integrity. In this way Pérez Turrent values the self-asserting values that Alma represents, whereas Ortega Mendoza criticizes them.

Who Benefits from the Films' Morals? Third-Wave Films and the Theory of Maternal Deprivation

The second part of the chapter relates notions of morality to the needs of children and mothers. A "good mother" is often defined as one who takes good care of children. However, exactly how much and what kind of care should a mother provide to be considered good? This question was inspired by Judith Warner's study on motherhood in United States in the 2000s. In *Perfect Madness: Motherhood in the Age of Anxiety* (2005) Warner, a well-established journalist and biographer, explains that during the 1970s feminist movement, women achieved a certain degree of self-actualization and self-esteem. Feminists understood that the social gains women had attained in the public sphere would eventually cause changes in their private lives. However, during the 1980s changes within the home did not materialize, and the emphasis shifted from caring for the well-being of mothers to caring for the well-being of children. By the end of the 1980s and into the 1990s, children, not mothers, became the focus of societal preoccupation. To empower children with self-actualization and self-esteem became the goal, and as the title of Warner's book suggests, it was a road to perfect madness for mothers.

Warner maintains that attachment theory was the means by which U.S. society in the 1980s shifted toward children-centered concerns. John Bowlby's theory of "maternal deprivation" was used in the United States to justify the new focus on children's psychological needs. In *Maternal Care and Mental Health* (1952) Bowlby, a British psychoanalyst and psychiatrist, studied homeless children or orphans who had been separated from their mothers during times of war. Bowlby's theory, also known as "attachment theory," demonstrates that separation from mothers affected the children's disposition and character during adulthood.

Attachment theory, Warner (2005) contends, was used in the 1980s to reinsert ideas about "bad mothers" (94). In the 1950s, before Bowlby's time, it was commonly understood that mothers were to take care of their children's physical needs (92). However, in the 1980s, mothers also became responsible for the psychological problems of their children. Warner argues that Bowlby's theory was misused in the 1980s: the theory that explained the traumatic experiences of children at the times of war was applied to children in families during peace time. "The linking of nightmare experiences of children lost and abandoned to mundane everyday situations of short-term separation became attachment theory's legacy" (94). Attachment theory was the scientific basis that allowed a return to notions of bad mothering; mothers who worked and thus had less time to take care of children were blamed for children's psychological problems, including their anxiety (94).

Warner's claim can be substantiated by examining Barbara Almond's (2010) *The Monster Within*. Sometimes, Almond is critical of the abuse of attachment theory. For example, she describes a daughter who told her parents, "If they did not let their grand-child sleep with them (when they were babysitting) it would interfere with his sense of security, possibly forever"

(229). While most possibly a grandson who is used to sleeping in his parents bed will have problems sleeping by himself, it is not clear that sleeping in his own bed will affect his sense of security forever. At other times, Almond is less critical. Assumptions derived from attachment theory are inserted into the interpretations she makes of her clients' problems. For example, when analyzing the reasons why thirty-five-year-old married architect Amanda has ambivalent feelings about being a mother, Almond writes:

> In her first year of life Amanda spent six months in a harness to correct her congenital hip dysplasia.... During this time her mother had severe arthritis in her hands, which made it difficult to "hold and diaper her baby girl." Normal cuddling and soothing were disrupted. This disruption of mother-infant intimacy was partially offset by the mothers' concern and presence. She might not have been able to pick the baby up, but she used her voice to soothe and comfort her. Amanda loved her mother, but something was still missing [66].

Almond's interpretation of Amanda's case leads the reader to believe that Amanda's aversion to motherhood comes from the disruption that took place when she was one year old. The "something" that "was still missing" is the attachment between Amanda and her mother. Although Amanda's mother was present with her voice, she could not cuddle her. In Almond's interpretation, attachment theory is taken out of context. As a baby, Amanda was not abandoned because her parents had died, like the orphans that Bowlby theorizes about; she was well taken care of. Besides, how could a one-year-old baby tell the difference between having the nurses change her diapers and cuddle her or her mother? And how could this change in caretakers create Amanda's aversion to motherhood?

In the light of analysis like Almond's, we need to ask: how are mother's needs accounted for in today's views of mother-children relations? While the concern for children, who are seen as helpless and unable to take care of themselves, is to a certain extent understandable, the balance between children's and mothers' needs requires examination. Thus, the question: How do classical and third-wave films balance the self-actualization of mothers and children? Two films that take place in the same dance hall, Colonia, are used to compare how each narrative justifies the investment in the care of mothers and children, the classical film *Salón México* and the third-wave film *Danzón* (1991).

SALÓN MÉXICO, A CHILD-CENTERED NARRATIVE

Emilio Fernández's film presents the life of an older sister, Mercedes, who cares for her younger sister, Beatriz, as a mother. *Salón México*'s protagonist follows the Ideal of Virgin Motherhood. In her one-room house, there is a portrait of the Virgin hanging on the wall, and during the film Mercedes is shown placing a flower offering under the portrait of the Virgin. Mercedes joins worship with imitation of the Virgin: she emulates the Virgin by being maternal, by taking care of her sister.

The moral status of mothers is brought up toward the end of the film, during Beatriz's final exam. When asked to talk about heroes, Beatriz includes saints, like Saint Francis and Saint Bernardine; wise people, like Pasteur and Madame Curie; and war heroes, such as battle fighters. According to Beatriz, mothers also belong to this group of heroes because they "fight against all odds to get their children one step up."

If we take Beatriz's words as a definition of classical morality, Mercedes would be a heroic mother because she works very hard to get her "child" an education that will open up possibilities beyond prostitution. Selfless Mercedes uses the money she makes at the dance hall, Salón Mexico, toward her younger sister's education. Paying for Beatriz's expenses in an upper-middle-class school is understood as a maternal act in *Salón México*. Mercedes' boyfriend, Lupe López, explicitly links Mercedes's care of Beatriz with the maternal when he tells Beatriz: "Your sister is more than a mother for you." Beatriz's fiancé, Roberto, also relates Mercedes's sacrifice for Beatriz to the maternal when he says: "[Mercedes] sacrifices for her younger sister like a mother." Mercedes's efforts, it seems at first, qualify her as a mother.

Mercedes's work, however, disqualifies her. *Salón México* orchestrates the dramatic tension around Mercedes's morality. This tension is created by the collision of what the film sees as two opposing worlds: Mercedes's work in the cabaret on the one hand, and her ambition to mother her younger sister Beatriz on the other. The difference between the world of the dance hall and the all girls' boarding school where Beatriz studies is hinted at by Mercedes's use of two sets of clothes. On the days in which she visits Beatriz at the school, Mercedes irons elegant and respectable clothing, unlike the more revealing clothes she wears to work. This moral tension is eventually resolved against Mercedes, when she is deemed unacceptable as a mother.

Toward the end of the film, the principal of Beatriz's school substitutes Mercedes in her role as mother. After Beatriz's exam, the principal embraces Beatriz and the viewer is lead to believe that Beatriz has gained a morally superior mother. At this emotional moment, Roberto, who is Beatriz's future husband and also the principal's son, returns from the morgue. While the camera takes a long shot of Roberto, the soundtrack announces the triumph of morality with festive music. The music alludes to Roberto's heroism as a pilot wounded in war and, simultaneously, anticipates a happy ending. A close-up of Roberto looking at Beatriz, in a shot reverse-shot fashion, follows a medium shot of the couple looking at each other. The audience is lead to interpret these looks as a sign of their love. Afterward, in a long shot, the principal gives away "her new daughter." Before leaving the principal's arms to go to Roberto's, however, Beatriz looks in her new mother's eyes for her approval. Beatriz's principal provides the stable home that Mercedes couldn't provide.

Salón México exemplifies a child-centered morality. The best interest of the child is given precedence over the interest of her mother. The focus on Beatriz's marriage is the reason why Mercedes has to die. After her death, Beatriz's life can improve. Mercedes's theft is the motive used in the narrative to justify substituting a sacrificing mother for the principal in Beatriz's school. In order to get rid of Mercedes, *Salón México* juxtaposes a scene in the cabaret in which one of the clients complains because Mercedes has stolen money from him, to Beatriz's final exam. By including the theft scene, *Salón México* makes clear that although Mercedes sacrifices herself for the benefit of her sister, she does not have the moral qualities of a mother. Classical morality requires that mothers be able to teach their children the differences between good and bad, and as *Salón México* illustrates, Mercedes does not know them.

From a third-wave point of view, *Salón México* uses a suspect morality: Mercedes's work at the cabaret, including her stealing, enables Beatriz to attend school and advance her social position. Yet, while the film's narrative disapproves of Mercedes's actions, it still allows Beatriz to marry Roberto, which is the result of these actions. This is possible because *Salón México* creates a child-centered morality in which the well-being of children takes center stage. The film ends with the anticipation of a better life for Beatriz and a token recognition of the efforts of the sacrificing mother. The line, "She shouldn't have died," in the final song is a nostalgic remembrance of Mercedes's efforts. Yet, at the same time, the line makes her death necessary. Mercedes has to die so that Beatriz can "get a step up."

In *Salón México* the best interest of Beatriz is so important that taking Mercedes's life is justified. Much like Stella (Barbara Stanwyck) in the much studied film *Stella Dallas* (King Vidor 1937), Mercedes is pushed aside and sees her daughter's marriage from the tomb. A mother should be willing to die to better her child.[19]

Mothers' Self-Actualization in *Danzón*

In *Danzón,* Novaro returns to a classical film scenario, the well-known Salón Colonia, to pay homage and question the 1949 cabaretera film *Salón México*. Julia attends weekly dances at the same dance hall where Mercedes worked. *Danzón*'s reference to Golden Age classics is reinforced by the sound track, which includes several hits by famous singers Agustín Lara and Toña La negra.

Though taking place at the same cabaret, *Danzón* and *Salón México*'s position on the morality of sex workers differs considerably. In *Salón México*, mother love and sacrifice are not enough for Mercedes to be considered a "good mother." In contrast, in *Danzón*, la Colorada's (Blanca Guerra) sacrifice and mother love, expressed in very tender scenes in which she bathes and puts to bed her two children, make her a good mother. *Salón México*'s concealed disapproval of Mercedes's profession and *Danzón*'s approval of la Colorada's illustrate radically different morals: in the third-wave film to be a sex worker is compatible with being a good mother; in the classical film it is not. However, the difference between classical and third-wave morality goes beyond the way in which each film established the sexual limits of mothers.

In *Salón México* the mother is created as a character without needs and thus without a need for self-actualization. All we know about Mercedes is that the most important thing in her life is Beatriz, and the same can be said of Doña Gracia or Doña Lupe. In contrast, in *Danzón* the mother's well-being and adjustment to a new cycle of life takes center stage. Julia, played by actress María Rojo, needs to adjust to Perla's request for more freedom. Teenager Perla is presented as a reasonable adolescent who has interests and friends of her own. As if she were a mother a la Sara García, Julia misses Perla; she does not welcome the extra time for herself and decrease in her maternal responsibilities. In several scenes Julia is portrayed as being moody and giving sharp answers to her coworkers and clients. A dance hall devotee and lover of danzón, a Caribbean-based dance, Julia feels bored and lonely. These feelings explain why when her long-time dance partner, Carmelo, stops coming to the dance hall without warning, she uses his disappearance as an opportunity to improve her life. Following a false tip about Carmelo's whereabouts, Julia travels to Veracruz. Thus, Perla's need for more breathing room gives Julia the opportunity to renew herself.

Salón México and *Danzón* differ in the amount of maternal care daughters need. In *Salón México* Beatriz is presented as someone in desperate need of maternal care; the film narrative is organized around the task of finding a better mother for naïve and inexperienced Beatriz. In contrast, in *Danzón*, teenager Perla, who is the same age as Beatriz, is savvy about life. On several occasions, *Danzón* shows Julia's frustrated efforts to take care of Perla, who is a telephone operator like her mother and works in the same office. For example, one day when they have an early shift, mother and daughter sleep in the telephone operators' ward. In preparation for sleeping at the ward, Julia explains to Perla, in the presence of their coworkers, how to hide her personal belongings under her pillow. Julia's coworkers respond to the mother's comment with "Don't exaggerate" and remind Julia that Perla already knows these things. On another occasion, Perla is shown amusing herself by reading a magazine and eating snacks. Julia asks her to be her partner and practice danzón, to which the adolescent daughter responds with a bored expression. In yet another scene, a coworker asks Perla: "What is wrong with Julia? Menopause?" she suggests. Perla is not in need of maternal care or guidance; what she needs is more freedom and time for herself. While in the case of *Salón México*, an attachment to mother is fundamental, in the case of *Danzón* it is unnecessary.

Perla's need for freedom makes possible a literal focus on the mother. The daughter is left a minor character in *Danzón*. The film focuses on the mother. In Veracruz, Julia enjoys the ocean, meets new friends like Sussy (Tito Vasconcelos), and has an affair with Rubén (Víctor Carpinteiro), an attractive sailor much younger than herself. Upon her return to Mexico City, Julia is, and looks, like a different person. When she meets her friend Silvia (Margarita Isabel) wearing her new wardrobe, Silvia is both surprised and happily suspicious. Although Silvia doesn't say anything, her gestures show what she is thinking: What happened to Julia's austere, traditional clothes?

Salón México and *Danzón* present contrasting views in regards to mothers' concerns. While Mercedes's death is justified and presented as commendable in the final song, Julia receives praise. The song "Antonieta" played during Julia's visit to the docks in search for Carmelo is an example of the film narrative's interest in *Danzón*'s mother. "Antonieta" sounds like many traditional Mexican love songs because its danzón rhythm fits in well with the rest of the film's songs. The lyrics come from a poem by the Mexican gay poet Javier Villarrutia, not from Mexican lore, and are directed toward Julia.[20]

The song begins as Julia walks along the docks, among huge boats with names that refer to romantic love, and ends in a close shot of the tugboat *See Me and Suffer* (*Me ves y sufres*). Love is described in multiple ways, as an "anguish," "a question," and as "a suspended and suspenseful shining doubt." In the tugboat is Rubén, the young handsome sailor with whom Julia will have an affair. Within the context of Julia's trip of self-discovery, this song is not about missing the loved one, Carmelo; nor is it about the new love to come, Rubén. Novaro turns romantic love into self-love, into the gratification and self-indulgence of the mother, so that she recovers from her boredom and loneliness and can adapt to a new cycle of life. The second part of the song makes this meaning clear. Love is about loving the other, but love is also about promoting self-love. Love is "closing your eyes" and leting "dreams flood your body." And most importantly, love is about indolence (*indolencia*). In Spanish, and in the particular context of the poem, indolence

3. The Qualities of Classical and Third-Wave Mothers 71

Julia at the docks (courtesy María Novaro).

has the meaning of self-indulgence in a positive way, of pleasure. Love is allowing oneself to feel pleasure in the presence of the other. Gratification and satisfaction is what Julia will feel in the presence of Rubén, who becomes a stop in her search for self-discovery. The love described in "Antonieta" is what Julia experiences during her trip in search of her new self. As the narrative develops, it is as if Julia could close her eyes in a luxurious state of comfort and pleasure, like a river of forgetfulness, as she sails aimlessly adrift.

Julia is in a very different position than the mothers in classical films. Unlike the exemplary mother that Beatriz describes in her final exam, Julia does not have to "fight against all odds to get their children one step up." The absence of a naïve child like Beatriz, the fact that Perla can take care of herself, and the recommendation of friends that Julia leave her daughter some space, allow the mother space to take care of herself. "Antonieta" restores the imbalance in classical films between mothers and children. In *Salón México* the only concerns that matter are those of "children"; in *Danzón* mothers are presented as vulnerable individuals who need care and, more importantly, love.

Warner (2005) explains that in the 1980s "attachment theory has become so main-stream that we pretty much take it for granted" (92). If that is the case, by restoring the balance between the needs of children and mothers *Danzón* takes a step in the opposite direction. Making attachment theory seem unnatural, questioning the misuse of this theory is fundamental for feminism. Only by restoring the balance between the needs of children and mothers, which *Danzón* does using the character of Julia, can the self-actualization of mothers become a reality.

Conclusion

Third-wave films redefine mothers' "goodness." Chapter 3 traces the core self-effacing characteristics of the Ideal of Virgin Motherhood to the Franciscan idea of humility and to the construct of the Virgin as Mother. An examination of *Una familia de tantas* from the perspective of the third-wave narrative *Ángel de fuego* shows that the Ideal of Virgin Motherhood that Doña Gracia represents is characterized by self-effacing values, especially humility and submission. In contrast, self-asserting values, like fortitude and justice, characterize *Ángel de fuego*'s third-wave mother.

Chapter 3 concludes that while the moral values of classical and third-wave films differ, third-wave films do not put forward amoral or unchristian values. The Angel of Fire's qualities of fortitude, justice and temperance are Christian values. What a self-affirming mother like Alma leaves behind is the misogyny in Christian thought that associates femininity almost exclusively with passivity, submission and obedience.

The change from self-effacing values to self-affirming ones benefits mothers. From Oliver's perspective, Alma's anger is healthier than negative feelings of shame. Third-wave films promote values that allow women to move away from alienation and the negative effects of shame. With her Exterminating Angel, Rotberg leads mothers away from depression, to feel that they too need self-realization.

Warner's warning, that attachment theory is an obstacle to mother's self-actualization, is used to read the classical narrative *Salón México*. From Warner's point of view, classical films appear as a child-centered narratives, narratives in which the well-being of the child is given the utmost importance but the interest of the mother is considered secondary or unimportant. Third-wave narratives stand out because they make the interest of mothers significant; in the case of *Danzón* by arguing that adolescents need more freedom. The comparison between *Salón México* and *Danzón* shows that the classical narrative, preoccupied mainly with the education of Beatriz, forgets the well-being of the mother. In contrast, the third-wave narrative puts Perla aside, to center on the troubles of a mother whose main focus needs to change once her daughter becomes an adolescent.

The two issues studied in this chapter, the characteristics of mothers and the benefits of morality, are related issues. From a feminist perspective, the characteristics of a third-wave mother promote the well-being of mothers, restoring balance between the interests of the child and the mother.

4

Sexuality in Classical and Third-Wave Films

Chapter 4 examines how the sexuality of mothers is represented in classical melodramas and third-wave films. Of all the attributes that are essential to the Ideal of Virgin Motherhood, the restriction on women's sexual freedom is the one which has received the most attention. During the 1970s and 1980s feminist scholars claimed that in classical melodramas women were given only two alternatives, "good mother" or "whore." In the 1990s, Latin American feminist scholars considered the "saintly mother" and the "prostitute" as two roles that restricted women's sexual freedom. These alternatives were seen as problematic; in order to be good, mothers had to give up being sexual. To counter this tendency, Ana López praised the previously vilified rumbera, which had previously been villified, making this stereotype into an icon of vitality.

This chapter moves from an analysis that emphasizes the transgression of sexual norms to an examination of agency, defined as the capacity to want objects and act toward goals. After summarizing the discussion of women's sexuality in classical films, the chapter clarifies the position of third-wave filmmakers. The examination of *El secreto de Romelia* (1989), *Danzón*, and *Los pasos de Ana* (1989) shows that third-wave filmmakers are respectful of women who hold conservative views of sexuality. The same is not true of agency; third-wave filmmakers give agency to their characters. There is no contradiction between both: a character can have conservative views about sexuality and she can make her own decisions (i.e., be an agent). The lack of connection between sexuality and agency in past analyses needs to be revised. To show the differences, the second part of the chapter examines the agency and sexuality of the three women in the classical melodrama *Señora tentación* (*The Temptress*, Diaz Morales, 1947).

Scholarly Approaches to the Study of Sexuality in Mexican Classical Cinema

In *La aventura del cine mexicano: En la Época de Oro y después*, Jorge Ayala Blanco uses two separate categories: mothers and women who are open about their sexuality. Mothers are studied in "La familia," while prostitutes are studied separately in "La prostituta" (Ayala Blanco 1993, 112). Included in "La prostitute" are rumba dancers, the B-girls, and vamps (such as the character played by María Felix in *Doña Bárbara*). Separating motherhood and sexuality shows that women in Mexican classical cinema cannot be mothers and openly sexual at the same time.

U.S. film scholarship uses a similar separation between motherhood and sexuality, but it adds Octavio Paz's reference to La Malinche. In *The Labyrinth of Solitude* (1950)[1] Paz describes the historical figure known as Doña Marina, who acted as an interpreter for the sixteenth-century Spanish conquistador Hernán Cortés. In the chapter, "The Sons of La Malinche," Paz explains that La Malinche expresses the rancor that Mexicans felt about being violated. Paz describes a displaced hatred: unhappy with being the product of rape, the Mexicans turned their hatred not on themselves, but on the raped mother (Paz 1961, 86–87). The writer proposes that through the scream, "Viva México, Los hijos de La chingada," Mexicans are in touch with this still unresolved identity.

Starting in the 1960s, feminist scholars wrote about the sexual restrictions of women in classical films. This discussion of women's sexual freedom in Mexican cinema was part of a broader discussion about the limitations imposed on women's sexuality around the world. During the 1970s and 1980s, the feminists asserted that Paz's stereotypes were based on a distorted notion of women's sexuality. In the 1970s, Chicana feminist scholars in particular contended that Paz's association of female sexuality with betrayal reinforced the machismo they experienced in their communities. Cordelia Candelaria (1980), in "La Malinche, Feminist Prototype," was one of the earliest to raise her voice against Paz's interpretation of La Malinche. In 1981, coinciding with the Mexican publication of Paz's revision of *Labyrinth*, Norma Alarcón attacked Paz's view of Malintzin for its historical inaccuracy, a critique that was further developed by Cherríe Moraga in 1986 and by Alarcón again in 1989.[2] Using historical accounts of the Conquest to support their arguments, these scholars proposed that Malintzin was sold as a slave before Cortés arrived, and she used her translating skills to gain power. Malintzin was not a traitor from this perspective.

The debate about La Malinche led by Chicana feminist scholars in the field of literature affected the way in which Paz's theories were discussed in U.S.–based scholarship of Mexican film. References to Paz, whether positive or negative, are mentioned in the most important studies on female stereotypes written during the 1980s and 1990s, beginning with Carl J. Mora's 1985 study. The legacy of Chicana scholars was felt in the 1990s, when Paz's female dyad was understood as part of a sexist discourse on female sexuality in Mexico. For instance, in *Cinema of Solitude*, Charles Ramírez Berg (1992) distances himself from Paz's discourse when he comments, "Because of her [La Malinche], Paz and others have argued, feminine sexual pleasure is linked in the Mexican consciousness not only with prostitution but with national betrayal" (24). From Berg's perspective, women are not by nature traitors; rather, female sexuality has been historically associated with treachery. In their analyses of Mexican film, feminist film scholars have placed the figure of La Malinche in historical context. In her study of images of women in classical melodramas, film scholar Joanne Hershfield draws on Tzvetan Todorov's *The Conquest of America* to argue that Malintzin's sexual relationship with Cortés was strategic and military rather than emotional (Hershfield 1996, 20). After 2000, ironically the fiftieth anniversary of *The Labyrinth of Solitude*, the debate about Paz's stereotypes in Mexican film studies seemed to unwind; Paz became a marginal reference in the discussion of Mexican female stereotypes, as example see the works of Elissa Rashkin (2001) and Susan Dever (2003).

Other studies have concentrated on counteracting the negative associations attached to female sexuality. Ayala Blanco critiqued the rigid morality and restrictive nature of Golden Age melodramas. For him, the prostitute, whom he considers the flip side of the maternal woman, was created to reestablish the familial equilibrium threatened by asexual mothers (1993, 108). The stereotype of the "good wife" limits husbands' access to their wives' sexuality, because, in order to be "good wives" women have to act virginally even after marriage. Prostitutes allow an outlet for husbands' sexual desires in a nonthreatening way. In a similar defense of open sexuality, U.S.–based feminist film scholar Ana López (1994) associates the female body with life and energy. In "Tears and Desire: Women and Melodrama in the 'Old' Mexican Cinema," for example, López admires images of women who are able to express their sexuality, as in the previously vilified rumbera; and she laments images that glorify women's repression, such as the stereotypes of the "good-mothers" or "bad-women."

Sexuality in *Una familia de tantas*

In *Una familia de tantas* Doña Gracia's unawareness of sexuality exemplifies the asexuality of a "good mother." In a scene in the kitchen, the maid

Guadalupe makes a sexual joke. She remarks that the adult son Hector had asked for chili pepper on his eggs at breakfast. Doña Gracia doesn't notice the link between chiles and sexuality and simply responds that it is unusual to have chile for breakfast. Guadalupe tries unsuccessfully for a second time to talk about Hector's sexuality by saying that he came in late last night. Doña Gracia responds that he was working. Guadalupe waits until the children leave the kitchen to try for a third time, saying: "Young Hector is old enough to be doing *his* things," only to be ignored once again with a "Come on Guadalupe, put more wood on for the bath." Understanding that Doña Gracia does not want to "see" Hector's sexual maturity, Guadalupe drops the subject. Doña Gracia is so innocent that she does not think about sexuality.

Framed as a medium eye-level shot, the scene portrays Doña Gracia and Guadalupe as equals by situating them at the same level. Their positions on sexuality, however, differ considerably; while Doña Gracia is a "blind" Virgin-like housewife, Guadalupe sees sexuality as something natural and therefore discussable. Watching *Una familia de tantas* from the perspective of its portrayal of women, one has to wonder: Why does the point of Doña Gracia's chastity have to be repeated so many times? What does chastity stand for? Warner (1976) proposes that in the bourgeois idealization of domestic life in the fifteenth century, chastity was seen as a sign of spiritual superiority (189). When applied to married women, who must have sex for procreation, chastity became control of the body, which was understood as essential for moral superiority. Within Catholic ideological discourse, a chaste person is a generous and empathetic being with the capacity to give to others.[3]

THIRD-WAVE FILMMAKERS AND SEXUAL PURITY: CORTÉS'S *EL SECRETO DE ROMELIA*

Third-wave filmmakers and film scholars do not see the sexuality of women in classical films from the same perspective. Unlike Ayala Blanco, third-wave filmmakers do not critique rigid morality, and unlike López, they do not put forward images of women who are able to express their sexuality. While third-wave filmmakers are aware of the limitations imposed on women's sexuality in classical melodramas, their relationship is one of understanding rather than criticism, Busi Cortés's *El secreto de Romelia* is the best example of a respectful look at the sexuality of a 1940s "good mother," like Doña Gracia in *Una familia de tantas*.

El secreto de Romelia is representative of the third-wave's position on sexuality; in the film a daughter leaves behind her 1970s ideas about sexuality in order to understand her mother's classical ideas. The film's narrative follows Romelia, a woman who was an adolescent in the late 1930s and early 1940s,

when Cárdenas was president. The film is narrated from the point of view of Romelia's forty-year-old daughter, Dolores, who considers her mother's 1940s notions about sexual purity from a 1980s perspective.

El secreto de Romelia compares the different approaches to sexuality of three generations of women. It centers on Romelia, a grandmother who was unfairly accused by her husband, Don Carlos, of having lost her virginity before their wedding. The accusation became known, and Romelia had to leave town. Forty years later, Romelia tells her daughter Dolores, conceived on the only night that she spent with her husband, that she kept the blood-stained sheets to prove to her that she was a virgin when she married. The film is narrated from the point of view of Romelia's forty-year-old daughter, Dolores, who considers her mother's 1940s ideas about sexual purity old-fashioned.

The narrative pivots on Dolores's effort to understand her mother's view of sexuality. For that to happen, Dolores has to accept Romelia's view, which in the film is represented by Romelia's defense of virginity. *El secreto de Romelia* begins with Dolores's disdain for her mother's ideas and ends with her respect for her mother. By taking Dolores's point of view, the film encourages the spectator to join in the painful process of accepting Romelia's view of sexuality.

During the beginning credits, the screen shows a medium shot of Romelia behind a window. She looks sad, and her image is frozen while the credits are written over her image. The shot that follows, in which her image unfreezes, further explains Cortés's intentions. Gazing at something the spectator cannot identify, a tired and worried Romelia moves her lips up and down in a mechanical and confused manner. *El secreto de Romelia* encourages the audience to engage in the process of understanding why Romelia looks so tired and sad and to participate in "unfreezing" Romelia.

Dolores's awareness of her mother's ideas establishes two separate psychological spaces, her own and her mother's. The film's narrative depicts Dolores's progressive understanding of her mother's ideas. At the beginning of the film, Dolores refuses to acknowledge any viewpoint other than her own. Dolores is furious with her mother when she discovers that her father, Don Carlos, had died, not many years ago, as her mother had led her to believe but only the previous month, Dolores is furious with her mother. She had wanted to meet her father. When she demands an explanation, she and mother and daughter go into the living room. There is a warm fire in the background. Despite the allusion to warmth suggested by the fire, the camera takes the two women in a series of shot-reverse-shots, thus underscoring their lack of empathy for each other's ideas. Their clothing and body positions visually reinforce their emotional distance: Romelia is dressed in an impeccable, old-

Opposite: Poster for *El secreto de Romelia* (Colección Filmoteca de la UNAM).

fashioned suit and sits properly on the front part of her chair, holding her back straight, her legs carefully together. Dolores is wearing casual clothes and leans back in her chair, lighting a cigarette. Their emotional distance is evident in their conversation: Dolores asks, "What was my father like?" and Romelia responds, "Aren't you going to work on your dissertation today?" and then expresses a wish to drop the subject and go to bed.

The turning point in their relationship comes when Dolores accepts her mother's 1940s views on sexuality. After the two leave the living room, they continue their conversation in the bedroom, a more intimate space, lit with warm light from a nightstand lamp. In contrast to the living room sequence (shot in a shot-reverse-shot fashion), the bedroom sequence is shot using a more intimate medium shot that includes both women in the same frame. As mother and daughter sit talking at opposite sides of the bed, Romelia's secret is revealed.

In *El secreto de Romelia*, the process by which Dolores comes to respect Romelia's point of view hinges on her understanding of why Romelia kept, for almost forty years, the sheets from her wedding night. When Dolores learns that her mother left town because she couldn't bear the gossip about her, Dolores accuses Romelia of caring only about appearances. Her disdain for her mother, as well as her guilt about her disdain, is apparent in her tone of voice. It comes from her unwillingness to accept that for women of her mother's generation, virginity was essential to social acceptance. When Romelia explains that she left her village because "everybody in the village thought that I wasn't a virgin," Dolores answers: "So what? Your virginity belongs to you, not to men." At this point, Dolores is unable to move beyond her own point of view, while her mother continues to insist, "No Loli [Dolores], you are wrong. A lady shouldn't think that way." For Dolores, it makes no sense that her mother kept the blood-stained sheets, and she asks incredulously: "To show to whom?" But although she cannot quite understand her mother at this point, her mother's openness to vulnerability moves her. When Romelia explains that she kept the sheets to show "you, your children, I do not know..." we can see, by looking at Dolores's face, that she finally can feel her mother's pain. Her compassion is also expressed in her posture; she bends forward, as if starting to carry her mother's burden. This movement brings her closer to the light coming from the lamp behind her mother, and her look of condescension changes to one of empathy. After asking for forgiveness, she asks: "Did you love him?" When her mother says she did, Dolores reaches to touch her mother and says softly: "Why didn't you tell me? I would have understood you."

Thus the film shows that Dolores is capable of accepting Romelia's point of view even though she does not accept the ideals of virginity for herself. Her identification still maintains a distance between them. To use Kaja Silverman's (1996) terminology, we could say that Dolores identifies with Romelia's "conditions and quality of being 'other'" (15). By the same token, the acceptance of Romelia's otherness establishes mother Romelia and daughter Dolores as two different individuals, the former subscribing to the ideal of virginity, the latter rejecting it.

To underscore the idea that each generation holds different ideas about sexuality, Cortés also includes in *El secreto de Romelia* one more generation: Romelia's granddaughters. Thus, while Romelia might think that virginity at marriage is essential, her daughter does not share this value, and her daughter's three daughters make fun of it. At the end of the film, the granddaughters overhear the conversation between Romelia and Dolores about the importance to Romelia of virginity. In trying to make sense of this discussion, Romi, the youngest, named after her grandmother, asks if her grandmother is a virgin. María, the eldest, doesn't want to answer, but Aurelia, the middle sister, explains that "single women without husbands are virgins." The eldest sister jokes that if that is the definition of virginity, then she is the Virgin Mary. This joke is especially significant in the Mexican context, where femininity is based on the model of the Virgin. In Mexican films of the 1940s and 1950s, female characters try to approach normative ideals by imitating the Virgin.

The Ideal of Virgin Motherhood that was taken so seriously in the 1940s has been transformed into a joke by the young generation. This comic sequence continues with another question from Romi: "Why did the sheets have blood?" Aurelia explains, "On their wedding night women get a little blood." Romi then wants to know where the blood comes from, and her sister tiredly answers: "From her nose." This answer, comically displacing the main concern of Virgin Motherhood from the vagina to the nose, shows that the granddaughters will not live by the ideals of their grandmother. By widening the scope of the film to include granddaughters, *El secreto de Romelia* reveals patterns of womanhood over several generations, showing that, while all may have children, for the older generation virginity will be fundamental, while for younger women, it will be a thing from the past. *El secreto de Romelia* takes the differences to an extreme by suggesting that women of different generations may not even understand each other. Yet, *El secreto de Romelia* promotes understanding of 1940s ideals rather than simply rejecting them. This understanding, however, does not mean that 1940s ideas apply to 1970s–1980s women like Dolores or that her ideas about sexuality are going to apply to her three daughters.

El secreto de Romelia does not make the case that Romelia lived under oppressive sexual ideals or defend the point that Romelia should have been freer. Rather, Cortés's film calls for the establishment of critical distance with regards to the 1940s Ideal of Virgin Motherhood. This distance means that while the ideal rings true for Romelia, it does not ring true for her daughter Dolores, and much less for Romelia's granddaughters. Critical distance brings acceptance; the film's position concerning 1940s ideals of sexual purity is not one of judgment but of respect. Thus, Cortés's position differs from that of López in her 1994 article. Romelia, whom the film tries to understand, is after all a "good-mother." While López wants sexual freedom for the 1940s, Cortés wants understanding. The filmmaker considers it important to understand the perspective of women in the 1940s.

Sexuality in *Danzón*

In *Danzón* María Novaro, like Cortés, returns to classical melodramas, this time by situating her narrative in a 1940s scenario, the famous dance hall, Salón México. In *Danzón*, Julia, a phone operator and lover of the dance danzón, is adjusting to having her teenage daughter Perla want more time for herself. Tired and discouraged, Julia (María Rojo) uses the disappearance of her dance partner Carmelo as an excuse to spend some days in Veracruz, where she has an affair with sailor Rubén. Despite having an affair, getting more close fitting dresses and shorter skirts, Julia is not a sexually liberated character, but a proper, naïve woman.

Novaro did not create a more sexually liberated character because she thought it would not be realistic: "It seemed truer to me that Julia not be a reckless character along feminist lines, but rather, the average woman next door." The shooting of the film confirmed this idea. Novaro was denied permission to shoot Julia working at a real switchboard. After reading the script, members of the phone operator's union denied the director access to the location because they considered Julia's conduct improper. The unionized workers thought that a phone operator having an affair with a young sailor was shameful and were afraid that people would think that phone operators had affairs, something they did not find true. Novaro's position is different from some feminist scholars who prefer a character to openly defend a woman's right to free sexuality.

María Rojo plays a forty-year-old conservative mother embarrassed by plastic breasts. For instance, Julia's face shows concern when she visits the changing room of a transvestite called Susy, who becomes her best friend. She is embarrassed looking at Susy's plastic breasts, her flowers, and dresses and also at the dolls with enormous breasts that decorate the wall of the cabaret where her friend dances.

Through Julia, Novaro portrays Mexico's position vis-à-vis with liberated sexuality. Talking about Julia's reaction to Susy's fake breast and the dolls in the walls, Novaro explained:

This embarrassment [Julia's] produces a great feeling of tenderness in me because it's not about antiquity, about the past, but rather, is a generous and quite naive feeling. The most amusing and greatest proof of the existence of this embarrassment at a national level came when *Danzón* was shown on television in Mexico, and these scenes were censored. They took out precisely the shots of naked dolls. This made me think that I wasn't wrong at all; my country is naive in that way. The censor's embarrassment was exactly as I portrayed it: he refused to let those plaster women with the enormous tits be seen on television [Arredondo 2013, 163].

Julia is embarrassed by Susy's plastic breasts (courtesy María Novarro).

Novaro makes Julia a naïve and conservative character because portraying a sexually liberated character would be untrue to national feelings.

Julia is also embarrassed by wearing the highly defined makeup that Susy uses for her shows. In the scene at Susy's *camerino*, the transvestite talks about different kinds of women and the kinds of makeup that go with each type. Then she asks: "Can you tell the difference? Since you are a summer woman reds, oranges, deep greens fit you very well." The *Danzón* script explains that Julia doesn't know what she fears, but she is afraid of going out with the makeup that Susy put on her.[4] In the same way in which Cortés takes critical distance with regards to Romelia's ideas about virginity, *Danzón* allows distance through a humorous view of Julia's naïveté. Speaking for her sister Beatriz and herself, Novaro explained:

> When Julia is primping, putting on make-up, dolling herself up, ready to go to the docks to look for the sailor she has seen in one of the tugboats, ready to say that he's her cousin in case anyone thinks badly of her, we were playing with our emotional upbringing.
>
> In playing, we explore all the things we have inherited. With this method, it doesn't weigh on you: "This is how I was raised, this is my tradition and I recognize it as part of me, but I'll make fun of it and won't let it run my life" [Arredondo 2013, 158].

Novaro may have a liberated sexuality, a reason why she laughs, but her character does not need to have it. The acceptance of the fact that naïve sexuality is common in Mexico is essential for Novaro's critical perspective, but it does not mean that she agrees with the status quo. The director clarified: "Through humor, we were able to accept our culture, yet, at the same time, we freed ourselves from what we were taught to feel when we were growing up" (Arredondo 2013, 157). Humor is a mechanism that helps the Novaro sisters acknowledge their emotional inheritance and, at the same time, challenge the predicament of having being raised Catholic. As if it were Dolores looking at Romelia, Novaro is respectful to an older mother who is proper, naïve, and easily embarrassed.

Sistach's *Los pasos de Ana*: Doubts About a Liberated Sexuality

Marisa Sistach does not propose a liberated sexuality either. She believes that we should not be too optimistic about the sexual liberation of Latin women. In filming *Los pasos de Ana* the director encountered a situation similar to the one Novaro experienced with the phone operators. In the script, Ana, a young divorced mother, was going to spend an enjoyable night with a man she met at a disco. However, the events that took place during the shooting made the director reconsider her idea:

> The person playing Ana — Guadalupe Sánchez, a non-professional actress — along with several members of the film crew, expressed such rejection of the idea that she [Ana] could find this casual relationship enjoyable that I decided to change the script. I didn't want to project so much optimism about the extent to which women's sexuality in Mexico had been liberated [Arredondo 2013, 130].

The reaction of Guadalupe Sánchez made Sistach reconsider the idea that women could in a short time overcome the sexual norms they have lived with for many years. Despite the fact that she could have maintained her original idea, she preferred to cast doubt on the possibility of easy sexual encounter:

> I changed the relationship so it functioned as a way for her to settle into her solitude, but it wasn't enjoyable. When I changed the script, it wasn't just because of theoretical pressures, but because the actress couldn't play the "games" written into the script. Maybe because she wasn't an actress by profession and found it was more difficult to place herself in that role, but she probably had a deeper reason [Arredondo 2013, 130].

The filmmaker gave the character the opportunity to have an encounter free of guilt, but that freedom was accompanied by loneliness, not pleasure. Sistach explained her decision to have Ana not enjoy a casual relationship:

> I sensed that for Latin women, a casual encounter could not be enjoyable because there are too many taboos for them to be able to enjoy a purely physical relationship. Besides, women's sexuality is complex. Women need a sensual, erotic, delicate, drawn-out prelude that, perhaps, most men aren't used to. Men's machismo, their tendency to think about their own pleasure and not the pleasure of both people, is a problem for women [Arredondo 2013, 130–131].

Sistach continued to be interested in issues of sexuality, and, in her second feature, she portrayed sexuality in two male adolescents, a very different sexuality from that of a young single mother.[5] If, as third-wave filmmakers explain, their films are a response to classical films, then we can conclude that the changing view of women's sexuality is not the most important issue for third-wave filmmakers. Third-wave filmmakers take a position of understanding and respect regarding old-fashioned views of sexuality. Sistach's view of Guadalupe Sánchez's difficulty with Ana's sexual role, Cortés request for respect for Romelia's notion of virginity, and Novaro's creation of an embarrassed, conservative yet generous character show that third-wave filmmakers prefer to accept the existence of an old-fashioned Catholic sensibility about sexuality rather than promulgating a sexual liberation not aligned with national attitudes. However, if third-wave filmmakers do not react against old-fashioned views of sexuality, how should we characterize their response? The notion of desire, used in feminist film studies can help us to see that while third-wave mothers have desire, they do not have an open sexuality.

Agency in Third-Wave Films

From the mid–1970s to the late 1990s North American feminist scholarship used the concept of desire, drawn from classical psychoanalysis, to address women's agency in classical Hollywood films. Among the most important examples of this type of analysis are Laura Mulvey's "Visual Pleasure and Narrative Cinema" (1975) and "Afterthoughts on 'Visual Pleasure and Narrative Cinema,' inspired by King Vidor's *Duel in the Sun*" (1999), and Mary Ann Doane *The Desire to Desire: The Woman's Film of the 1940s* (1987). Mulvey and Doane asked: is the woman in the film narrative an object of desire or a desiring subject? In Doane's examination, the ability of the female character to look at someone is taken as a sign that the character is a subject, an agent, the carrier of the look. In contrast, the inability to look, the passive role of being looked at, is considered as a sign that the character does not have agency.

The notion of objects of desire that Doane uses comes from classical psychoanalysis. Object-relation psychoanalysis, which developed during the 1930s and was widely used in the 1970s, went back to biology's study of an organism and its surroundings in order to discuss human relations. Freud, for example, focused on the way in which instincts are directed toward objects (Laplanche-Pontalis 1974, 278).[6] He distinguished between an object, its source, and its aim and used words such as object cathexis, object-choice, object-love, and object-tie to describe the subject's attachment to objects (Freud, 1921). Feminist scholars used Freud's ideas because he differentiated between men and women's relations toward objects. He believed that while the majority of men develop objects, women rarely do so, remaining at an intermediate state called the narcissistic stage.[7] Doane and Mulvey brought Freud's differentiation between masculine and feminine relations to objects into film studies; they wanted to counter Christian Metz's non-gender-specific way of understanding cinematic spectatorship. Metz assumed that males and females in the audience responded to the film in the same way. In contrast, Doane and Mulvey maintained that spectatorship depended on the sex of the person watching the film, because males and females went through different identificatory processes.[8]

During the 1970s, psychoanalytic approaches to film theory moved away from classical psychoanalysis's emphasis on instincts; instead, the notion of object is most often used in relation to the Lacanian concept of desire, based on lack. In her 1974 essay, Mulvey uses Freudian and Lacanian psychoanalysis to claim that in the classical Hollywood system, female characters are the objects of desire for the male gaze.[9] In *The Desire to Desire*, Doane uses Freudian theory, seen through Lacan's notion of lack, and thus distinct from Freud's preoccupation with instincts. Doane is less interested in learning about female instincts than in understanding the conscious wishes of women and their representation in cinema. Her notion of the subject and object of desire are widely used in the study of classical films, including Mexican films of the Golden Age.[10] Mulvey's and Doane's works led to new questions in the analysis of classical films: if desire is defined as the capacity to want objects and the ability to work toward the fulfillment of that want, then is desire present in the context of Mexican classical and third-wave films? The question developed from Mulvey's and Doane's idea of desire is very different from the one asked in the first part of the chapter. In the case of *Danzón*, previous approaches will ask: Does Julia comply with established sexual norms? Is Julia a liberated character or not? The following section uses Doane's and Mulvey's notion of desire to examine Julia's character. These analyses reach very different conclusions.

Danzón's Reversal of the Process of Identification

In classical Hollywood cinema and in Mexican melodramas of the Golden Age, female characters are the objects of the male gaze; they are the ones that spectators look at, not the ones that look. *Danzón* does more than acknowledge the importance of classical melodramas for Mexicans; it responds to them.

In order to change the way the audience identifies with the Julia, *Danzón* revisits three scenarios associated with Golden Age films. The film includes scenes at the dance hall, where Julia spends several evenings a week; the cabaret, where her friend Susy performs; and the harbor, where Julia looks for Carmelo. In Mexican classical cinema, the docks of Veracruz are a well-known locus of dangerous love, where beautiful women fall in love with forbidden sailors. For example, in *La mujer del puerto* (*The Woman of the Port*; Boytler 1933) Rosario (Andrea Palma) unknowingly falls in love with her own brother.[11] In *Danzón,* the names of the boats that Julia sees along the docks as she looks for Carmelo allude to classical film scenarios. For instance, the boat *Black Tears* refers to a famous romantic song from the classical period by Toña la Negra. The wardrobe in *Danzón* also suggests a connection to classical Mexican melodramas: Julia walks along the docks wearing a bright red dress, red lipstick, high heels, and a matching red flower behind her ear. On this sunny, windy afternoon, Julia's dress swirls in the wind and the intense red is in sharp contrast to the deep blue sky.

Tug boat *Me ves y sufres* (courtesy María Novaro).

In her red dress, walking along the Veracruz docks Julia is a visual reference to classical melodramas; however, the way in which the camera is positioned and the organization of the scene does not establish a Golden Age viewpoint. In classical narratives, women are the objects of the look; that is, the film is shot making the spectator look at women (in psychoanalytic terms, women are the objects of the look). Novaro's second long-feature film responds to a classical structuring of the gaze by organizing the scene from the point of view of the woman; making women into subjects who do the looking.

The most compelling scene that reverses the classical gaze takes place as Julia encounters several sailors in their boats. The scene consists of three shots organized in a continuity style that shows an exchange of looks between Julia and the sailors. First, in a extremely low angle, the camera takes a long-shot of the sailors looking down at Julia from the boat railing. Then the camera takes a point-of-view shot of Julia who is both shy and delighted looking up at the sailors. In this shot, there is a close-up of one of the sailors resting his arms over the railing as he looks at Julia. The shot is taken from a very low, almost vertical angle. The scene is organized from Julia's perspective: the extreme positions of the point-of-view shot assure the audience that the scene is seen from the dock where Julia is. The scene is also organized around Julia's feeling of enjoyment in men's gaze. The scene makes sense from a woman's perspective. The second shot shows the protagonist's interest in men and her capacity to actively look at the sailors; the first and third shots attest to Julia's desire, to her (hidden) longing to be looked at. The capacity to look and the fulfillment of her desire — to be looked at — attest to Julia's position as a subject who has objects. Unlike the female protagonist of classical films, Julia has the capacity to look and thus to desire; she is the subject who has objects. She is an agent.

Julia's love for danzón, a dance that evolved from Cuban habanera and became very popular in the city of Veracruz, might seem symptomatic of her passive role in life. In this Caribbean dance, the male dancer takes the active position: he holds the woman and directs her steps. The woman takes the passive role: she follows the lead of her male partner. Can we reconcile Julias' love for a dance in which she does not take the initiative and her capacity to be agent? Novaro addresses Julia's agency when she says:

> Julia dances the danzón and does so following the man, because that's the way one really enjoys this dance. What's the problem there? Julia is a woman with a passion for the danzón and is able to follow its rules — to dress like a real woman, to be the one who obeys in the dance, who follows the man. Nevertheless, she is also totally and absolutely the master of her own life — that is, according to how her life has shaped up and the possibilities she would logically have, given who she is. She lives her life according to what she is given and she is so open, so generous, and so full of life.... She is so willing to take

what comes to her in life and to react accordingly that, ultimately, she's in charge of her life. She's more in charge of her life than she even realizes. Julia shows this ability to choose on her trip to Veracruz, when she chooses her young lover and when she leaves him, and also by dancing with Carmelo, this very elegant gentleman [Arredondo 2013, 166].

Novaro convincingly puts forward the argument that Julia's love for danzón does not undermine her agency. The director distinguishes between dancing and deciding, and clarifies that while Julia takes a passive role when she is led in the dance, in everyday life she takes an active role. *Danzón*'s protagonist initiates the trip to Veracruz, following what she knows is a false tip. She also decides to initiate a romance with Rubén and to end it, and she even chooses to dance danzón. Because of her ability to make decisions, the director considers her "a master of her own life," someone "in charge of her life." This is another way of saying that Julia is an agent. So, for Novaro, Julia's love for danzón does not put her agency in question. Julia loves dancing, and while men may direct her dancing, they do not direct her life.

The analysis of Julia using Mulvey's and Doane's ideas of desire lead to a reconsideration of prior conclusions. Previously, we concluded that Julia's conservative sexuality only marginally challenges Golden Age norms. The opposite is true when we examine Julia by using the idea of desire. Julia is a character who looks and who is an agent. Because of this, she directly challenges the dynamics of classical melodramas, where women are looked at and take a passive role. Mothers in third-wave films are created as a response to the limitations imposed on women's capacity to act on their own in classical films, to be subjects, in classical films. Third-wave filmmakers' creation of characters who have agency demands a reconsideration of previous studies of Mexican classical film. Is the transgression of sexual norms the most important limit women and mothers face in Mexican classical cinema?

Sexuality in the Classical Canon: Señora tentación

This section includes two analyses of the same classical film. Following the ideas put forward by López in "Tears and Desire," the first analysis looks at the character's relationship to classical norms regarding sexuality. The second analysis is based on the notion of desire used in feminist film studies. When analyzing the stereotypes of the classical melodrama, most scholars have examined films directed by El Indio Fernández or Fernando de Fuentes. However, unlike the better-known films by Fernández, Díaz Morales's *Señora tentación* offers the possibility of looking at the classical canon as a whole because it includes three clearly differentiated kinds of women in one film.

In "Tears and Desire" López puts forward a topography of the most common spaces that appear in Mexican classical melodramas and organizes them according to female sexuality. In López's topography, the center is inhabited by those female characters who do not have sexual desires. Those who are sexually liberated live at the margins. The further away one goes from the center, the more a person is sexually free. The feminist scholar uses specific actresses to discuss these spaces; for example, in the central space of the patriarchal home live *madrecitas queridas* (beloved mothers), asexual women who suffer and sacrifice themselves, best represented by actress Sara García (López 1994, 153–154). *Malas mujeres* (bad women), as played typically by actress María Felix, share the same central space as the beloved mothers, because they also are asexual. In López's espatialization of desire, women who become prostitutes because of economic hardship live one step away from the center (156). Beyond them live *rumberas* (women who dance in cabarets).

In *Señora tentación* the three female characters live in clearly demarcated spaces to which the protagonist, the musician Andrés (David Silva), has access. Andrés lives with pianist Blanca (Susana Guizar), works with rumbera Trini (Ninón Sevilla) in a cabaret, and falls in love with diva Hortensia (Hilda Sour), a famous South American couplé singer and musical entrepreneur. Blanca, who stays at home playing the piano most of the time, represents an asexual woman. Her name, which in Spanish means white and is thus connected to purity, and her blindness, which can be read as a sign of her inability to "see" sex, reinforce the idea that she is a character who abstains from sexual relations. Following López's topography, we could say that Hortensia, the musical entrepreneur who stays in expensive hotels, has a similar position to Blanca. Because of her love for luxury, she is situated in the same central spaces related to the patriarchal home; in sexual terms, the "good-woman," Blanca, and the "bad-woman," Hortensia, share the same patriarchal space. Despite being the "Lady Temptation" that gives the title to the film, Hortensia's body is not overtly displayed; she is not presented as someone who transgresses sexual norms. There are no examples of prostitutes in *Señora tentación*, but further away from Blanca and Hortensia lives rumbera Trini, played by Ninón Sevilla. So, if one considers the freedom with which woman display their bodies, as López does, the center of *Señora tentación* is occupied by asexual characters Blanca and Hortensia, the space of the prostitute is empty, and beyond that is the space of rumbera Trini, whose body vibrates with sexual energy. If we read *Señora tentación* following López's ideas, we will praise the rumbera's display of sexual energy, while questioning the lack of sexual energy in Blanca and Hortensia. When looking at classical films, López's analysis finds the restriction posed on women's display of their own bodies problematic. For that reason, she praises rumba dancer Ninón Sevilla, whom she sees

4. Sexuality in Classical and Third-Wave Films 91

Blanca in *Señora tentación* (Colección Filmoteca de la UNAM).

as the female character most closely associated with an overt sexuality. According to the U.S.–based scholar, rumberas "project a virulent form of desire into the screen" (158).

Although López mentions the word desire in reference to Sevilla and in the title of her article, "Tears and Desire," she is not really talking about the same notion as the one used in feminist film studies. Doane's notion of desire refers to the capacity to want objects and the ability to work toward the fulfillment of that desire; López's does not. López praises Sevilla for projecting a sexualized image, for being a sexual icon. However, in most films, the rumbera is almost exclusively locked into the position of being desired, a position that undermines her agency. For instance, in *Señora tentación*, the rumbera Trini, played by Sevilla, is a character with vibrant sexuality: when performing at the center of the stage, she offers her body as a sexual spectacle. Trini's tight top covers her breasts but leaves her belly exposed; her long satin skirt with shiny embroidery opens on the side so that the musicians who accompany her — and by extension the men in the audience — can enjoy her long legs that end elegantly in delicate high-heeled shoes. According to López the rumberas are women who desire. Yet, despite Trini's lack of sexual inhibition, what we see is not Trini's desire, but the desire of others for Trini's body — the musicians, the males on stage and those at the cinema. Moreover, in *Señora tentación*, Trini is depicted in what Freud calls the narcissistic stage. Trini does not have what object relation theorists like Freud call objects; her love for Andrés is presented as filial rather than erotic.[12] For instance, when Andrés decides to leave Blanca and follow Hortensia on a tour, Trini accompanies him as a friend. To emphasize her nonsexual, childish nature, Trini speaks with the voice of a child and acts with the naïve personality of a young girl.[13] Trini's desire, as it appears in *Señora tentación*, is very close to what Freud calls narcissistic love. Trini does not have any object of desire except her own body. In the film we do not know of any desires Trini might have because her character is not created as an agent.

The narcissism in Trini is a sharp contrast with Hortensia's desire. At the hotel, Hortensia has multiple desires: she wants Andrés, her own elegant and luxurious lifestyle, and most significantly, her career as a musical entrepre-

Trini in *Señora tentación* (Colección Filmoteca de la UNAM).

neur. Interestingly, female desire, when it exists, as in the case of Hortensia, is negatively represented and thus, it is not recognized as desire. The film is called *Lady Temptation,* which hints at the attraction-repulsion that Hortensia's desire produces, because Hortensia, the Temptress, uses her passionate look and seductive voice to lure Andrés. At the same time, Hortensia's irresistible sex-appeal is linked to evil intentions and danger, and this is portrayed as repulsive. This diva's desires are in sharp contrast to Blanca, who sacrifices what she wants for Andrés' desires. She gives the money she has saved for an eye operation to Andrés, so he can publish his songs. In *Señora tentación,* the agency of the good-wife and the bad-woman are remarkably different, while that of the rumbera is somewhere between them.

An analysis based on desire reaches very different conclusions than the one López proposes. Applying López's analysis to *Señora tentación* we can conclude that asexual characters Blanca and Hortensia occupy the center, the space of the prostitute is empty, and beyond that is the space of rumbera Trini, whose body reverberates with sexual energy. In a desire-based analysis, such as Doane's, the center is occupied by the good-wife who does not have objects and who does not desire anything for herself. Next is the narcissistic desire of the rumbera, who desires her own body. Still further away from the center is Hortensia, the bad-woman, who has her own objects of desire. While in López's analysis based on the transgression of sexual norms the bad-woman shares the center with the good-wife; in a desire-based examination the bad-woman is a transgressive character who lives at the margins of the system.

A desire-based analysis brings new light to an understanding of classical melodramas. If the bad-woman, the one who represents agency, is the trangressive character, then we have to conclude that the real prohibition in classical films is not about sexuality but about agency. If the characters in *Señora tentación* represent a polarity whose opposing ends are a woman without agency and a woman who is a subject or agent, then we need to pay attention to desire and agency, and also to compensation. In *Señora tentación,* the characters' level of agency is closely related to their fate: Blanca's avoidance of personal desire is compensated, while Hortensia's agency is punished by death.

From the perspective of agency, third-wave films clearly challenge the classical canon because they praise the type of femininity that is punished in classical films. The femininity praised in *Danzón* is very similar to the one condemned in *Señora tentación.* Julia has sailors as objects in the same way as Hortensia has Andres; Julia makes decisions about her life just as Hortensia does; Julia is an agent as is Lady Temptation. Third-wave films, however, give their female characters different outcomes; instead of punishing Julia for her agency, she becomes happy. In terms of desire, third-wave and classical films oppose each other: third-wave film rewards agency; classical films punish agency.

Conclusion

Third-wave filmmakers did not share the same concern as Latin American scholars about sexual purity. Interviews and film analysis show that third-wave filmmakers were aware of the demands for sexual purity in the characters of classical melodramas. Third-wave filmmakers did not respond by creating sexually liberated mothers in their films. For instance, Sistach learned that a sexually liberated woman would not be a realistic portrayal for Guadalupe Sánchez. Mexican women directors believe that women themselves were not yet ready to overcome sexual restrictions. Since open sexuality was not realistic, Sistach changed the scene she wrote for Ana. Similarly, *El secreto de Romelia* is respectful of Romelia's ideas of virginity. These limitations are also clear in *Danzón*. Julia has an affair with a handsome sailor but is portrayed as naïve because she is embarrassed by Susy's plastic breast. Third-wave filmmakers find the morality inherent in classical models of the good mother and the prostitute old fashioned, but their focus is not on changing the characters' acceptance or rejection of conservative sexual norms.

Rather than creating sexually uninhibited characters like the ones played by Ninón Sevilla, *El secreto de Romelia*, *Danzón* and *Los pasos de Ana* center on women who, educated within a conservative morality, feel uncomfortable being openly sexual. Third-wave films take a distance from the socially established norms for women regarding sexual behavior and structure their films so that the audience can respect sexually conservative female protagonists. If we only take into account the film's challenge to established sexual norms, we will conclude that third-wave films do not defy classical norms of sexuality. In third-wave films, conservative views on sexuality are only marginally challenged. From this perspective, third-wave films do not respond to classical films. The problem with this analysis, the chapter argues, is in how we understand desire.

Rather than measuring the films' defiance of sexual norms, chapter 4 examines the film's identificatory processes. Third-wave films respond to the way in which the gaze to express female desire is structured in classical films to express female desire. The examination of *Danzón* from Mulvey's and Doane's idea of desire concludes that Julia is the bearer of the gaze, that her look expresses her desire. Unlike classical films, in which female characters do not have agency and are unable to look, Julia is an active agent who looks. Her gaze expresses the character's desire for the sailors she sees. From the point of view of desire, third-wave films like *Danzón* challenge the way sexuality is structure in classical films.

To show the differences between reading classical melodramas from a consideration of agency or from the point of view proposed by López, chapter 4 analyzes *Señora tentación*. It contrasts two readings, one that emphasizes the transgression of sexual norms and one that focuses on agency. Looking from third-wave films to classical films, it is clear that classical films pose clear limitations on women's agency. Díaz Morales' *Señora tentación*, for instance, punishes women who have agency; Hortensia, the bad-woman, is a woman who is an agent and actively desires. In fact, Hortensia is bad precisely because she wants people and things. Chapter 4 concludes that agency is an essential element in the analysis of classical films, and that third-wave films respond to classical narratives by making their female characters agents.

5

Reconsidering Mothers' Autonomous Identity

This chapter poses the question: how do mothers in classical and third-wave films negotiate their identities in regards to having a separate identity while fulfilling the role of caretakers? Given the lack of attention the topic has received, it might seem that the issue of a separate identity versus a caretaking identity is not important enough to need a whole chapter. Quite the contrary, this chapter demonstrates that there is not only a fundamental difference between classical and third-wave films, but that its study reveals the underpinnings of the constructions of motherhood in third-wave and Golden Age Mexican films.

Negotiation of a separate identity emerges as an important theme when one analyzes third-wave films in their own right. Films such as María Novaro's *Una isla rodeada de agua* (*An Island Surrounded by Water*, 1985); Cortés's *Las Buenromero* (*The Buenromero Sisters*, 1979–80), *Un fragil retorno* (*A Fragile Return*, 1980), *El lugar del corazón* (*The Heart's Place*, 1984), *Hotel Villa Goerne* (1981); and Marisa Sistach's *Los pasos de Ana* raise the issue of how women in general and mothers in particular can have their own separate identities (often as professionals).

My chosen methodology of studying third-wave films as a response to classical films motivates me to pose the same question of Golden Age films. If the negotiations between a separate identity and caretaking are prominent in third-wave films, and if third-wave films are a response to classical films, then how can mothers, in a classical film context, negotiate an identity as individuals and as caretakers? In classical films, the answer to this question is: no, mothers cannot negotiate a separate identity, since it is assumed that mothers are exclusively caretakers. This response raises further questions, such as: what is so feared in the narrative that women who create a separate identity for themselves must be punished? At the same time, the prohibition against mothers who establish separate identities poses another question to third-wave films. If it is true that women in third-wave films create a separate identity for themselves, do they do so at the expense of their role as caretakers? In the end, then, the problem of having a separate identity is seen in relation to, or even impinging upon, the role of caretaking. Thus, the fundamental issue that emerges when we stage a dialogue between these sets of films is this: are having a separate identity and being a caretaker mutually exclusive or compatible?

A Separate Identity in Classical Films

If one examines specific classical films such as *Una familia de tantas*, what stands out is a prohibition against bodily display and sexuality and not a prohibition against having a separate identity. It is easy to reach the conclusion that ideal mothers in classical films need to be pure. However, if one moves away from films that can be considered "good" examples of the Ideal of Virgin Motherhood and examines "bad" examples, the conclusion can be different.

Portrayals of deviation are helpful in understanding norms. The bad woman stereotype, especially in its vamp, or *"devora-hombres,"* version, is mainly a phenomenon of the melodramas of the classical period, and most people agree that it is best represented by actress María Felix — the grand dame of Mexican cinema and the best-paid female actress of the time.

In *Doña Bárbara* there is a scene in which Marisela, Doña Bárbara's daughter, appears in a white flowered dress riding side-saddle. Following Marisela's shot, the camera cuts to a long-shot of Doña Bárbara (María Felix) in a black pant-skirt riding "the masculine way," with a leg on each side of the horse. The colors, white for Marisela and black for "La Doña," give us the idea that the film approves of Marisela's gender norms by associating it with white (purity, innocence). Following the same logic, the film rejects Doña Bárbara's gender norms by associating it with black (evil, bad intentions). Why is the character played by María Felix bad?

In López's (1994) article "Tears and Desire: Women and Melodrama in the 'Old' Mexican Cinema" she leaves this question unanswered. She studies norms of sexuality by looking at the roles in which Mexico's most prominent actresses are cast and relating their roles to the spaces these actresses inhabit in the film. In López's topography, the center is inhabited by those female characters who respect norms of female sexuality, while at the margins one finds those women characters who transgress these norms: the further away from the center, the more a character transgresses. The center is, thus, inhabited by the "good wife," represented by actress Sara García (153–154). Interestingly, in López topography, *malas mujeres* (bad women), typically played by actress María Felix, share the same central space as the good mothers, because neither of them transgresses sexual norms (153–154). This affirmation makes sense because López bases her topography in bodily display, and neither beloved mothers nor bad women display their body. López's explanation, however, leaves us with a question. What makes María Felix's characters part of the "bad mother" category? Mexican melodramas are intentionally educational, and thus the possibility of having good and bad together, sharing the same metaphorical space, seems incongruent. If the "good mother" and the "bad woman" share the same central space, marked as the normative space, what distinguishes the "bad woman" as bad?

Doña Bárbara's Mature Development

One of Felix's best known portrayals of the bad woman stereotype is Doña Bárbara. In a superficial reading of *Doña Bárbara* audiences can conclude that the protagonist is bad because she loves passionately. Unlike normative women who passively love, Doña Bárbara desires actively, an idea that the film portrays through series of scenes featuring her beloved's photograph. After meeting her neighbor Luzardo, who has been away studying law in Caracas, Doña Bárbara falls madly in love with him. The film shows Doña Bárbara cutting a photograph of Luzardo from the local newspaper and putting it in the altar in her room. In order to add negative connotations that can guide the audience into understanding the mistake that Doña Bárbara makes in desiring actively, the film includes a scene in which her active desire is associated with witchcraft and presented as manipulative.[1] At the altar, as Doña Bárbara lights three candles to "Lucifer, Satanás and Belcebú," she puts Luzardo's photograph upside down and says: "I look at you with two, my eyes, without which, you will feel like blind, your reason and your pride will go head over heels." By relating the photograph to the devil the viewer is led to interpret active love in women as bad.

Doña Bárbara's narrative links the protagonist's unfeminine behavior to trauma. In a series of flashbacks at the beginning of the film, the audience learns that Doña Bárbara's violent and unfortunate rape when she was young caused her to develop into a woman with masculine traits, an aberration. Among other things, Doña Bárbara's rape affected Doña Bárbara's love life. The film explains that her way of loving Luzardo, shown in the way she responds to Luzardo's photograph, is mistaken. Doña Bárbara loves as a man would, for which she needs correcting.

A more profound reading of the film shows that there are other reasons why Doña Bárbara is bad or more precisely, that Doña Bárbara's way of loving is a sign of a more significant problem. When examined through Freud's view of development, Doña Bárbara's active desire can be interpreted as a sign that she has matured. Having matured in a Freudian paradigm implies that she has created a separate identity for herself. Thus, it is logical to conclude that what Doña Bárbara has done that is bad enough to warrant putting her in the "bad-woman" category is to create a separate identity for herself.

During what has been termed his "first period," Freud approached human psychological development from an object-relations perspective, looking at the ability of men and women to develop objects. In "On Narcissism" (1914), "Instincts and Their Vicissitudes" (1915), and "Group Psychology and the Analysis of the Ego" (1921), Freud saw the ability to have objects in developmental terms, suggesting that having objects is an ability that humans develop as they mature. In "On Narcissism," for instance, Freud described narcissism as "the attitude of a person who treats his own body in the same way in which the body of a sexual object is ordinarily treated — who looks at it, that is to say, strokes it and fondles it until he obtains complete satisfaction through these activities" (73). Freud postulated that good-looking women are in love with their own bodies and that the energy invested in loving their own bodies impedes their ability to love men. Thus, he concluded that women who do not have true objects are not fully mature; they are at a narcissistic stage, their development is halted.[2] Freud sets up a process of development by negation in which developing as a matured individual consists in objectifying the other. Thus, when applied to the film we can say that the norm that Doña Bárbara breaks is not only a prohibition against active desire, but, more importantly, a prohibition against having a separate identity.

From a Freudian perspective, the scene at the altar indicates that Doña Bárbara is a mature individual. At a developmental level, the photograph indicates that Doña Bárbara has developed an object, visualized in Luzardo's photograph. Within this context, the introduction of the devil in the altar scene can be understood as a warning to the audience against active desire. The presence of the devil reminds the audience that women should stay at a stage in which their bodies are their main objects; only men should mature and have objects. By implication, however, the scene shows that Doña Bárbara has matured, and if she has matured, she can see herself as a separate person. Interestingly, by the time the audience watches the altar scene, they had already been told that Doña Bárbara has a separate identity; although, this message came visually and not verbally.

The scene at the altar needs to be read in conjunction with the fence that surrounds Doña Bárbara's property. The film begins as "La Doña" has demarcated her property by setting up a fence that separates her territory, El Miedo,

Domineering Doña Bárbara (Colección Filmoteca de la UNAM).

from Santos Luzardo's land, Altamira. Thus, the protagonist's separateness is represented in the film through a device that visually demonstrates that the protagonist has created a boundary around her self-hood; the space within the barbwire fence is her separate space.

Doña Bárbara traces the steps that a bad woman, who has wrongly created a separate identity for herself, takes in order to return to normative femininity. The steps involve giving up active love, but most importantly giving up the fence. The film ends with scenes of a boundless land, thus reinforcing the idea that the cornerstone of Doña Barbara's problem was the fence, representative of her separate identity.

As in many other melodramas of the Golden Age, in *Doña Bárbara* the bad woman learns to behave in an Ideal of Virgin Motherhood way. The turning point for Doña Bárbara is when she decides to return some of Luzardo's cows. Doña Bárbara is presented in the film not only as someone who has imposed boundaries, but also as a thief. During her neighbor's long absence from Los Llanos, Doña Bárbara has stolen some of his cows. Thus, her first good deed is to lasso some of the cows that are at El Miedo, and return them to Altamira. As the lassoing scene progresses, Doña Bárbara accepts being "illuminated" and protected by a male with superior moral qualities. The film depicts Luzardo—whose first name, Santos (saint), suggests a generous character—as a morally superior character by situating him standing up while Doña Bárbara is sitting down. Luzardo restores Doña Bárbara to her original ideality by healing the wound of her rape. After, Doña Bárbara explains, looking up to Luzardo, that "brutal men took advantage of her, and that she will make men pay for it." Luzardo, looking down, answers: "The violence you have been a victim of does not justify your own violence." Later Luzardo adds: "Have you thought about how much harm you have done to yourself?" Doña Bárbara is illuminated by Luzardo's words and concludes: "I have harmed myself enough with this violence." Afterward, she goes back to her altar and turns the photograph up again while she repeats Luzardo's words: "Have you thought about how much harm you have done to yourself?" Next, Doña Bárbara takes the photograph out of the altar and lovingly presses it against her heart. Under the guidance of the patriarch, Luzardo, Doña Bárbara gives up her object, a step that will mark her return to a nonindividuated identity.

Giving up Luzardo as an object leads to the return of a boundless identity. The film finishes in the opposite way in which it began; in the final scenes, the camera first shows a broad land without fences and then an old fence and a dead cow in fading out. The off-screen voice clarifies, "El Miedo doesn't exist anymore," "the man-eater has disappeared," and the film shows a very low horizon line broken by only a few trees. By reading the fence in conjunction with Doña Bárbara's process of individuation, we can conclude that the fence visually reinforces Doña Bárbara's reverse process of individuation; at the beginning of the film Doña Bárbara has matured, in Freud's terms, and is an individuated person; by the end of the film, she has given up individuation and she is back to narcissism.

The film's end is clear in regards to its prohibition that women have a separate identity. In *Doña Bárbara* the return to a land without fences, to boundless femininity, is associated with hope and peace. In the last scenes of the film, while the audience sees a shot of open space, mostly sky, the voice-over announces "All is Altamira now," and then the voice-over continues: "Broad and expansive land, all horizons and roads of hope." In this scene the film associates the boundless land, representative of boundless femininity, with hope. The narrative organization of the film helps the audience realize that the prohibition against active desire is in reality a prohibition against a separate identity. This is the reason why, in the narrative development, the scene in which Doña Bárbara gives up her object comes before the scene in which she gives up her separate identity. Giving up her object is a prerequisite for returning to a nonindividuated identity.

While it is obvious that this film imposes severe limits on women's separate identity, it is important to know why. In other words, why do classical films insist that women don't have a separate identity? The next section argues that the fear that women may become professional entrepreneurs plays an important role. That argument emerges clearly in another classical melodrama that includes a "bad-woman" character.

HORTENSIA IN *SEÑORA TENTACIÓN*

Hortensia (Hilda Sour) in *Señora tentación* is another "bad-woman" character with traits similar to Doña Bárbara. Like Doña Bárbara, she has clearly developed objects; she has made Andrés (the male protagonist) fall madly in love with her. In *Señora tentación,* a woman who has individuated is also associated with evil; the film is called *Lady Temptation* because Hortensia, the Temptress, uses her direct look and seductive voice to lure Andrés. Hortensia's irresistible look is linked to danger, evil intentions and harm, and is portrayed as repulsive. Thus, we can conclude that Doña Bárbara and Hortensia are "bad," not only, or primarily, because they violate norms of feminine chastity, but because it is evil of them to make men into objects, as this means that they have individuated and have a separate identity.

What *Señora tentación* adds to our discussion of the dangers of a separate identity for women is the link between having a separate identity and becoming a professional. The issue of a profession already appears in Doña Bárbara, who is a rancher and landowner, but it is more prominent in the urban context of *Señora tentación*. In Díaz Morales's film, Hortensia is portrayed as a famous South American couplé singer and musical entrepreneur; that is, she has two professions, one as singer and another one as musical entrepreneur. It may be that the very reason why women are forbidden from creating a separate identity for themselves is because being separate is linked to being a modern woman and having a professional role, as Hortensia does dreaming about being a musical entrepreneur. This link, between having a separate identity and danger, is in agreement with López's view of the role of Mexican melodramas of the Golden Age. For her, melodramas dramatize the changes in societal values that Mexico went through in the process of modernization after the Mexican Revolution. López believes that melodramas expose the contradictions and desires within Mexican society, especially in three areas: "The clash between old (feudal, Porfirian) values and modern (industrialized, urban) life, the crisis of male identity that emerges as a result of this clash, and the instability of the female identity that at once guarantees and threatens the passage from the old to the new" (López 1994, 511). The establishment of new values, women's potential to enter the workforce and play a role in the urban industrialized society, and the instability that these changes will impose on a male identity are all reasons that explain why Golden Age films view woman's separate identity as a threat.

Doña Bárbara allows us to reach important conclusions in regards to María Félix's role as "bad woman." Focusing on the prohibition against displaying the body, López concluded that the "bad woman" played by Felix inhabited the same central space as the "good mother." However, when we focus, as my analysis does, on normative femininity and the creation of a separate identity, the "good woman" and the "bad woman" inhabit opposed spaces. The good woman, who has not individuated and loves passively, inhabits the center; the bad woman inhabits the margins. In fact, the association of María Felix with the margins is represented in the film itself. It is no accident that Fernando de Fuentes chose to adapt a Venezuelan novel to represent a character who stands for female aberration.[3] Such characters can only live in places that in the Mexican imagination are considered further away from the Mexican nation, as Venezuela is. The locus of *Doña Bárbara* is also "far away" for Venezuelans, who consider Caracas the central space, and the Venezuelan Plains (Los Llanos), where the film takes place, far away. Thus the *devora-hombres* lives far away from the central space occupied by the good-mother, because she has become an individual.

A "bad" woman is bad because she has created a separate identity for herself. *Doña Bárbara* and *Una familia de tantas* portray mothers who are prohibited from creating separate identities for themselves. The mother in *Una familia de tantas*, Doña Gracia, provides a positive example of this idea; Doña Gracia's mediating role exemplifies the mother who relinquishes a separate identity in order to be a mediator between her husband and the children. *Doña Bárbara*'s mother is a negative example of the same idea. Doña Bárbara's bounded self-identity is portrayed as inappropriate for women in general and for mothers in particular.

Separate Identities in Third-Wave Films

Third-wave films respond to classical films by portraying a woman's separate identity in a different light. One way to establish the differences is to look at the classical film *Doña Bárbara* in conjunction with Novaro's third-wave film, *Una isla rodeada de agua*; both films use physical space to visually represent personal space, but the way in which each film values having a separate identity is very different.

In María Novaro's graduating thesis from CUEC, a woman's mental space is metaphorically represented by an island. Paintings of islands appear several times in the film. As Edith, the protagonist, is about to enter a studio of photography, the camera stops at the door, showing a painting of an island with palm trees. The metaphor of an island is especially prominent during Edith's fifteenth birthday celebration. She goes to the studio to have her picture taken and the backdrop for the photograph is an island of luxurious palm trees surrounded by crashing waves. As she poses for the photograph, Edith aligns the upper part of her body with the island. This scene represents Edith's entrance into adulthood (fifteen in Mexico) by visualizing her separate identity; the perimeter surrounding the island represents the boundaries of her identity; her physical and psychic space ends where the water begins.[4] Her personal identity has limits; she is like an island.

The island, in the case of *Una isla rodeada de agua,* and the fence in the case of *Doña Bárbara* represent the protagonist's separate identity by demarcating physical space.

Edith poses in front of a backdrop of an island (courtesy María Novaro).

Despite the fact that both films use physical space to represent an autonomous identity, the associations that each film attaches to female separateness are distinctly different. *Doña Bárbara* links a separate female identity with aberration, the devil, manhood and fear. Doña Bárbara's creation of a separate identity is presented in the film as a cause for masculine anxiety. The name of Doña Bárbara's ranch, El Miedo (Place of Fear), and her nickname of *devora-hombres* (men-eater) are signs of this anxiety. In the film, men fear Doña Bárbara's control over them, a fear that La Doña herself addresses when she says that she "takes men when she needs them and, once she is done with them, throws them away in pieces." The term devora-hombres reflects the threat to patriarchal power associated with María Felix's character; men fear that their masculinity is going to be "eaten up." The negative connotations established in the classical film context are in sharp contrast to the connotations attached to a separate identity in third-wave representations.

Una isla rodeada de agua differs from classical films by establishing a positive association between femininity and a separate identity; Edith is encouraged to see herself as separate. In *Una isla rodeada de agua* the space that represents a separate identity has positive associations. In the original backdrop, the island is represented as a green luxurious place. In other parts of the film, Edith's autonomous identity is associated with pleasure and is shown as synonymous with seeing the world in luxurious colors. In a humorous scene, the protagonist's separate identity is expressed through her sense of vision. The scene begins with the question of a four-year-old girl who, surprised because Edith's blue eyes are an unusual trait among the local population of the state of Guerrero, where Novaro's film takes place, asks the protagonist: "Do you see everything blue? A series of shot-reverse shots shows what Edith sees. After a shot of Edith's very blue eyes, the camera cuts to a shot of the ocean in which the water is magenta and the sky is yellow. This sequence suggests that Edith takes pleasure in the richness of the magenta contrasting with the yellow. The main character's capacity to see is surprisingly and refreshingly associated with pleasure and playfulness, and never associated with masculinity. When Edith looks, she sees and enjoys luxuriant colors. This scene also tells the audience that Edith sees the world differently from other people. We know that people with blue eyes do not see a magenta ocean, but the film relates Edith's separate identity with her capacity to see the world that surrounds her in a way that is specifically hers, and this in turn is like being an island. In contrast to classical films, third-wave films create women who have a separate identity. They are not made to return to normative femininity, like Doña Bárbara.

Mothers' Relations to Other Family Members

In classical films mothers' creation of a separate identity for themselves is seen as dangerous; it is feared that a separate identity would decrease mothers' devotion to taking care of the unity and well-being of the family. In *Doña Bárbara*, for instance, the protagonist has created a separate identity for herself that the film views as detrimental to her role as mother and wife. The opposite is shown in *Una familia de tantas*; Doña Gracia is "good" because, having given up a separate identity, she is involved in the family, connecting father and children.

When we put third-wave films and classical films in dialogue, the demand that women, like the Virgin, take a mediating role between father and children stands out. The Virgin Mary's identity is based on her mediating role, on her relation with others, and so is Doña Gracia's identity. The main role of the mother in *Una familia de tantas* is to mediate in order to connect the father with his children (see chapter 3). Father and children are portrayed as two groups that stand apart from each other. Mothers intercede for the children, and at the same time they subject them to the father. In *Una familia de tantas* Doña Gracia's identity is through her role of connecting her children to Don Rodrigo. In classical films, the Virgin and Doña Gracia's identities are reduced to being conduits between father and children. Such identity "empties them out," so to speak, of a personal identity. That is, we do not know anything personal about the Virgin and Doña Gracia, such as their likes or dislikes. Why, could we ask, do films of the Mexican Golden Age not give mothers a separate existence?

In classical films, a mother's separate existence and an identity based on that separate existence is seen as detrimental to her role as a mediator within the family. So, although it is not obvious on a superficial viewing, within classical films, mothers' acquisition of a separate identity is seen as impinging upon their roles as mediators. Doña Bárbara is a case in point, because her separate identity is shown to be in opposition to her role of caring for her husband and daughter.

Wifehood and Motherhood in *Doña Bárbara*

The actions of women characters in films of the Golden Age are often motivated by an implicit fear that if a woman takes an identity other than a caretaker, it will detract from her main role of connecting the father and the children, and nurturing them. In *Doña Bárbara,* the protagonist's sense of separate self disqualifies her from the role of wife. Doña Bárbara's psychic space, represented by the fence, prevents her from having a relationship to

Lorenzo Barquero, Marisela's father. This disjunction can be seen in a scene in which she refuses to consider anything "ours," meaning hers and Lorenzo's. When Lorenzo tells Doña Bárbara that she needs help for "our daughter," she responds: "Can there be anything in the world that is yours and mine?" This dialogue shows that Doña Bárbara's sense of autonomous self is an obstacle to her role as wife and mother. Not only is her communication with her husband at stake, but also her ability to have effective communication with her daughter. Lorenzo Barquero cannot communicate well with her about their daughter because Doña Bárbara has built a separate identity for herself. This one incident with Lorenzo is not an isolated case. Doña Bárbara also refuses to use the plural pronoun with her new potential husband, overseer Balbino Paiba. When Balbino asks her for a cigarette, she responds, "Smoke yours," showing that she is unwilling to share even a cigarette. This is something, the film implies, which is normally done, even with strangers. The cigarette incident helps us understand the next scene, in which Balbino proposes marriage ("We should formalize our relationship"), and Doña Bárbara responds by wanting to whip him. She is presented as unwilling to be part of an open masculine landscape, and her selfishness and irrationality disqualify her as a wife, according to the film's logic.

Doña Bárbara's creation of a psychic space for herself also disqualifies her from being a mother. Again, according to the film's logic, Doña Bárbara's separate sense of self contains the emotions she might otherwise feel toward her daughter. The scene that follows Doña Bárbara's meeting with her exhusband shows the way in which Doña Barbara's autonomous identity prevents her from fulfilling her role as a mother. Knowing that her daughter needs help, Doña Bárbara visits her and, from her horse, throws her a bundle containing money. This suggests that Doña Bárbara thinks that money can replace the love and care that a mother should provide. The incident is an example of inappropriate nurturing behavior. Although well intentioned, Doña Bárbara is not able to take care of her daughter appropriately. The film lets the audiences know that a mother is supposed to give love, not money.

Seen from this standpoint of the Ideal of Virgin Motherhood, Doña Bárbara's separate identity negatively affects her role as mediator; it keeps her love from reaching her husband and daughter. Classical films' rejection of an independent identity for women is based on the presumption that self-identity is detrimental to women's role as caretaker for their family members. Interestingly, third-wave films don't argue that mothers should give up their relationship to others in order to develop an independent sense of self. Rather, third-wave films present self-identity and a relationship to others as compatible.

Relations Between Mother and Daughter in *Una isla rodeada de agua*

In Novaro's *Una isla rodeada de agua*, having a separate identity and relating to others happen simultaneously. This is referred to metaphorically in the second part of the film's title. If we accept that Edith's identity is represented by the island, as the film suggests, then we can say that the teenager's separated identity is the perimeter of the island. However, her identity as an island is not an isolated one; the *rodeada* (surrounded) in the film's title suggests that despite being an island, Edith's perimeter is surrounded by water. In other words, she is distinct, but in relationship with the ocean.

In *Una isla rodeada de agua* Edith is associated with her mother, Lucía. In the first scenes, Lucía, a guerrilla fighter, leaves Edith, then one year old, in the care of her neighbor. Despite her neighbor's advice to "Think about Edith.... Don't be unreasonable," Lucía paddles away to join a Marxist-Leninist guerrilla group, the Lucio Cabañas front. She is never seen again in the film, but her presence is constantly felt.

In order to emphasize Lucía's presence, the film traces an association between Lucía and the ocean. In a sequence in which Edith is looking out at the sea from a balcony, early memories of Lucía come back; she sees herself holding onto Lucía's waist with her legs by the seashore. These images are played with the sound track of Agustín Lara's famous song "Piensa en mi" (Think about me). The narrative context, Lucía remembering her mother, reframes the heterosexual love alluded to in the song; through the song the protagonist imagines her mother's love for her. In this way, Lucía remains by Edith's side and accompanies her through feelings of sadness (*ganas de llorar*) and deep sorrow (*un hondo pesar*). Lucía is absent, working on a political project, but still manages to be a crucial affective presence in her daughter's life. We can then conclude that *Una isla rodeada de agua* responds to classical films by making an independent identity, such as Edith's and Lucía's, compatible with a relationship to others. In other words, Edith can see herself as an island and at the same time have a close relationship with her mother.

There still remains one question. After a Freudian analysis of *Doña Bárbara* we have concluded that Doña Bárbara has a separate identity because she has objects. We have also seen that Edith in *Una isla rodeada de agua* has a separate identity. Since Edith, unlike Doña Bárbara, does not have objects, then it must be that having a separate identity involves other things besides having objects. What do third-wave films associate with having a separate identity? And what are the benefits that third-wave films associate with this?

Self-Expression in Third-Wave Films

Third-wave films identify having a separate identity with self-expression. Novaro's *Una isla rodeada de agua,* for instance, presents this idea by relating Edith's separate identity to seeing the world in a personal way. It is not coincidental that Edith, the person who in the film is portrayed as being like an island, is given the capacity to see the world in a unique way. Her view of the world in magenta is directly related to being herself; Edith is an island (has a separate identity) because she sees the world in her own personal way.

In third-wave films, it is important that the personal way in which one sees the world is communicated, since it is in this way that it becomes self-expression. In *Una isla rodeada de agua* Edith's separate identity is communicated to the audience, who also sees the world is magenta, as she does. Then the question is: why might third-wave filmmakers see this as a positive alternative to the sort of separate identity modeled by Doña Bárbara?

Self-expression is important because it leads to fulfillment and away from depression. In *Tales of Love* (1987) Julia Kristeva reflects on what causes what Freud terms melancholia (depression). In trying to help clients who are depressed, Kristeva asks: what makes depressed people depressed? She concludes that a lack of the ability or possibility of self-expression leads to melancholia. Kristeva refers to this idea with the concept of "psychic space"; she associates depression with flattened space and opposes it to opening psychic space, a state in which drives can be articulated into symbols and affects can be expressed through words; in other words, self-expression is communication.

Kristeva's notion of psychic space offers another way to discuss the notion of self-hood. Unlike Freud's account, it does not define self-hood in terms of negating the other by making the other into an object. For Kristeva self-hood is established in communicating a separate identity to others (articulating drives into symbols). However, for the particular case that we are analyzing, the dialogue between classical and third-wave films, it is important to establish a distinction between connection and communication.

Classical films emphasize that mothers need to be connectors, and third-wave films emphasize that mothers need to communicate. Although both terms imply a relationship with others, communicating includes self-expression and connection (in this sense) does not. For instance, in classical films, mothers like Doña Gracia connect father and children, but connection does not involve expressing themselves. In fact, in classical films, being a good mother does not leave any room for self-expression. By contrast, in third-wave films women's relationships to others involve not connection, but communication. For instance, in Edith's case, her relationship to others, and in particular to the audience, includes showing them traits that are specifically hers. We can then conclude that third-wave filmmakers are interested in establishing a separate identity through self-expression. We can also understand the problem that classical films pose from a third-wave perspective: if, as Kristeva argues, a flattened psychic space is a sign of depression, then making women become boundless, as in the case of Doña Bárbara, or making them center their identity on mediation, like Doña Gracia, is leading them to depression because in both cases self-expression is taken away from these women.

There is another characteristic of third-wave films that allows us to further understand why third-wave films value having a separate identity. In third-wave films, having a professional life is positively valued. In contrast to Hortensia's demise as a result of her desire to be a musical entrepreneur, in *Los pasos de Ana*, the protagonist finds value in making her own films. She finds in them a way to express herself.

Filmmaking as a Way to Open Psychic Space for Women

Los pasos de Ana literally puts emotions into images by recounting the first steps third-waver filmmakers took to enter into the film industry. Ana, the protagonist of the film, a graduate from the CCC, has to earn her living as an assistant director to a male director who worked for television. The making of the film shows traces of the first steps Sistach took to enter the colonized world of 35 mm filmmaking: Sistach directed her first feature-length film in the late eighties, a time in which film school graduates were unable to find subsidies for making their own films. For this reason, she had to shoot the film in 16 mm and then blow it up to 35 mm.

Often, opening up psychic space in third-wave films involves bringing the experiences of the filmmakers to the screen. *Los pasos de Ana*, for instance, is a semibiographical film in which Sistach creates the protagonist as her alter ego. Ana, like Sistach herself, is a CCC graduate and, also like Sistach, works in television. Sistach incorporated in her "opera prima" the experiences she has had in her professional life. In 1985, Sistach worked in UTEC television series about Mexican writers. Her assignment was to conduct research and write a program about Sinaloan poet Gilberto Owen. In *Los pasos de Ana*, Ana's most important assignment is to work on a television program entitled "Gilberto Owen, el recuerdo olvidado" ("Gilberto Owen, the Forgotten Memory"). Ana, again like Sistach, is a divorced mother in her thirties with two children, Juan and Paula, who are played by Sistach's own children. *Los pasos de Ana* includes Sistach's experience as a mother by showing Ana videotaping the day to day life of herself with her children. Furthermore, in an interview the filmmaker mentions another autobiographical element that she included in Ana's character: "I reproduced my own emotions in Ana's love of work and in the type of work that she does" (Arredondo 2013, 126). Filmmaking was a way to reflect and think about her emotions, and at the same time, making films produced its own emotions.

For Sistach, making a film, and more precisely a film about her own life as a filmmaker and a mother, is a joy. According to the director: "Making *Los pasos de Ana* was the fulfillment of a double dream: in making the movie, I was making Ana's dream a reality. And, at the same time, I was also realizing my own dream" (125). Kristeva's notion of psychic space is helpful to understand Sistach's filmmaking. Filmmaking is for Sistach a way in which affects, the emotions Sistach had as a mother and a filmmaker, can be expressed through images. By putting her life into film, Sistach opens up her own psychic space. The results of opening up psychic space are not surprising. Sistach added: "The work you like to do makes you a more complete individual, it fills you up.... Work, for me, is essential to my well-being as a person. When I'm working, I feel better than when I'm not doing anything" (133). Filmmaking, then, leads away from depression into meaningful existence.

The analysis of third-wave responses to classical films has focused on the discussion of a separate identity, showing that while in classical films women are not allowed to have a separate identity, in third-wave films women are encouraged to have a separate identity. In other words, in terms of the creation of a separate identity, classical and third-wave films are in opposition; the first discourages women from having a separate identity, while the second encourages it. The notion of psychic space explains why third-wave filmmakers are interested in establishing a separate identity for women; the prohibition in *Doña Bárbara* to have a separate identity is associated with depression, whereas Edith's open psychic space in *Una isla rodeada de agua* is linked with well-being, a state in which communication and expression are possible. Also, third-wave films like *Los pasos de Ana* show that filmmaking itself is a way of establishing a separate identity, a medium for self-expression. However, psychic space is not simply given to women; according to Busi Cortés, one must fight for it.

Psychic Space and Violence

In Cortés's shorts, having access to psychic space is not a given, but requires violence. Her imaginary, psychic space, the space from which women speak and create, is already owned by men, and women do not own any of that space. Thus, women must use violence to obtain justice. In an interview with the author published in *In Our Own Image*, Cortés reflects on the fact that, in all of her shorts and medium length films, men die.[5] We can interpret the deaths of male characters as necessary deaths; women literally or figuratively have to kill men to open up a psychic space for themselves.

Cortés's acknowledgment of the necessity of violence needs to be read in conjunction with Kelly Oliver's redefinition of psychic space. Bringing Kristeva's notion from the realm of the individual to the realm of the social, Oliver (2006) defines psychic space as *a set of conditions* that allows affects to be expressed in words and drives to be articulated as symbols (54). Oliver's definition includes social parameters; according to her, society opens up or flattens psychic space. Psychic space does not exist by itself.

The violence in Cortés's work should be seen in connection to the social conditions of filmmaking for women in the 1980s, when a group of women filmmakers like Ana entered the filmmaking industry by studying in state-funded schools. Sistach acknowledges that filmmaking is a male-colonized arena when she says: "For a woman in Mexico, in a medium dominated by men — as is the world of filmmaking ... becoming a film director is practically a dream" (Arredondo 2013, 125). Novaro's account of making films includes the violence she felt when entering the male-dominated world of filmmaking: "In my first movie the electricians would look at me as if I were mentally retarded. For them, a woman directing is just like a child directing. It's as if they were saying, "How could she possibly direct?" (Arredondo 2013, 187). Cortés's films portray the violence that Sistach and Novaro describe.

Killing Male Characters to Open Up Psychic Space for Women

In Cortés's shorts, women begin by decolonizing psychic space within the private sphere and expanding their area of influence to include the arts, where men have taken the role of producers of art. *Las Buenromero* was made as a class exercise at CCC. A still shot of the three Buenromero sisters in the end credits shows them as if they were three nineteenth-century melancholic sisters on a sofa, their heads laying softly on each other's shoulders and their eyes lost in space. Yet, they are clearly more active than that. They live in a house in an old provincial Mexican town, away from the elements of the outside world. Inside the house, they have designed their own entertainment: they kill their lovers. In an interview, Cortés pointed out that the Buenromero sisters kill men who symbolically represent power in different areas of society. Josefina kills a painter, who represents the arts; Matilde kills a sexton, who represents the power of the Church; Refugio kills a political candidate, who represents the power of politicians. Unlike many classical melodramas, where women's fulfillment comes in the form of marriage or romance, in *Las Buenromero*, fulfillment comes from killing. It is as if the death of the father and the killing of males who represent the symbolic order is necessary in order for these sisters to be content. By killing their lovers, the three Buenromero sisters make a physical space (the house) into their own psychic space, into a world that belongs to them. The Buenromero world, now emptied of men, allows a new subjectivity or sense of self to emerge. In Cortés's shorts, all women have the ability to plot, not only the young and more open-minded ones. *Las Buenromero* attacks the basis of the symbolic order: the church, the political party, the arts.

The world in which the Buenromero sisters live is a colonized one. In Kelly Oliver's "Psychic Space and Social Melancholy" (2002) and in *The Colonization of Psychic Space*, (2004), the author reads Kristeva's notion of psychic space together with Frantz Fanon's *The Wretch of the Earth* (1961). Fanon was a psychiatrist from Martinique who worked in North Africa, mainly in Algeria. Based on his experience treating inhabitants of French colonies, Fanon wrote about the way in which colonization affects the self-image of the colonized. His studies of the effects of colonization on the individual's psyche have been fundamental for postcolonial feminist commentators. Expanding Fanon's concept of colonization, in *The Colonization of Psychic Space* Oliver proposes that mothers of all continents are colonized subjects. If indeed mothers in particular and women in general are colonized subjects—if their private space is already owned by the colonizer—then the colonizer's death, whether it be literal or figurative is necessary in order for women to have their own psychic space. This idea applies to the story of Buenromero sisters, who kill three men who represent the symbolic order.

Cortés's (1980) *Un fragil retorno* (*A Fragile Return*) dramatizes the important role the death of the colonizer plays in women's access to psychic space. Filmed while she was still a student at the CCC, this short associates the physical space of an office with psychic space. The short takes place at Luis's office, where his wife Elia helps with secretarial tasks. *Un fragil retorno* begins as Elia is preparing a candlelight dinner for Luis, who is returning from a trip. She prepares the dinner at the office instead of their home because Luis is in the habit of coming back to his office first. The husband's office symbolizes Luis's priorities and also the ways in which women are used as workers but not given credit for the work they do; Elia organizes the office, does the errands, and provides new ideas, but all the credit goes to Luis.[6]

When Elia, who suffers from heart problems, is told by her sister Silvia that Luis has died in an airplane crash, her heart survives the shock. With

Luis's death, the physical space of the office becomes vacant. This vacant space becomes Elia's psychic space; she decides to enjoy the dinner that she had prepared for Luis and make plans for the future with Silvia. Now that Elia, who spent most of her time working for Luis, has more time, the two sisters can make their own plans. Thus, the colonizer's death creates an empty space from which women's psychic space can emerge. If, as Oliver (2006) suggested, psychic space involves "a set of conditions that allows affects to be expressed in words and drives to be articulated as symbols" (54), then in Elias's case, the set of conditions is to have an empty office space; it is only when the office is empty that she may cultivate psychic space. In *Un frágil retorno* however, Cortés chooses to emphasize the idea that women live in a colonized space more than she portrays their joy or contentment in owning it. When Luis, who was actually not on the fatal flight, shows up, Elia's fragile heart gives out: she has a heart attack and dies. The mistaken announcement of Luis's death opens a space for Elia which his reappearance closes. With Luis' return, Elia's psychic space disappears, and she literally dies.

In Cortés's (1984) *El lugar del corazón* (*The Heart's Place*) it is the space in which history is written that needs to be decolonized. Cortés filmed this medium-length feature film when she was a film teacher at the Universidad Iberoamericana in Mexico City. In *El lugar del corazón*, a group of high-school girls "kill off" their male history teacher to take revenge on him, because he ridicules them in class. The killing begins as a game: to get rid of the anger they feel at being ridiculed, the friends pretend to use witchcraft, sticking pins in a doll that represents their teacher. Through this game, however, the students get what they wish for: when they stick pins in the doll's legs, the teacher becomes an invalid. The film's title, *The Heart's Place*, refers to the "voodoo" practice at the climax of the plot: when the students stick pins in the doll's heart, "the heart's place," the teacher dies.

In *El lugar del corazón* the high-school girls take possession of a space that has symbolic value. Significantly, the teacher is a history teacher, so his death metaphorically means the death of a history made from a male perspective. At the end of the film, the three female students are left to tell the story and to make history; it is understood that this will be history from their perspective. *El lugar del corazón* can be seen as a development of *Un frágil retorno*. Three friends actively open up a psychic space; sticking pins in the heart's place opens up a symbolic space and leaves them in control. Half innocently, half purposely, these students fight to reappropriate a space from which to speak and make history. It is understood that as they grow up, these students will write a history of Mexico that includes the work and the presence of women.

Cortés portrays several scenarios (the home, the office, the school) in which women have to use violence in order to make a space to express themselves. Another context in which women need to use violence is in the arts and, more specifically, in the world of literature.

Cortés's *Hotel Villa Goerne*: Decolonizing the Arts

Hotel Villa Goerne, Cortés's (1981) thesis for the CCC, draws on some ideas already outlined in Cortés's previous shorts. As in *Las Buenromero*, in *Hotel Villa Goerne* the centrality of the male artist as the maker of meaning is challenged. And as in *El lugar del corazón*, plotting women — an adolescent girl, Fernanda, and her three aunts — kill a man in order to take control of a space delineated as masculine. The space to be conquered this time is the space from which literature is written. The male protagonist, writer Eligio, arrives at the hotel with the intention of staying for an extended period to write stories. Since Eligio lacks the inspiration to write his own stories, he hopes that he can turn the personal stories of the women living in the hotel into stories that will win him a literary prize. However, the women of the hotel do not acquiesce to his plan; whenever Eligio asks questions, he gets vague and contradictory responses. The film presents a garbage can full of rejected pages, which shows that Eligio has not made much progress.

As in the other films Cortés created, in *Hotel Villa Goerne* the death of a man facilitates the creation of women's psychic space. In this case, the writer is not literally killed, but the story that he writes is. Fernanda, the youngest of the women, goes to Eligio's room, steals his manuscript, and disposes of it. She goes to the park and makes paper swans out of the manuscript pages and quietly watches the swans float away. The scene has a mischievous, perverse tone, half playful, half malicious. After the audience sees Fernanda taking Eligio's manuscript from his room, the camera cuts to a shot of the pond in the park. As the change from an indoor space to an unfamiliar outdoor space is very sudden, it is disconcerting, and so it is easy to miss that is the swans floating on the water are paper swans and not real swans. A third cut, a close-up of a paper swan juxtaposed against a real swan, makes it clear that Fernanda has created paper swans out of the manuscript. The real swan and the paper swans enjoy a tranquil dance, which gives the impression that opening up psychic space is mischievous game. By its association with beauty and peacefulness, the decolonization of female spaces is presented as enjoyable entertainment.

In order to enter into the colonized space of literature writing, in *Hotel Villa Goerne*, Cortés literally gives the women protagonists control of the narrative. This represents a change in Cortés's narrative strategies. In the shorts described previously, women take control within the narrative; for instance

Las Buenromero sisters make an impact within the social institutions that surround them. In *Hotel Villa Goerne*, Cortés uses a formal technique to emphasize that women are the creators of the film's narrative. As if the film were a book, *Hotel Villa Goerne* is divided formally into sections; each section has a title that appears on the screen and is read by an off-screen female voice. The section titles, which are assumed to be the chapter titles of the story the women in the hotel are writing, announce the actions that follow. For example, after the spectator sees and hears "The Arrival," Eligio enters the hotel. Cortés uses titles to underscore that *Hotel Villa Goerne* is a story written by women and not a story written by a male writer about women.

Hotel Villa Goerne opens up psychic space for women in Kristeva's and Oliver's sense. In Kristeva's sense, the women in the hotel have opened up psychic space because they are writing about themselves, turning their affects into words. Cortés's thesis from CCC also creates psychic space in Oliver's sense: the owners have controlled the male writer and "killed" his story in order to write their own story. If in *Las Buenromero* the artist is killed, in *Hotel Villa Goerne* his work is destroyed and women take control of writing within the social.

Overall, Cortés's shorts lay out a gradual process of decolonization of the social sphere. First comes the disappearance of obstacles, the death of men or their work — whether lovers (*Las Buenromero*), husbands (*Un frágil retorno*), history teachers (*El lugar del corazón*), or writers (*Hotel Villa Goerne*). Afterward, Cortés has women "own" the vacated physical spaces. In *Un frágil retorno*, for instance, Luis's emptied office allows Elia and Silvia to make their own plans. A step further, in *Hotel Villa Goerne,* women create their own art in their physically owned space in which they can control the conditions under which they transform affects into words.

Since this book establishes a dialogue between third-wave films and classical films, and since classical films also include women characters like Doña Bárbara who also use violence, it is important to ask: is Doña Bárbara's violence similar to that of Cortés's protagonists?

Doña Bárbara and Violence

Doña Bárbara uses violence in a very similar way to the way that Cortés's characters use it; it is by violence that she has created a place for herself in society and within society's power structures. She has her own land, El Miedo, and a considerable herd of cows; she is in charge of her economic life, through owning both cattle and feather businesses; she has taken control of religion, through her alliance with the Devil; and most importantly, she is in charge of political institutions. We could say that at the beginning of the film Doña

Bárbara has gained what Cortés's characters are looking for: a space of her own and a place of power in society. However, the values that the narrative of *Doña Bárbara* associates with achieving psychic space are very different from the ones presented in Cortés's films.

Doña Barbara's violence is related to barbarism (a relationship established through the name of the protagonist). Doña Bárbara's actions are devalued by their association to political barbarism and unruliness. Rómulo Gallegos (1929), the author of the novel *Doña Bárbara*, script-writer of the De Fuentes' film, and president of Venezuela in 1948, creates Doña Bárbara with traits associated to José Antonio Páez,[7] a Venezuelan caudillo widely reputed in Los Llanos (the same place where *Doña Bárbara* takes place) to be barbaric. Doña Bárbara and Páez share the same "sin" of ignoring the constitution and establishing their own rules. For instance, at the beginning of the narrative the sailor who brings Santos Luzardo back to Los Llanos warns him that he is entering a territory governed by the laws of Doña Bárbara, and later on in the film, the audience learns that the local authorities rule by Doña Barbara's law. Given the allusion to Venezuelan politics inscribed in the novel, it is not a surprise that Santos Luzardo, a lawyer, comes to Los Llanos to "restore" Venezuelan law. The male hero is in charge of ending the terror created by a woman who is destroying Venezuela.

Another difference between Cortés's shorts and *Doña Bárbara* is that in the latter violence is associated with trauma and portrayed as revenge. In the scene in which Luzardo and Doña Bárbara talk while they are taking Altamira's cows back, the protagonist explains that brutal men took advantage of her, establishing rape as the cause of her violence. Her use of violence is devalued by its association with revenge: Doña Barbara continues talking of her rape by saying that she will make men pay for the violence of which she was a victim. In order to call attention to the film's association between violence and revenge, Luzardo responds, "Have you thought how much harm have you done to yourself?" Luzardo's question implies that revenge is a negative feeling and harms the protagonist. For all the violence Doña Bárbara causes, the film's logic argues, she is "thrown out," so to speak, from her place of control within the society and from Los Llanos. Violence, then, is another reason that makes Doña Bárbara bad and one that is used in the narrative to explain why she has to be punished and made to leave.

Classical and third-wave films present two different worlds; Cortés's shorts portray society as a colonized world where women do not have a space, while in *Doña Bárbara* the protagonist is the colonizer who has wrongly colonized the land (with the use of fences). This view of the world is tied to the need to use violence; in Cortés's colonized world, violence is the only way in which women are able to reach the goals that are otherwise denied to them.

If the goal is a world where communication and self-expression, rather than connection, are possible, then using violence is not only useful, but also necessary. Luzardo's suggestion that violence is just an emotion that perpetuates itself and creates more violence assumes that the use of violence does not have an end and is therefore useless and unnecessary. Yet violence in Cortés's shorts has an end: its underlying goal is to decolonized the societal space from which women have been expelled and to make it available to women.

The different views of classical and third-wave films in regards to women's use of violence are to a certain degree expected. What is perhaps more remarkable is the fact that both types of film cast the establishment of a woman's separate identity as an act related to violence. This association brings to the foreground women's entitlement to a separate identity: if women's separate identity is only achieved through violence, then we can conclude that in both sets of films, women are portrayed as not enjoying entitlement to a separate identity.

Conclusion

Classical and third-wave films conceive caretaking differently. In films of the Golden Age, being a caretaker is associated with being a mediator, and this role is seen as incompatible with an independent identity. A mother's separate existence and an identity based on that separate existence is seen as detrimental to her role as a mediator within the family. Mothers' acquisition of a separate identity is seen as impinging upon mothers' roles as mediators. In contrast, in third-wave films caretaking is not defined in relation to mediation, and consequently, autonomous identity and caretaking are compatible. Third-wave films redefine the ideal qualities of mothers, getting rid of the idea that a mother should act as a mediator between the father and the children. In part, as chapter 8 will show, because fathers are absent.

The bad women of classical cinema, such as María Félix and Hortensia, are bad because they have agency, and also because they create a separate identity for themselves. The capacity to act has a spatial representation in classical and third-wave films. A woman's separate identity is represented in *Doña Bárbara* by a fence and in *Una isla rodeada de agua* by the image of an island. Classical and third-wave films take opposing positions in regards to the establishment of autonomous identities for women. While Doña Bárbara is discouraged to maintain her fence, Edith is encouraged to maintain her separate identity. Having an autonomous identity is related to pleasure in the third-wave films, where Edith can see the world in different colors. In contrast, having a separate identity in *Doña Bárbara* is related to evil, and thus to displeasure.

Her wired territory is associated with fear; her land is called El Miedo (the Land of Fear). Because of her actions as an independent woman and her autonomous identity, Doña Bárbara is banned from Altamira, the original space conceived without fences, without women who have autonomous identities.

Classical and third-wave films associate the establishment of an autonomous identity for women with violence. Doña Bárbara's name suggests that the protagonist of *Doña Bárbara* has a violent personality. Similarly, by admitting that all the female characters in her shorts kill the male characters, Cortés acknowledges that women have to commit a violent act in society in order to establish their own identities, their psychic space. The difference is that classical films present the violence associated with having an autonomous identity as despicable, while third-wave films find it necessary. The Buenromero sisters, Elia in *Un frágil retorno*, Fernanda in *Hotel Villa Goerne*, and the high-school girls of *El lugar del corazón* use violence to decolonize a space that should be theirs but is not. To open up women's psychic space in the church, in politics, in Mexican history, women have to kill.

This chapter proposes new readings of classical and third-wave films by analyzing women's entitlement to a separate identity. For instance, when looking at classical films from a third-wave perspective, the prohibition against women establishing separate identities is prominent. This prohibition is not always obvious. When reading a classical film narrative like *Una familia de tantas*, what stands out is the film's call for purity, and the prohibition against mothers having a separate identity often goes unnoticed. This chapter has taken the example of the bad woman stereotype to demonstrate the extent to which women are violently forbidden from creating separate identities. A new understanding of classical films emerges from looking at the issue of women's entitlement to separate identities; this chapter demonstrates the enormous weight that the prohibition against having a separate identity plays in classical films, and thus it changes our understanding of classical films. To our examination of classical films' depiction of women's sexual restrictions we add the view that classical films restrict women's creation of an identity independent from caretaking.

The dialogue between classical and third-wave films has also resulted in the examination of aspects of third-wave films that have been neglected. Because a woman's identity as a mother is something that 1980s and 1990s generations of women did not find pressing as a topic of feminist discussion, critics have paid little attention to the issue of motherhood in third-wave films. This chapter's examination of the representation of motherhood in third-wave films from a classical film point of view has revealed new perspectives; for instance, the fact that third-wave mothers do not reject caretaking but, like classical mothers, embrace it. Third-wave films however introduce the transformative idea that caretaking is compatible with having a separate identity.

What is at stake in third-wave and classical films is women's entitlement to a separate identity, and also the possibility of being lovers, mothers and professionals at the same time. Having a separate identity, as Cortés's shorts show, is not an entitlement women currently enjoy but a goal that women may have to gain violently.

6

Looking Back at Classical Idealization

Many feminists have argued against the idealization of women and mothers. It is common to read in feminist articles of the 1980s published in North America and Mexico that real mothers have been idealized by mainstream culture into ideal, unreal mothers. In *The Riddle of the Sphinx* (1977), for example, Laura Mulvey and Peter Wallen respond to women's idealization in mainstream film by avoiding ideal images of women completely. The goal of these analyses is to create an awareness of the process by which patriarchal society controls women's behavior.

Chapter 6 moves away from previous approaches and looks at idealization in relation to a personal desire to be seen as ideal. In chapter 2 of *The Threshold to the Visible World*, "From the Ideal-Ego to the Active Gift of Love," postcolonial feminist Kaja Silverman (1996) reflects on idealization.[1] She begins her deliberation with Freud's notion of ideal ego (39–81). Roughly speaking, the ideal ego is a mental image of the ego that has been idealized, that has been made, so to speak, beautiful. However, Silverman gives the notion of ideal image a corporality that is more Lacanian than Freudian. In Lacan's explanation of psychological development, Freud's ideal ego (which for the most part is considered a mental image), gains corporality; it becomes the image of the child who, helped by his mother, recognizes his reflection in the mirror. According to Silverman's interpretation of Lacan, this image is ideal because when seeing her or his body reflected in the mirror, the child experiences a sense of corporeal cohesion that his or her body alone does not provide. Silverman claims that the search for that first ideal image continues through adult life; we attempt to get the same feeling of cohesion by surrounding ourselves with ideal images that we imitate, in the hope of being like them (41–45). It is this sense of idealization, as the personal desire to see oneself as perfect, that is at the core of this chapter. Chapter 6 examines the degree to which women are asked or ask themselves to excel in their job as mothers. Is the idealization in classical and third-wave films the same? If idealization differs, how do third-wave films respond to the idealization in classical films?

Idealization in Classical Films: María Candelaria

In my analysis of the idealization of mothers I have used Emilio Fernández's well-known film *María Candelaria*. Although the protagonist of Fernández's film is not a mother, within the classical film discourse, to be a woman is to be a mother to be. In this sense, although María Candelaria is unmarried and has not had children, she is considered in the same category as a mother. Typically, a mother's strive toward perfection is illustrated by films such as *Cuando los hijos se van*, in which a mother is so perfect that she gives everything to her children. While we associate the stereotype of the "good mother" with Sara García's films, I have used *María Candelaria* because it exemplifies the dangerous side at the core of idealization.

In the specific context of Mexico, the ideal image that all the other images of women refer to is that of the Virgin Mary; she is the feminine model or ideal image that organizes the Ideal of Virgin Motherhood. *María Candelaria* is a key film in the discussion of idealization because in it the protagonist is led by the film narrative to reach the ideal, to become like the Virgin. The approximation of the ideal is conveyed visually through several series of parallel shots between the main character and the Virgin.

At the beginning, María Candelaria is very different from the Virgin. After she complains that God plays favorites, the priest reprimands her and reminds her that she is hurting the Virgin. As the priest says that her anger is like a knife in Mary's heart, the camera pans to the left, simulating the movement of María's eyes as they discover a statue of La Virgen de los Dolores. A medium shot of a Virgin that resembles a Stabat Mater (a Virgin with a knife stabbed in her heart) adds a literal dimension to the priest's words; it is as if María's anger had literally thrust a knife in Mary's heart.[2]

When the camera pivots to show this Mater Dolorosa, María Candelaria's behavior "pivots" as well. She enters a transitional period in which she progressively learns to act like the Virgin. First, a high-angle shot of the Virgin is matched by parallel shots of her. Thus juxtaposed, the shots stress the similarities between the two female figures: María's hands, like those of the Virgin, are crossed on her chest, and her shawl is in the same position as that of the Virgin. Yet, the parallel shots still posit a difference: the Virgin is on the top edge of the shot, while María, now on her feet, is at its bottom. Later, as

María learns to sublimate her pain, alternating close-up shots of Maria and the statue of the Virgin on the same level indicate to the audience that María's moral status is now similar to that of the Virgin.

As the series of parallel shots comes to an end, a new element is introduced: the Virgin's tears. A close-up of the Virgin's face, emphasizing her tears, is paired with a similar shot that shows María's tears. María's face, lit with tears, invests her Virginity with ideality, represented metaphorically as light.[3] When María Candelaria becomes more like the Virgin, the parallel shots show an even increased proximity between María Candelaria and the Virgin. It is at this point that we need to ask: are ideals reachable? How close can María Candelaria get to reaching the ideal of being like the Virgin?

María Candelaria's Death

In Fernández's film, the protagonist becomes the ideal image she wants to be. A redundant misunderstanding leads to María Candelaria's death.[4] The film's insistence on creating a narrative explanation for her death seems superfluous, since María Candelaria's incarnation of an ideal requires death; ideals do not exist, and thus one can only be ideal if one is not human. After María has learned to act like the Virgin, she needs to leave her human condition and ascend to Heaven in order to further her resemblance to the ideal.

The parallels between the Virgin and María Candelaria escalate toward the end of the film, culminating in María Candelaria's ascension to Heaven. Her ascension begins as Lorenzo Rafael takes the body of his betrothed slowly around the spectacularly beautiful Xochimilco canals in a canoe at night. Xochimilco's peasants, standing by the canal banks with their torches, throw light on María Candelaria's body. The diegetic sound of church bells and an extra-undiegetic choral music invest the scene with ideality. Afterward, the camera cuts to a long shot of the canoe followed by several medium and close-up shots in rapid succession taken from Lorenzo Rafael's perspective. Surrounded by white flowers, María Candelaria looks like the Virgin herself. If we compare the trip in the canoe to the earlier sequence inside the church, we note that in the final scenes, there are no parallel shots of the Virgin. The shots, which were crucial in the earlier scene, have now become unnecessary, because in her entrance into eternity María Candelaria, as her name announces María Light, has become the Virgin of Light. The absence of a burial scene and the duration and illumination of the shots create the sense that María Candelaria is ascending to Heaven. The shots are brief and composed of sharply contrasted light, and the glow of her face and flowers against the dark waters gives the impression that the Virgin of Light has ascended to Heaven.

It is important to look at María Candelaria's death, and the film's suggestion that she becomes the Virgin herself, from Silverman's (1996) perspective: "The ideal image is impossible to approach except in moments of mania or delusion. For the most part, the subject who yearns to approximate it experiences not repletion, but insufficiency, not wholeness, but discordance and disarray" (39). Silverman explains that to become one with the ideal, to reach ideality, is an aspiration that can't be achieved. She stresses that there are several ways in which idealization can take place, one of which is narcissistic idealization. In this term, coined by Silverman, the word "narcissistic" is not related to primary narcissism but rather refers to a love for the perfect image. Narcissistic idealization is the desire to become one with the ideal image, like Narcissus's love for his image projected in the water, and I will argue, like María Candelaria. The series of parallel shots between the Virgin and María Candelaria expresses the protagonist's longing to become like the Virgin, and the scenes of her death show the completion of her desire. *María Candelaria* is an example of narcissistic idealization, because in it the main character becomes the ideal image.

To Silverman, the attempt to achieve ideality leads to frustration and negative feelings about the self. At first, it might appear that *María Candelaria* puts forward the opposite message: that through sacrifice and learning, one can incarnate the ideal and feel good about it. However, by using Silverman's (1996) critique of narcissistic idealization in chapter 5 of *The Threshold of the Visible World* we can reach very different conclusions. Silverman dedicates the section called "The ideal ego and the fantasy of the body in bits and pieces" (45–55) to illustrate the cruel effects of narcissistic expectations. She exemplifies her point by using Ulrike Ottinger's (1979) *Bildnis einer Trinkerin (Ticket of No Return)*. In Ottinger's film the protagonist, generically named "Madame," incarnates society's narcissistic ideals for women. She is determined to become one with the ideal. Madame is guided, the voice-over suggests, by "Medea, Madonna, Beatrice, Iphigenia, Aspasia," the ideal figures of womanhood of the society in which she lives.[5]

Silverman's (1996) critique focuses specifically on the consequences of narcissistic idealization. As the narrative develops, Madame's ego deteriorates; since Madame cannot incarnate the ideal, she begins to select parts of herself that match the ideal image ("fetishism," in psychoanalytic lingo). Yet this endorsement of ideal parts and rejection of the rest produces anger and frustration and leads to her decline. By the end of *Ticket of No Return*, Madame's image has been transformed from a beautiful and graceful figure with an elegant walk to a woman in rags falling to the floor. Silverman concludes that narcissistic ideals lead to the disintegration of women's egos; visually, these narcissistic ideals turn Madame into a stumbling tramp.

María Candelaria and Madame pursue similar goals: both of them try to become one with the ideal. Madame wants to turn into the ideal image of woman that appears in the media. Similarly, María Candelaria wants to become the Virgen de los Dolores. Despite having similar goals, the character's quest in each film renders very different results. In *Ticket of No Return* Madame turns into a degraded image of herself; whereas, María Candelaria re incarnates, so to speak, into the Virgin of Light. Yet, while the light and the melodious music are intended to be read as signs that María Candelaria has finally reach her goal and is the Virgin herself, Fernández's film can be read differently. The protagonist did not reach her goal because it is an impossible one.

If one reads the ending of *María Candelaria* without having the Christian belief in the Assumption, then the scene in which the body of María rides triumphantly through the canals of Xochimilco is an example of a failed attempt to become the Virgin. María Candelaria is dead, and therefore her attempt to become the Virgin has failed. If one understand her death in a literal sense, as the end of the character's life, then Ottinger's *Ticket of No Return* and Fernández's *María Candelaria* are very similar. In both films, narcissistic idealization leads to death and disintegration of the ego. The title of Ottinger's film, *Ticket of No Return*, hints to the fact that Madame does not need a ticket to return, because her pursuit of narcissistic idealization will lead her to death; neither does María Candelaria, because she is not coming back from her narcissistic trip. Yet, what is more telling when we compare both films is the difference in the films' position toward narcissistic idealization. While Ottinger's film clearly denounces this type of idealization, Fernandez's film lauds it. *María Candelaria* needs to be read against the grain so that the audience can realize the emotional and physical cost of narcissistic idealization.

Fernandez's film posits that women can, like María Candelaria, become Virgin-like. The conclusions to be drawn from *María Candelaria* reach further than the death of the film's protagonist. Not only do women who idealize narcissistically die psychologically, but also the construct of the Virgin Mary, taken as a narcissistic ideal, is deadly. Women who attempt to mimic the Virgin have to die to become as "good" as the Virgin. The problem is not only with Fernández's film, but with idealization in classical films, where the Virgin is the model of womanhood.

It is not possible to be like the Virgin, as being the Virgin is an unachievable construct. In "Stabat Matter" Kristeva (1986) explains that if we make the Virgin the One, other women cannot compete, because they will never be close to the ideal represented by the Virgin (107–109). Kristeva ends "Stabat Matter" suggesting that one of the solutions to overcome the negative effects of the construct of the Virgin is to free ourselves from the desire to be unique.

The title of Marina Warner's (1976) book, *Alone of All Her Sex*, hints at the same problem: the Virgin is alone among all women because she is perfect, while other women, according to medieval understanding, are imperfect. After all, the Virgin is a woman but is not human. Reading Fernández's film through Silverman's analysis of narcissistic idealization points to the complexity and the contradictions within the construct of the Virgin. *María Candelaria* tellingly shows that the only way in which women can become like the Virgin is by leaving behind the human condition.

Idealization in Third-Wave Films: Lola

The protagonist of María Novaro's (1989) *Lola* literally turns her back to the Ideal of Virgin Motherhood. The move away from classical idealization is alluded to during a trip Lola and her street vendor friends take to a beach in Veracruz. The friends stop en route to change a flat tire and Lola wanders away. She is then shown in the town's plaza, leaning on a marble statue dedicated to "The Mother." The white marble statue of a mother with a breast exposed on the left side and holding a child on her right stays in the background. A medium shot of Lola drinking beer at the foot of the statue with her back turned to "The Mother" is in the foreground.

The substitution of a statue of the Virgin for a human mother indicates that, by the 1980s, the Ideal of Virgin Motherhood is something of the past; Mary is no longer the icon of ideal motherhood. The normative ideal of the late 1980s has less religious connotations than the 1940s' normative ideal. Ideal motherhood is centered on more practical issues, such as the physical nurturance and care of children, signified by the exposed breast and the child. However, Novaro's opera prima does more than substitute a religious ideal for a secular one; it questions idealization itself.

Lola has her back literally and metaphorically turned away from ideal motherhood. The position of Lola's body, with her back to the statue, indicates that Lola does not care for what the statue represents. Her beer drinking, in the middle of the day, in a public place, without a glass, reinforces Lola's deviation from ideal motherhood and underscores the distance that separates her, in the foreground, from the morally superior mother represented by the statue, in the background.

From my analysis of Lola seated at the foot of the statue of "The Mother," one could conclude that idealization does not play an important role in third-wave films like *Lola*. Quite the contrary, *Lola* also idealizes mothers, but not

Opposite: Poster of *Lola* (Colección Filmoteca de la UNAM).

6. Looking Back at Classical Idealization

in a narcissistic way. The problem third-wave films addresses is not that mothers are idealized in classical films, but rather that ideals are unreachable, that women, like María Candelaria, cannot incarnate ideals.

Imperfect Mothers

In an interview with María Novaro that appears in *Lola*'s DVD the director calls Lola an imperfect mother.[6] There are multiple examples in the film that support Novaro's assertion. In a country where mothers' care for their children is expressed by making sure their off-spring wear appropriate clothing, Ana is inappropriately clothed. And thus the viewer can conclude that Lola is an imperfect mother because she does not take care about Ana's appearances.

During a recital for Mother's Day at Ana's school, Lola and her mother, Chelo, sit separately, their position in the audience foretelling their emotional distance. After the show, mother and daughter talk to each other. Chelo tells Lola in a reproaching tone that Ana is dressed inappropriately: Ana's hula skirt, Chelo explains, is not "like the skirts of the other girls." A high angle cut to Ana's back visually explains what Chelo is referring to: Ana's skirt is not long enough to wrap around the child's back, leaving her underwear exposed. From Chelo's perspective, Lola is an imperfect mother because Ana's clothes are not like those of the other girls.

Lola's imperfections are shown again in a visit to Ana's teacher. Casually dressed, Lola goes to school wearing flip-flops, which in Mexico is considered unsuitable footwear for a mother's visit to school. Inside the classroom, the teacher complains about Ana's unkempt appearance and lack of hygiene: "It hurts to see her so untidy" the teacher comments.[7] The audience understands the teacher's complaint because in previous scenes Ana has been shown in a skirt several sizes shorter than what she needs.[8] The teacher also admonishes Lola for her daughter's lack of personal care when attending class: her hair is not well combed. And finally, the teacher complains: Ana's homework is not neat. From the teacher's point of view, Lola is an imperfect mother because she does not take care of her child's appearances or homework.

Lola's imperfections indicate that Novaro's mother challenges narcissistic idealization: Lola's caretaking is not perfect. Yet, idealization is still present. Despite her inability to keep Ana's appearance to standard norms, Lola is not portrayed as a failed mother, for that implies a condemnation on the part of the film narrative, an attempt to tell the viewer that Lola is a "bad mother."

Each of the previous examples of Lola's imperfections is combined with a loving gaze on the part of the film's narrative. In the example of the Mother's Day recital, Lola does not respond to Chelo's comment with shame; instead, the look in her face suggests perhaps lack of interest but surely, exhaustion. The spectator is lead to believe that the length of the skirt is not important and to feel compassion for Lola. A mother as exhausted as she is, the film narrative suggests, requires the spectator's sympathy; she has not time to take care of small things.

The same request to understand the protagonist is present when Lola visits Ana's teacher. In an interior shot of their living room, Lola attempts to respond to the teacher's complaints about Ana's untidy homework. To protect Ana's notebook she clears the table of objects and covers it with a tablecloth. After having placed the notebook in the clean space that she has prepared, she proceeds to do the homework herself. In a medium shot, Lola is shown gesturing as she pronounces the letters that she is writing in Ana's notebook. Doing the work for Ana undermines her position. Yet, because the incident is presented as humorous, with Lola opening her mouth as she writes the letters, she is not censured. Instead, the humorous incident requests the audience to react with a laugh and feel kindness toward Lola.

There are multiple instances in which the use of humor creates a distance between daily life and ideal motherhood. At one time, Lola is shown dyeing a streak of blonde hair; afterward, unsupervised Ana dyes a streak of her hair too. *Lola* presents Ana's imitation of her mother as funny and not as dangerous. According to the logic of the film, Ana is simply imitating her mother, as six year olds do. A similar situation occurs when Ana is shown preparing a ketchup sandwich for herself in the kitchen, while Lola, in another room of the house, is unable to move, overcome by her depression. Within the logic of the film, the ketchup sandwich is a wink to the audience. Ana has refused to eat meatloaf that Lola has labored over, and she is presented as a normal kid who prefers junk food to healthy food. In another instance, Ana drops the house keys from the top of a bridge onto oncoming traffic; this is understood within the film's logic as an example of children playing with adult objects as toys. The streak of golden hair, the ketchup sandwich, and the missing keys underscore the distance that separates Lola from ideal motherhood. However, Lola's imperfections are not presented as shortcomings. Instead, these incidents raise awareness about the hard life a single mother faces and demand empathy.

It is because these incidents are presented in a humorous way that some people in the audience will feel compassionate toward Lola. Silverman (1996) refers to the link between idealization and love when she explains: "Those of us writing deconstructively about gender, race, class and other form of 'difference' had made a serious strategic mistake. We have consistently argued against idealization, that psychic activity at the heart of love, rather than imaging the new uses to which it might be put" (2). Silverman believes that idealization is necessary for love; we cannot love something or someone without idealizing it first. Silverman's approach complicates the process of idealization by making it at the same time unavoidable (it is the process by which we love) and dangerous (narcissistic idealization ends in fetishism, death).

Third-Wave Film's Idealization-at-a-distance

Silverman's (1996) analysis of Cindy Sherman's *Untitled Film Stills* (207–227) helps to understand the type of idealization that is present in third-wave films. In her still photographs Sherman depicts several women trying to appear ideal. The second still (Silverman 1996, figure 77), for instance, shows a woman who is looking at herself in a bathroom mirror. The woman is positioned at the center of the photograph, posing in a classical fashion. If we only look at her reflection in the mirror, we could conclude that she is ideal. However, the photograph is framed to include many objects that are not reflected in the mirror. One sees the ordinary backdrop of the whole bathroom wall, which includes an old-fashioned sink with a glass of water and even part of a trash can below the sink. Silverman (1996) calls attention to the contrast between the woman's pose, striving to mimic the ideal, and the framing of the photograph in a long shot (208–209). Because the photograph is taken as a long shot that includes the sink and trash can, it exposes the woman's effort to appear ideal. Despite her positioning of the body to appear ideal in the reflection in the bathroom mirror, the sink and the trash can in the backdrop show that she is a fake. For Silverman, the contrast between the pose and the framing underscores the distance between the woman's aspiration to ideality and the reality of her everyday life.[9] Silverman continues her analysis of Sherman's stills by paying attention to another element that is prominent in the stills: the personal desire to be seen as ideal. The philosopher explains that in Sherman's stills the women's distance from the ideality is not used against them; rather than degrading the women for having aspirations that they cannot reach, the stills put forward a generous way of identifying with the woman's desire for ideality. Silverman writes: "But the *Untitled Film Stills* go even further: they promote our identificatory relation not with the ideal imago which the women they depict fail to approximate, but rather with the women themselves, and they make this identification conducive of pleasure rather than unpleasure" (207). Silverman calls attention to the process of identification: the reason why we identify with the women Sherman portrays is because they make us come to terms with our own desire to be seen as ideal. Similarly, by reiterating that Lola is an imperfect mother, Novaro is inviting the audience, and especially its mothers, to identify with Lola and thus to come to terms with their own desire to be perfect mothers.

DIFFERENCES BETWEEN NARCISSISTIC IDEALIZATION AND IDEALIZATION-AT-A-DISTANCE

Idealization-at-a-distance is the opposite of narcissistic idealization. It refers to an alternative way to idealize, which promotes the awareness that ideals are unreachable. María Novaro's *Lola* invites us to empathize with Lola when she is at the foot of the statue. The distance between Lola and normative ideals is explicit in this scene; unlike the mothers of classical melodramas, Lola clearly fails to live up to the ideal depicted by the statue. However, her failure is not "conductive of unpleasure." Rather, the film empathizes with Lola in her difficult task of being a mother. This empathy is a gift of love, not for an idealized woman, but for an imperfect mother.

Lola responds to the idealization in classical films by acknowledging the desire to be seen as ideal, but maintains that reaching the ideality is impossible. These differences are apparent in the way in which María Candelaria and Lola position their bodies in relation to ideal images. *María Candelaria* and *Lola* have shots in which the protagonists are at the foot of statues of exemplary mothers. However, the relationship between the films' characters and the statues could not be more different. While in the case of María Candelaria the protagonist is on her knees praying, in the case of Lola she is sitting with her back to the statue. The protagonists' bodies express their ideological position toward narcissistic ideals. By praying and standing on her knees looking at the statue, María Candelaria's body tells the audience that she is desperately trying to become like the Virgin. In contrast, Lola has her back to the statue, communicating a distance from the ideal mother represented by the statue of "The Mother." The message conveyed in this scene is clear: Lola is not attempting to become the ideal mother. Thus, while María Candelaria is willing to die to reach the Ideal of Virgin Motherhood, Lola doesn't even try. Novaro's position on motherhood was quite controversial.

REVIEWER'S REACTIONS

Many aspects of María Novaro's mother stirred passionate sentiments in film critics and audiences. From November 22–30, 1989, when *Lola* was being shown at the Muestra, newspapers in Mexico City published fourteen reviews. Proportionately, more women than men liked the film. From the four women who reviewed the film, three of them (Vega, "Lola"; Velázquez; Cato) liked the film, while one (Murúa) did not. Susana Cato summarized the reaction of the female audience by saying that women either identify or reject identification with Lola. According to Cato, some females in the audience felt relieved with the demystification of motherhood, while others were afraid that people abroad would think that all Mexican women were like Lola. Female critics had similar reactions to that of the audience described by Cato; some critics, such as Sara Murúa, rejected Lola, while others such as Carolina Velázquez identified with her. Murúa disdained Lola for not trying hard enough and contended that Lola chose self-realization, "enjoying herself," over motherhood.[10] For Murúa, to be a mother is to reach as far as possible toward perfection. This necessitates leaving behind personal needs and desires.

From the ten men who reviewed *Lola* in 1989, six (Pixel, Rodríguez Pineda, Barriga Chávez, Barbachano Ponce, Johnson Celorio) liked the film, while four (Albarrán, Viñas, Ayala Blanco, Marín Conde) did not. Male critics who attacked the film felt that Lola lacked the willingness to fight or lacked a sense of direction. Bothered by Lola's depression, one of Mexico's most well-known critics, Jorge Ayala Blanco, calls her a "being drifting," because Lola did not know who she was or what she wanted. Ayala Blanco seems to ask: is Lola doing her best? By saying that Lola is a being drifting, he answers this question negatively: Lola is letting herself go, not putting enough effort into what she is doing.

Other male critics expressed their contempt toward Lola by arguing that she became depressed and "irresponsible" rather than selflessly "maternal." Tomas Pérez Turrent takes a similar stand to Murúa. For him, Lola is somebody "attempting to elude her role as a mother." By not trying hard enough, Perez-Turrent suggests, Lola is not fulfilling her role as mother. Moises Viñas (1989) concurs with Pérez Turrent in remarking on Lola's unwillingness to fight the odds; for him, Lola "wrongs her young daughter without even making a minimal effort to alleviate her pain." Morúa, Pérez-Turrent and Viñas are dissatisfied with Lola's level of commitment to her role as mother. The reactions of Mexican audiences and film critics show that Novaro's request to empathize with Lola in her difficult task of being a mother was a challenge for many people.

The Price of a Loving Image: Luz Cruz's Trial Against Cazals

The first part of chapter 5 examines the perils of idealizing narcissistically and the need to be aware of our desire to be seen as ideal. The second part studies the importance images play in identification. More specifically, it focuses on the response of a real mother who sued a filmmaker for her deidealization in film.

In August 1982, Elvira Luz Cruz was accused of strangling her four children. The twenty-six-year-old indigenous woman lived in a town of shanty houses without electricity or sewage, taken illegally by homeless people. With no clear evidence to prove whether she killed her children, she was sentenced to twenty-eight years in prison.[11] Felipe Cazals based his film *Los motivos de Luz* (*Luz's Reasons*, 1985) on the case of Luz Cruz.

In *Los motivos de Luz,* the protagonist is an ignorant and irrational woman and a failed mother. Luz Cruz is presented as an illiterate woman who believes in witches and apparitions and is a psychotic. For instance, when she is asked if she killed the children or not, she responds that she can't remember. Her mother-in-law—Luz Cruz explains—is a witch and gave her a potion, which explains why she does not have a memory of the events of that day. Believing in witches and potions is used as a sign of Luz Cruz's lack of rationality. Her religious belief is put to the same use: to demonstrate that the protagonist lacks the capacity to think rationally. Luz, the protagonist, is presented in a cell having a flashback in which she reports to the village priest that she has seen an apparition. Her religious convictions and her belief in apparitions become the argument for why she cannot tell the difference between reality and imagination.

Luz Cruz did not like Cazals's interpretation of her life. Awaiting her sentence, she sued the director from jail. The trail lasted four years, 1985–1989, and went through several appeals. Initially, the accused wanted to increase her chances of having a fair trial.[12] As *Los motivos de Luz* made her appear guilty of matricide, Luz Cruz wanted to postpone the showing of the film until the verdict had been reached. To stop Cazals from showing the film, Luz Cruz sued him for defamation.[13] Cazals's lawyers responded to Luz Cruz's lawyers' argument by saying that it was not defamation because most films were just a filmmaker's interpretation of reality. The person with the authority to make the decision, then director of Radio, Televisión y Cinematografía (RTC), Fernando Macotela, decided that the film should be released. He argued that pulling the film would violate freedom of expression. Thus, in 1986, commercial exhibition of *Los motivos de Luz* began. Luz Cruz responded by changing her appeal and charging Cazals for "moral damages, slander and defamation" ("daños morales, tergiversación y difamación," Vega 1996, 25). In response to the suit, the exhibition of *Los motivos de Luz* was halted, so that the film would not damage Luz Cruz's image for her trial.

Luz Cruz did not find that stopping the exhibition was enough, so she continued to sue Cazals because she "was not satisfied with the fact that they were making a movie about the tragedy [she] went through."[14] The young indigenous mother sued the director because the image of her that the film offered mattered to her. The case against Cazals for defamation, slander, and moral damages continued until 1988, at which point it was overturned because Luz Cruz did not have the money needed to pursue it.

Feminist journalist Patricia Vega wrote eleven columns in one of Mexico's leading newspapers, *La Jornada* about Luz Cruz's legal process.[15] After their publication in the newspaper, Vega compiled them in a section of her book that she titled "Elvira Luz Cruz, sus motivos."[16] Thanks to Vega's dedicated attention to the trial and her compilation of information, we have accessible information about the case today. After reading "Elvira Luz Cruz, sus motivos" the question emerges: what were Luz Cruz's reasons for taking up a legal battle?

Revising Lacan's Theory of Identification

Frantz Fanon's analysis of the effects of colonization on the individual psyche can help to understand why Luz Cruz battled against the director for four years. His description of the problems of colonized subjects focuses on self-image: colonized people do not have a positive image of themselves to love.

Postcolonial theorist Kaja Silverman (1996) has explained the process pointed out by Fanon in Lacanian terms in the section "Fanon and the Black Male Bodily Ego" (27–31). Revising Lacan's theory of identification, Silverman argues that society plays an important role in the way in which the subject interprets the image that appears in the mirror. In her opinion, the role of society is not fully accounted for in Lacan's theory. In Lacanian psychoanalysis, the ego forms by looking into the mirror, where it finds a coherent image of the self. Silverman argues that when reading Fanon's (1967) *Black Skin White Masks*, it is obvious that the image that a black person finds in the mirror is often not a coherent one, because it is tinted by society's interpretation of a racially marked body. Silverman concludes that the reluctance of a racially marked person to recognize the reflected image as his or her own impedes the ego development described by Lacan.

Silverman's interpretation of the way in which racially marked individuals have difficulty gaining their identity in a discriminating social context helps to understand Luz Cruz's legal battle. If Cazals's filmic representation is a mirror for Luz Cruz, then we can understand why Luz Cruz rejects Cazals's image. She does not want to identify with the image of a violent irrational mother portrayed by Cazals, and she manifests her rejection in the legal process. She finds Cazals's portrayal of herself in *Los motivos de Luz* morally damaging to her idea of herself.

Luz Cruz's reaction against Cazals points to the importance of idealization in the representations of mothers in film. She fought to defend her dignity; she struggled to retain an image of herself that she could love. That an illiterate mother resorted to lawyers to fight back against her portrayal in a film reminds us that idealization is an unavoidable process for identification and self-love. The battle should not be against idealization, but against narcissistic idealization, the idealization that demands perfection.

Fighting Back: Cruz's Second Appeal

Losing the first case did not stop Luz Cruz; she made a second appeal. This time she sued Cazals and the Producing House Chimalistac for moral damages only, arguing that she had never given permission to have her life portrayed in a film (Vega 1996, 24). In 1992, Cruz won her case. The judge found forty-two coincidences between her life and the life of the person represented in *Los motivos de Luz*. These coincidences, the judge ruled, did not respect Luz Cruz's right to a private life. Producers and distributors had to pay Cruz seventy million old pesos, a pay-back for the income generated by the exhibition of the film, and in 1996, Cruz received sixty-two thousand pesos in compensation (20). Vega considers the outcome of Cruz's battle only partially successful. Her voice was finally heard, although the people involved in making the film (Cazals and the scriptwriter Xavier Robles), as well as the ex-director of RTC (Macotela), who did not stop the exhibition in 1985, suffered no penalties. By suing Cazals and winning, Luz Cruz got back an image of herself that she could love and identify with. Only three years later, on July 9, 1993, she was released from prison for good conduct, having served only half of her initial sentence.

Conclusion

Chapter 6 examines classical idealization from a third-wave perspective focusing on the extent to which mothers in classical films are expected to live up to an ideal that is impossible to achieve. Classical films promote narcissistic idealization, in which a person attempts to be one with the ideal. The analysis shows that in *María Candelaria* the film's imperative to achieve the Ideal of Virgin Motherhood proves deadly; María Candelaria has to die to become as "good" as the Virgin.

Third-wave films respond to classical films by bringing critical distance to the process of idealization. Chapter 6 does not argue that ideals have disappeared, but rather that everybody's personal desire to be seen as ideal needs to be accounted for. Rather than the narcissistic idealization of *María Candelaria*, third-wave films propose idealization-at-a-distance. When aware, one can recognize and accept one's own desire to be seen as ideal and take a distance from that desire. The imperfect mothers portrayed in the positive light of third-wave films promote self-reflection: not about the idea that ideals are unreachable, but about the personal desire to be seen as ideal. *Lola*'s imperfect mother brings some critical distance to the personal desire to be seen as a "good mother."

Staying away from narcissistic idealization does not mean staying away from idealization altogether. Films such as *Lola* do not argue against the process by which an object or a person increases its value, but instead explore new uses of idealization. Likewise, Luz Cruz's compelling battle to restore her self-image damaged by *Los motivos de Luz* tellingly shows how idealization is fundamental to identification.

Chapter 6 incorporates Silverman's explanation of the process of idealization to locate the desire for perfection at the intersection of society and the self. That is, the chapter understands idealization, on the one hand, as a process in which society creates ideal images, normative ideals, that are used as standards for mothers. On the other hand, mothers, being part of society, may internalize the ideals, or more importantly, the desire to see themselves as ideal. Third-wave films bring the discussion of idealization to a more private realm, showing that mothers need to question their own desire to be ideal.

7

Maternal Affectivity in Mexican Films

"Maternal Affectivity in Mexican Films" examines mother love, the emotional ties between a mother and her children. The actress Sara García is the focus of the three films examined in chapter 7: the 1941 classic, *Cuando los hijos se van* (*When Children Leave*) by Juan Bustillo Oro; the 1971 film *Mecánica nacional* (*National Mechanics*) by Luis Alcoriza; and the 1989 third-wave film *Los pasos de Ana* by Marisa Sistach. The chapter compares these films, ranging between the 1940s and the 1980s, in which García played the role of mother because many consider her the icon of mother love in Mexican cinema. Julianne Burton-Carvajal (1997), for instance, calls García the "prototype of national maternity" (196), and Marisa Sistach explains that "Sara García is an actress who always played the role of the self-sacrificing mother in the movies: she is always 'the mother of...' and has a relationship of very affectionate acceptance with her children" (Arredondo 2013, 129).

The three films selected illustrate the process of transformation in the concept of mother love. In *Cuando los hijos se van,* where mother love is tied to moral motherhood, maternal affect has social validity. In *Mecánica nacional,* where García dies on screen, the idea of mother love, represented as obsolete and related to oedipal feelings, goes under attack. In the third-wave narrative *Los pasos de Ana,* a film that compares the protagonist to the Sara García of *Cuando los hijos se van,* some of the aspects of mother love that were deemed old-fashioned in *Mecánica nacional* are recuperated.

Several of the questions raised in chapter 7 are inspired by Rebecca Jo Plant's analysis of maternal affectivity in United States. Plant's (2010) examination in *Mom: The Transformation of Motherhood in Modern America* begins in the nineteenth century. The Victorian mother, referred by Plant as "Mother," is a pillar of morality and uses mother love as a tool in teaching moral values (11). In the Victorian period moral motherhood and mother love are dependent from each other: mother love is used to achieve morality, and morality is the goal that necessitates mother love. Plant's study of mother love in the context of the United States raises the questions: Can the Mexican perceptions of mother love in films of the 1940s be similar to the one described by Plant? Are there examples in cinema of close affective bonds with "Mother," in which ties to "Mother" assure moral rectitude?

Plant traces a history of the concept of mother love in the United States and explains that, by the end of World World II, most people in the United States did not perceive a direct link between mother love and moral motherhood. In the aftermath of World War II in the United States, a close link between mother and son is seen as a sign of maternal overprotection (Plant 2010, 11). Furthermore, backed up by Freudian psychoanalysis, mental health specialists suspected that the close emotional ties between mother and son were oedipal and therefore unhealthy. Plant's contention that after War World II mother love becomes linked with oedipal desire raises the question: are the close ties between mother and son also looked at with suspicion in Mexican cinema after World War II? And if classical mother love lasts longer in Mexico than in the United States, what could be the reasons to explain that mother love has social validity for a longer time in Mexico?

Mother Love in the Classical Period: Cuando los hijos se van

Mother love and moral motherhood appear closely linked to each other in *Cuando los hijos se van*, resembling the Victorian ideal described by Plant. Mother love was imagined as a "silver cord" that emotionally tied children to "Mother" assuring that they would follow the path of moral rectitude. Victorians idealized "Mother," Plant (2010) explains, because "she sacrificed herself for the good of her children and because her moral guidance was deemed so indispensable to proper character formation" (88). The Victorian model provided moral guidance to sons who were considered more at risk of bad character than daughters. Something similar to what Plant calls the Victorian ideal is illustrated in *Cuando los hijos se van*: an aged mother not only nurtures her children but also gives them moral guidance.

In *Cuando los hijos se van* the awareness of children's morality is gendered. The father (Fernando Soler) is blind to the moral status of his children, while the mother (Sara García) is aware of it. Mother, Lupe Rosales, is not only a pillar of morality; she can see through her children's behavior. By contrast, Pepe Rosales, although well intended and a moral person himself, is unable to evaluate moral values.

7. *Maternal Affectivity in Mexican Films* 139

Doña Lupe and Don Pepe (Colección Filmoteca de la UNAM).

Cuando los hijos se van's narrative is structured to underscore Don Pepe's inability to grasp his children's morality. The audience first sees José (Carlos López) stealing a wallet full of money from a visitor to the Rosales's home. He hides the empty wallet in Raimundo's room. Afterward, Don Pepe accuses Raimundo (Emilio Tuero) of being a thief and punishes him. As the audience has witnessed the incident, they know that the culprit is not Raimundo but Don Pepe's other son, José Rosales.

Though Don Pepe shows his moral standards by punishing the theft, Father throws the wrong child out of the house. Don Pepe does not learn that Raimundo is innocent and José guilty until the very end of the film, which emphasizes his lack of moral sagacity. For most of *Cuando los hijos se van* Father is unable to understand his children's morality, a characteristic that disqualifies him as an educator.

The opposite can be said about "Mother." Although Lupe is powerless to overturn the father' verdict, she knows that Raimundo is being unfairly accused. Because of her close ties with her children, and especially with Raimundo, Lupe knows the truth even without seeing it. Mother's special

Doña Lupe and Don Pepe with their son (Colección Filmoteca de la UNAM).

sensitivity to the moral status of her "children" explains why the mother is responsible for moral education. In a classical text like *Cuando los hijos se van*, the stand bearer for mother love, Sara García, is a moral model for her children.

Mother Love as Enhancer of Morality

In Golden Age films mother love plays a fundamental role to teach morality. Bustillo Oro's film establishes a direct relationship between mother love and morality: the more mother love a child receives, the higher standard of morality he or she will have. For that reason, the children who are distant from their mother, Amalia Rosales (Marina Tamayo) and José, receive less nurturance and are weaker morally. Amalia marries a much older man for money, and Jose is a liar and thief. In contrast, Raimundo, who is closer to Lupe, has high moral standards.

The link between Raimundo and Lupe is made explicit on Mother's Day.

On the day dedicated to mother love, Raimundo, who no longer lives in the Rosales home, sings a song that he has composed for Lupe on the radio. In the song, Raimundo expresses his desire to re-establish the mother-son bond by singing: Mother "who could be nurtured in your arms like I was before." It is Mother's love, the nurturance alluded to in the song, that has taught Raimundo to be a superior moral being.

The mother love of the Victorian period and of Mexican classical cinema shares similarities. Lupe's close relationship with Raimundo is similar to what Plant refers to as "silver cord." Furthermore, we could say of Bustillo Oro's film that it expresses "the belief that mothers should forge emotionally intense relationships with their children, especially their sons, to keep them on the path of virtue" (Plant 2010, 87). In addition, Raimundo's song shows gratitude. We could say that it expresses the idea that "children owed a debt to their mothers that could never be repaid" (87). Also, in classical Mexican cinema and in the Victorian ideal, Mother's position of high moral standing derives from the gratitude that her children, like Raimundo, have for the love they have received; this love gave them strong moral fiber. Despite their similarities, the mother love of the Victorian model and of the Golden Age remain valid for different periods of time. In Mexico the idea of classical mother love (the dyad mother love/ moral motherhood) is brought down in the 1970s; in the United States, three decades earlier.

Plant (2010) proposes that the antimaternal sentiments that lead to the disillusionment with mother love developed in two overlapping stages (11). The first stage, which began after World War I, removed mothers from their high moral plain; they became like other human beings. This process directly affected the relationship they had with their children. Plant explains that the Victorian ideal of mother love was based on "the conviction that mother love was the purest of all human sentiments, entirely unrelated to sexual desire" (87). Mothers can maintain strong bonds with their children as long as their love is thought of as asexual. However, with the demotion of women from "Mother" to mother, their love came to be seen as sexual, and so, the strong emotional ties were no longer seen as positive. Plant explains that "Until the 1930s, most childrearing experts sought to restrain maternal affectivity by urging women to adopt 'scientific' schedules that would serve to regulate the child's biological needs, while also mitigating the emotional intensity of the mother-child relationship" [11]. By the 1930s the Victorian "silver string" is no longer a valid concept for educating children.

The second attack to mother love started in the 1940s, when mother love began to be perceived as pathological. In Plant's (2010) chapter "Pathologizing Mother Love: Mental Health and Maternal Affectivity" (86–117) the author examines dismissal letters from young soldiers fighting in World War II. Her examination concludes that mother love began to be perceived as incestuous. She contends that Freud's theory of the oedipal love, in which there is a posited unconscious sexual desire of sons for their mothers, played an important role in pathologizing mother love. Mental health experts, according to Plant, interpreted the soldiers' mental problems as directly affected by the strong emotional attachment to their mothers. As a solution, these experts recommended that soldiers shift ties from mother to wife/girlfriend and from mother love to heterosexual love.

Mexico's history of mother love considerably differs from the one described by Plant. In Mexico, Freud's Oedipus Complex did not played as important a role as it did in the United States. Also, in the 1940s Mexican context, psychologists and psychiatric experts did not play a role in determining the emotional ties that connect mothers to their sons. Mexican Catholicism, and especially the cult of the Virgin Mary, explains why the classical model of mother love, illustrated by *Cuando los hijos se van*, had a much longer life in Mexico than in the United States.

The Virgin and Mother Love

Kristeva's analysis of the Virgin helps one to understand why classical mother love lasted longer in Mexico. Kristeva uses a Freudian psychoanalytic approach to study the myth of Mary.[1] She situates the image of the Virgin within Freud's most famous scenario, the Oedipus Complex, and explains the ways in which the construct of Mary has been created to satisfy the psychological needs of men. Thus, she counters scholars who interpret Mariology, the cult of the Virgin, as important mainly to women.[2]

The Virgin, commonly represented with a child in her arms, Kristeva argues, tries to resolve issues pertaining to the relationship between men and their mothers. The myth of the Virgin avows and disavows primary narcissism, the attachment to and identification with the maternal body. On the one hand, the myth of Mary perpetuates the desire for the inseparability of the mother and the child. On the other, it disavows primary narcissism by taking the Virgin's sex and bodily functions out of the equation. With the figure of the Virgin, Kristeva claims, men have access to the heart and breast of the mother but they are saved from her sexuality. The Virgin stands for the inseparability of mother and child, in a safe way that can be accepted by society. In "Motherhood According to Giovani Bellini," Kristeva (1971) examines the Virgins painted by Bellini to demonstrate that the Virgin is a displacement of the painter's love for his mother. According to Kristeva, this displacement is not exclusive to the painter; other men, including the Church Fathers, use the Virgin for the same purpose, to avow and disavow primary narcissism.

In *Cuando los hijos se van* mother love is portrayed as asexual, and therefore there is nothing threatening in a filial relationship between mother and son. In the same song that Raimundo composes for Mother's Day, the line "Mother, for one of your kisses I would give my life," articulates the degree to which the affective ties between mothers and sons are seen as filial. The asexuality of the Virgin, model for "good" mothers like Sara García, explains how Raimundo, who is in his thirties, can ask his mother for a kiss. Lupe, like the Virgin, is constructed as an asexual being.

In trying to create a history of mother love in Mexico it makes sense to relate the concept of classical mother love to Catholicism. As long as Catholicism is not questioned, mother love does not come under attack. In the first six decades of the twentieth century, the cult of Mary as Mother flourishes. During the 1940s and 1950s the importance of Mary as Queen intensified, culminating in 1954, when the Vatican gave the title "Queen of the Church" to Mary.

In the same years in which Mexicans were watching for the first time *Cuando los hijos se van*, in the United States mother love is suspected of being oedipal. The Virgin's asexuality makes mother love safe in Mexico, where men can have very strong ties with their mothers without fear of oedipal desires. Bustillo Oro's film exemplifies the importance Catholicism had to shape mother love in Mexico.

Cuando los hijos se van as a Rendition of the Stabat Mater

A convoluted series of clues in Bustillo Oro's film lead to the revelation that Raimundo is another Christ. Lupe uses the house to get credit to cover up for her son José's theft at work. The agent takes advantage of her, having her sign an empty form and then doubling the amount. When Raimundo tries to clear up the debt, the agent kills him.

In *Cuando los hijos se van* Raimundo's death parallels the death of Christ. In a scene that takes place at the last Christmas Eve dinner of the film, Lupe looks at Raimundo's empty chair and tells her husband: "Raimundo paid for you and for all." She then adds: "Raimundo died as Christ on the cross, paying for the sins of all." It may appear that *Cuando los hijos se van* is about the death of a son, Christ/Raimundo, but it is not.

Cuando los hijos se van uses Raimundo's death as a foil for Lupe's sorrow, which is the cornerstone of the film. The use of a son's death to point to mother love is part of a well-known Catholic tradition. The death of Christ has carried different associations in its two-thousand-year history. Up until the fifteenth century Christ at the Cross was a reference to the death of the population in Europe.³ However, after the Holy Places were recovered in the fifteenth century, the Crucifixion became a symbol of mother love. The passion in its post–fifteenth-century interpretation was less about Christ's death than about the Virgin's love for her dying son. As Warner (1976) reminds us, "The Crucifixion, the Deposition and the Entombment came to life" through Mary's eyes (112). Catholics are moved by the pain a mother feels for her dying son.

A displacement of blood, the signifier for suffering, allows the focus to shift from the sufferings of the son, to those of his mother. Initially, Christ at the cross is associated with blood, which represents his sufferings. After the fifteenth century, the Virgin is also associated with blood. Bloody knives stabbing the Mater Dolorosa's heart are representative of her sorrows and sufferings when her son dies.⁴ The death of Christ/Raimundo in *Cuando los hijos se van* has a post–fifteenth century referent; Lupe is presented as a "Stabat Mater" in Raimundo's song on Mother's Day. The son who has unfairly been thrown out of the home dedicates his song to "those seven knives that the Virgin, mother of the Redeemer, has stabbing her."⁵ This line connects Lupe to the sorrowful mother at the foot of the cross. In addition, there is a reference to blood and pain in the red thorny flowers that Doña Lupe cultivates passionately. The thorns puncture the skin like a knife; the red color of the roses also reminds the audience of blood. Thus, the red roses in Doña Lupe's garden are used to express the same emotion as the knives in Mary's throbbing heart: the pain of a mother for the fate of her children. Within Mexico's Catholic discourse, the Stabat Mater and Lupe's red roses are part of the same discourse on mother love. The emotions in Doña Lupe are a rendition of the Virgin in the role of mourning mother. And so, the central issue in *Cuando los hijos se van* is not Raimundo's death, but rather Lupe's response to his death, which exposes the maternal love and the suffering she feels for Raimundo and her other children.

Cuando los hijos se van visualizes the anguish of the Virgin at seeing her son die, literally via satellite television. The film was sold to many other Latin American countries, and thus a wide audience of Catholics were able to enjoy García's twentieth-century portrayal of the Virgin's maternal affect. In this light, the melodramas in which Sara García has performed are manifestations of popular Catholicism. Indeed, they use techniques similar to the evangelical methods used by the Franciscans in the fourteenth century: symbolism, emotions, and nonverbal language. And, like the Franciscans' sermons, these melodramas were popularly acclaimed. Given the essential role Catholicism plays in the formulation of mother love in Mexico and the role that Sara García had in attaching a face to the mother-son bond, it is no surprise that in the

1970s reassessment of mother love is a combined attack on both Catholicism and Sara García.

Mecánica nacional's *1970s Attack on Mother Love*

The criticism of motherly stereotypes came from a prolific male filmmaker, Luis Alcoriza, who was born in Spain and worked in Mexico since 1940. For his critique of the classical system Alcoriza brings actress Sara García to the screen, not as a regular character, granny Lolita, but as her star persona. By 1971, García had played the role of mother numerous times—from 1933 through the 1940s—and also grandmother during the 1950s and 1960s. In 1968 she was named by the press the "Official Mother of Mexico" (Peña 2000, 53).

In *Mecánica nacional* after eating too many tacos, granny Lolita, played by Sara García, dies of indigestion. The actress's celebrity and the fact that she plays her own star persona allow the director to point directly at the roles that García had previously played. The death of the "Official Mother of Mexico," the undisputed icon of mother love, indicates the "official" end of the Ideal of Virgin Motherhood.

Alcoriza's *Mecánica nacional* marks the turning point at which classical definitions of mother love become outdated.[6] While the love of "Mother" guides Raimundo in *Cuando los hijos se van*, in *Mecánica nacional* it is an unnecessary burden for Lolita's son, Eufemio (Manuel Fábregas). *Mecánica nacional* is an incisive parody of the ideas that held together the classical system. Alcoriza's film makes a direct connection between motherhood and the cult of Mary, and criticizes both. Given the national stature of Sara García, as well as development of the Marian cult within international Catholic culture, Alcoriza's film is not only a critique of the classical canon, but more importantly of the Ideal of Virgin Motherhood.

THE CROWN: THE MOTHER AS VIRGIN

Mecanica nacional reminds its audience that the Mexican notion of mother love and the religious discourse attached to it is, indeed, a visually codified one. This is especially true in the scenes depicting the wake of granny Lolita in the middle of the Acapulco-to-Mexico-City auto race. With the cars of the people attending the race blocking access to the road, Granny's family decides to celebrate her wake at the races, because there are so many cars all parked one next to the other that it would be impossible to take Lolita out.

When the people surrounding the family find out that Eufemio's mother is dead, they make a tinfoil crown for her. The crown is part of a larger effort to satirize classical cinematic codes; it makes the connection between motherhood and the Virgin explicit. The crown is a burlesque prop critiquing a whole system of thought. It refers to Sara García's acting career, establishes a connection between the actress and the Virgin, and it is used to mock the cult of Mary and García's motherly roles.

The Virgin had officially received her crown as "Queen of the Church" in 1954; the actress, over a decade later. García had been crowned "Mother of Mexico" only three years before *Mecánica nacional* was released. In 1968, the journalist from *La Ultima Reseña de Acapulco* named García their queen and made her a paper crown (Muñoz 1998, 66). By making a crown for the "Mother" of classical cinema, *Mecánica nacional* directly addresses the association between mothers and the Virgin, and between motherhood in film and Sara García. The crown reminds the audience that the idea of classical mother love has been naturalized (made natural) to such an extent that spectators are no longer conscious; it makes the Ideal of Virgin Motherhood visible. However, granny's crown is a twofold sign: it reminds the audience that Lolita is a queen and it also makes fun of her royalty. The crown is made out of tinfoil and not silver, and this makes the notion of mother love, which the crown refers to, laughable. To further add to the deidealization effect suggested by the tinfoil, the long shot of the group of mourners is directly followed by a close-up of an unidentified person frying eggs. The connection between the mourners and the eggs makes García's "Virginity," her likeness with the Virgin, seem banal and grotesque.

Mecánica nacional has several scenes in which cinematic conventions relating to classical mother love are blatantly lampooned. In one of these, the press, amazed by the death of one of the spectators, takes a break from reporting on the auto race to attend Lolita's wake. A crane shot of the race is followed by a shot of the family and friends attending the funeral. The presence of an on-screen camera within the film reinforces the idea that what is being discussed are cinematic codes, ways of approaching the "real." While the camera focuses on the family and friends, the broadcaster commands: "Go down to the old woman, make sure you take the crown," and to the relatives and bystanders the broadcaster orders: "Don't look at the camera," thus further erasing a distinction between the real and the cinematic.

Mecánica Nacional also parodies the organization within the shot and the gestures of classical films, making them look artificial and exaggerated. After giving orders to the crew member to take the crown, the director commands: "Go down all the way to her hands." The out of screen spectators can see that the broadcaster wants to focus on granny's hands, held together in

Sara García's wake in *Mecánica nacional* (Colección Filmoteca de la UNAM).

prayer. *Mecánica nacional* highlights that mother love has a codified system that includes body positions, camera angles, framing and the organization of the shot around granny's corpse.

Mecánica nacional pokes fun at Catholic rituals. In preparation for shooting the wake, the broadcaster gives directions to family and friends: "All you women, pretend you are praying." His command makes fun of the ritual of praying; an example would be that of María Candelaria kneeling at the foot of the statue of the Virgin, her eyes directed toward the upper part of the frame (where the Virgin is), and her hands held together in prayer. Through imitation and caricature, *Mecánica nacional* aims to expose the Catholic discourse on mother love as outdated.

Cuando los hijos se van and *Mecánica nacional* take radically different positions on mother love. Bustillo Oro's film takes for granted that mothers are superior moral beings and that sons become superior moral beings by being close to Mother; Alcoriza does not. Moreover, in *Cuando los hijos se van* mother love has a positive effect; it makes Raimundo into a model son who cares for the well-being of the family and who is willing to give his life for the family.

Unlike Raimundo, Eufemio does not become morally superior by being close to his mother; rather, Lupe is a heavy burden that Eufemio has to dispose of.

From the very beginning of *Mecánica nacional* negative somatic associations express the need to leave mother love behind. Having the "Mother of Mexican Cinema" die of indigestion after having eaten too many tacos is already a somatic sensation; the displeasure of the body increases as the making of the tinfoil crown is cut next to the frying of eggs; the annoyance peaks near the end of the film, when granny's corpse begins to rot in the heat. As the well-attended race comes to an end and traffic starts to flow, Eufemio puts the body of Lolita in his car to begin his triumphant though sluggish march. The funeral is shot at a very slow rhythm, reflecting the pace at which the cars advance in the traffic jam, with long shots in which hardly anything happens. A sense of boredom is increased by the sounds of the funeral march, consisting of high-pitched, histrionic, disorganized sounds. In addition, the heat makes the spectators get a feeling of disintegration. While Eufemio is given priority to exit the race because he carries the "Queen of Mexican Cinema," homage is accompanied with a sense of breakdown. In the heavy heat

Participants attend the race at *Mecánica nacional* (Colección Filmoteca de la UNAM).

of a mid-summer afternoon, granny's decomposing corpse starts to smell. The flesh that so many times had embodied the self-sacrificing mother "rots" onscreen. It is this smell, as well as the impossibility of a fast exit from the race traffic, that creates a sense of collapse. Through negative somatic sensations—the rhythm, the heat, the noise, the smell—*Mecánica nacional* makes the spectator separate from the mother love that García represents. And thus, 1971 marks the point when García's motherly role is considered ossified, and also claustrophobic and dangerous.

Mother love is especially dangerous for sons like Eufemio, who are easier targets than daughters of mother love. *Mecánica nacional,* a film which describes the "mechanics" of the Mexican mind, how the Mexican mind works, directly addresses Mexico's nationally constructed masculine roles. This allusion to national stereotypes is reinforced by the jacket worn by Eufemio, which has the word "México" written on the back. The jacket helps the audience identify the character with a symbol; Eufemio's machista attitudes are to be understood as representative of the attitude of Mexican males in general. Despite the film's superficial critique of Eufemio's machismo, Alcoriza's film is a defense of Mexican masculinity as represented by Eufemio. And in several occasions, the love that García became famous for is presented as a threat to her son's masculinity.

Alcoriza's film suggests that García's mother love has oedipal overtones. When the press is shooting the wake, the broadcaster directs Eufemio on how to pose for what we could call an "Ideal of Virgin Motherhood shot." He tells Eufemio to "kiss your mother, then raise your face and look at the sky." As the broadcaster's directions materialize, spectators see a medium shot of Eufemio in the lower part of the frame, with his eyes directed toward the upper right and his hands held respectfully together as though praying. The audience is directed to laugh at his effeminate gestures: Eufemio prays like a woman. Alcoriza's portrayal of Eufemio has points in common with the dismissal letters from World War II soldiers that Plant mentions: both consider that mother love has damaging effects for the soldiers/Eufemio, and both recommend to become healthy by having sex. Lolita's death frees Eufemio from Mother's strong emotional ties and restores his masculinity, as shown by a scene in which Eufemio has an affair with a woman in a nearby group. Although his wife complains and makes a fuss, the spectator is directed to celebrate the restoration of Eufemio's sexual potential, once restricted by mother love. In *Mecánica nacional* classical mother love is portrayed as dangerous for male sexuality.

The End of the Ideal of Virgin Motherhood

Catholicism, and especially the multifaceted construct of the Virgin, plays a fundamental role in shaping mother love in Mexico. For that reason,

Alcoriza's frontal attack on mother love includes a criticism of Catholicism, the ideology from which the cult of mother love emerges. The film directly mocks the most prominent Catholic gestures, rituals and codes used to represent mother love in cinema in an attempt to decouple the link among motherhood, the Virgin, and Sara García's star persona.

The important role Catholic culture plays in Mexico explains why mother love lasted so long; only after Catholic ideals had been attacked did classical mother love fall apart. *Mecánica nacional* shows that by the 1970s the dyad mother love/moral motherhood was rare in Mexico. We can conclude, then, that classical mother love lasted long after the 1940s in Mexico. As a result, the history of mother love in Mexico is different from that of the United States. The two attacks on mother love Plant mentions (the attack on moral motherhood after World War I and the attack on the oedipal desire of mother love after World War II) coexist in the case of Mexico. Alcoriza's assault on mothers as superior moral beings takes place at the same time as the assault on mother-son ties. In *Mecánica nacional* moral motherhood, represented by García, is associated with putrefaction. Simultaneously, Eufemio's sexual liberation after his mother dies portrays classical mother-son bonds as obstacles for male sexuality.

Alcoriza's film marks not only the end of the mother love/moral motherhood dyad, but most importantly the end of the Ideal of Virgin Motherhood. After the 1970s, the Virgin is no longer a model of motherhood for women. This is especially true for the films of third-wave filmmakers. Interestingly, it is not the end of Sara García or mother love.

1989's "New" Feminist Mother

Los pasos de Ana compares film graduate Ana, the film's protagonist, to Sara García. The scene takes place in a bookstore where Ana and Carlos, a friend of the protagonist, are looking for information for their new television program. In the conversation, taken in a close-up, thirty-year-old Ana confides that she has decided to let her thirteen-year-old son, Juan, go to live with his father in San Diego. Ana, however, does not feel liberated about the departure of Juan. She tells Carlos that it breaks her heart to see him go. As the camera pulls away, Carlos tells Ana: "You better modernize yourself, or you are going to end up like Sara García in *Cuando los hijos se van.*" Despite Carlos's suggestion to modernize herself, Ana has an intense love for her children that certainly reminds the viewer of Sara Garcia's maternal affect. Is this retrieval of García's star persona a conservative return to nuclear family values in the 1980s or quite the contrary, it is a new feminist view on motherhood?

Los pasos de Ana is neither a restoration of classical morality nor a return to the nuclear family. When interviewed, Sistach talked about the differences between both mothers as one of principles: "although Ana and Sara García might fundamentally be mothers, their principles separate them," and the director added, Sara García and Ana "are truly at opposite ends of the spectrum. Everything Sara García believed in, Ana cannot (Arredondo 2013, 130). In this quote, Sistach presents the differences between the two mothers as one of ideas, not of roles. While both characters love their children, they have very different values. For the third-wave director, this is what makes the difference.

In *Los pasos de Ana*, it is Carlos who lays out the principles that separate the protagonist Ana from García's star persona. He tells Ana: "You fuck freely; you smoke pot whenever you can; you have to work hard to make your living; and since your husband left you, you don't have the slightest idea of what your future will be like." The first difference that stands out in Carlos comparison is a difference in morality. Smoking pot and fucking freely are clearly not the classical standards of morality that García stands for. In an interview Sistach reiterates the same idea when she says that Ana's "sexuality is overt and liberated" (Arredondo 2013, 130). Also, from a classical film standpoint, Ana could not fulfill motherhood's most important function: guidance. How could a mother who uses drugs and has free sexual relations ensure that her children stay on the right path?

Ana and Sara García stand for different principles related to the family. In most classical films the "Mother of Mexico" belongs to a nuclear family and is married to a responsible father, like Don Pepe in *Cuando los hijos se van*. The same is true of other classical melodramas; in *Una familia de tantas* for instance, Doña Gracia is happily married to Don Ramiro. As Julianne Burton and others have shown, these are paternal melodramas, melodramas in which the family centers on the father. In contrast, in third-wave films like *Los pasos de Ana*, fathers are absent. Mothers are the heads of the household in most third-wave narratives, like Dolores in Cortés's *El secreto de Romelia*; Julia, Ana and María in *Conozco a las tres*; Alma in *Ángel de fuego*; and Lola. The presence and absence of fathers posit a different style of family life; while most classical families are nuclear, third-wave film families are not.[7]

In *Los pasos de Ana* Sistach uses depth of field to represent the distance that separates Ana from Sara García's principles. After a close-up in which Carlos and Ana converse, the camera pulls away to a medium and then a long shot, leaving Carlos and Ana in the upper right part of the background. The camera focuses on a stack of books in the foreground, which represent, metonymically, the history of film in Mexico. Literally, then, the spectator sees Ana's motherhood from the historical perspective represented by the books.

By looking at *Los pasos de Ana* from *Mecánica nacional* as representative of the 1970s, we add one more chapter to the history of mother love in Mexico. In third-wave films mother love is clearly separated from oedipal desire. *Los pasos de Ana* separates the protagonist's heterosexual desire for her lovers, which is seen as sexual, from the protagonist's love for her child, nonsexual. These two loves coexist within the protagonist without impinging upon each other. Examining *Los pasos de Ana* side by side with *Mecánica nacional* also shows that mother love can exist in Mexico in a non-Catholic version. The Virgin, which does not appear in the whole film, is not Ana's model of motherhood; instead Sara García is Ana's image of maternal affect.

Sistach's Reinvestment in Maternal Affect

Sistach brings Sara García into *Los pasos de Ana* in order to recover maternal affect for feminism. There are, of course, some differences between García's and Ana's mother love. In *Cuando los hijos se van*, for example, García is not shown playing with her children; she is a much older mother than Ana, and her "children" are adults. García's age is related to her role as mother; 1940s mother love assures that children will stay on the path of moral rectitude. Its 1980s counterpart does not intend to be a moral guide for children; the end of the century mother love assures that children are an important part of the life of mothers.

When Sistach created Ana's identity, she gave motherhood a primary role: "I wanted Ana to have a three-part identity. Her affection toward her children is the part I thought was the most fundamental" (Arredondo 2013, 129). Sistach changed the film's initial script to make Ana's love for her children stronger. "I really liked the script," she explained, "but I felt it lacked Ana's passion for her work and her tenderness toward her children" (127). At a workshop she attended at the film school in San Antonio de los Baños, Cuba,[8] Sistach had the idea of having Ana make a home video about her children within the film (128). The video within the film, Sistach thought, would express the love Ana feels for her children, Juan and Paula. In the film, the divorced mother's video recording of her children's daily activities fulfills a double function: it shows the protagonist's love for her children and her passion for filmmaking. Mothers' affection toward their children plays a fundamental role in *Los pasos de Ana*, as in other third-wave films.

Maternal Affect in Third-Wave Films

In *Ángel de fuego*, Alma goes through penance and sacrifice because she loves her child. In other films, the world of children is also important. The

Alma and her puppet child (photograph by Daniel Daza, courtesy Dana Rotberg).

ubiquitous presence of toys signals the importance of mother love in María Novaro's *Lola*. Children's toys lighten Lola's household. In an establishing shot at the beginning of *Lola*, the camera slowly pans the apartment. What catches the eye of the spectator is the arrangement of Ana's toys: dolls and puppets are carefully organized along the walls of the room and fill the space.

The bright colors and diverse shapes of the toys speak about the gaiety children bring into a mother's life. A scene depicting Ana's trip to the beach with another mom illustrates the challenges of living with toys. A point-of-view shot taken from Lola's perspective in her apartment looking down at the car parked on the street humorously depicts the difficulty of closing the trunk when the car is full of inflatable beach toys. Upon Ana's return to the apartment, the beach toys raise Lola's spirits once more. The orange inflatable floaters still in Ana's arms bring a smile into Lola's otherwise gloomy face. In *Lola*, children and their toys are associated with happiness.

Similarly, engaging in children's play is positively associated with affect in several scenes at the playground. Lola relates to Ana by participating in children's games, as when they both pretend they are ballerinas. From dancing in the playground to playing with Barbie dolls, the time that Lola spends playing with Ana brings fresh air into the depressed life that Lola lives in.

Novaro's careful depiction of toys and games is not accidental; it is a way of hinting that mother love can be to the benefit of the mother as well. In classical films, mother love is aimed at benefiting the children, not the mother. Lupe's love in *Cuando los hijos se van* is associated with pain and blood; it is a sacrifice the mother makes for the good of her children. The same is not necessarily true of mother love at the end of the 1980s decade. Playing with Ana alleviates Lola's deception with heterosexual love and the harsh economic conditions caused by Mexico's 1985 earthquake. The unexpressed emotions Lola feels when burdened with earning a living and preparing Ana for school are offset by the rewards that having Ana brings to her life. Although seriously depressed, Lola does not commit suicide because of Ana. From a feminist point of view, it makes sense to have mother love when it benefits the mother.

In conclusion, mother love, although always present, is conceived very differently. Third-wave films selectively recuperate mother love from the 1940s and 1950s by getting rid of the association of mother love and moral motherhood. Third-wave films recover mother love by bringing it into a new setting: the family headed by a single mother, in which fathers are absent and romantic love is not available. Furthermore, the 1980s mother love takes into account mothers, not just children. Third-wave mother love brightens a mother's difficult existence, thus recovering and giving new meaning to maternal affect. Third-wave mother love, represented by toys, signifies joy, instead of the sacrifice represented by García's red roses or Mary's knives. The new meaning Mexican women filmmaker give to maternal affect is much in line with the efforts of feminist analyst Julia Kristeva.

Kristeva's Resemantization of the Semiotic

Kristeva (1986) wrote "Stabat Mater," a study on representations of the maternal in music and painting, when she was pregnant.[9] In "Stabat Mater" Kristeva tackles the semiotic, a phase of human development dominated by instincts in which the child has not yet acquired language.[10] Kristeva poses that this presymbolic, preverbal stage governed by bodily drives does not disappear with the acquisition of language but rather re-enters the symbolic. To make her point, she gives symbolic and semiotic accounts of motherhood on the same page. The symbolic account contains a history of the Virgin as a mythical figure, as a human construct. The semiotic account, visually differentiated from the symbolic account by the use of bold characters, describes how the maternal body feels to a pregnant mother. Although the semiotic and symbolic accounts of motherhood are separated from each other by the type of font used, both accounts relate to each other. For example, on the same page, the semiotic account talks about the experience of being pregnant on the left side, and on the right side the symbolic describes paintings of the Virgin's tears and milk.

Kristeva argues not only for considering the semiotic and symbolic as separate but coexisting, but most importantly she also defends that the semiotic has been excluded from the symbolic. For example, the Catholic Church does not approve of representations of a pregnant Virgin. In a sense then, the semiotic aspect of Mary is excluded from the symbolic. However, the many paintings of the Virgin's tears and milk show that the semiotic is a driving force in the discourse on Mary. It is Mary's bodily attributes—the tears, the milk—that drive the maternal cult of Mary. Thus, Kristeva points to a twofold discourse on Mary: while the Virgin's pregnant body is rejected from representation, bodily aspects of her maternity are a fundamental part of the symbolic: many churches have portraits of a Virgin crying and showing her breast. Kristeva has explained that in the case of the Stabat Mater, the tears, otherwise associated with the semiotic and abject, are resemanticized as nurturance.

Sara García receives a prize for *Mecánica nacional* (Colección Filmoteca de la UNAM).

Thus, the visual and verbal discourse on Mary allows positively valuing motherly affect (tears) and motherly nurturance (milk). "Stabat Mater" contributes to the missing discourse on motherhood by giving an account of the symbolic that includes the female body.

Kristeva's "Stabat Mater" can be used to explain Sistach's appropriation of Sara García. The scene at the bookstore illustrates the surprising position third-wave filmmakers take on to mother love. Despite Carlos's words of caution, Ana loves her two children with as much affection as Sara García does in *Cuando los hijos se van*. The affective ties between mothers and their children are just as strong in third-wave films as they are in classical films.

In *Los pasos de Ana,* Sistach, like Kristeva, brings the semiotic into the symbolic. Third-wave filmmakers' recovery of maternal affect is similar in many aspects to Kristeva's recovery of the semiotic. In Kristeva's case, the analyst recovers the pregnant body and brings some of its signifiers, the tears and the milk, into the symbolic. In the case of third-wave filmmakers, they recover García's maternal affect as a valid component of the maternal. Sistach does not use the Virgin per se, but uses García's star persona, a manifestation of the cult of the maternal. Like the Virgin, Sara García owes her success to creating a star persona that brings aspects of the semiotic into the symbolic. By watering her rosebushes with her own tears, García wins the hearts of Mexicans and brings rejected aspects of the maternal into Mexican film.

Tears and Excess in Scholarly Articles of the 1970s–1980s

Sistach's recovery of "Mexico's Mother" is in sharp contrast with the position taken by specialists writing on Mexican film. These scholars for the most part reject maternal affect, what Kristeva calls the semiotic. From the 1970s to the 1990s, García's films, precisely because of her excessive maternal affect, were excluded from what was considered "good Mexican cinema." In 1977, Aurelio de los Reyes wrote a section entitled "Madre solo hay una: la del cine mexicano" ("Mother There is Only One: Mexican Film Mother"). De los Reyes suggests that Orol's role for Sara García in *Madrecita querida* (*Beloved Mother*, 1935), the first of García's motherly performances, is reductionary and lacks depth. According to De los Reyes, Orol creates "A figure born beyond and above anything else, solely to shed tears and to suffer, an androgynous and asexual being whose only function, whose only reason for living is this: To Be Mother" (De los Reyes 1977, 109). De los Reyes calls attention to García's excessive tears and suffering, and considers Orol's understanding of the maternal simplistic.[11]

Carl J. Mora (1985) criticizes *Cuando los hijos se van* for its melodramatic excess; according to Mora, Bustillo Oro's film contains "139 minutes of unrelenting melodrama and nostalgia" (229). He also writes that Orol in the film *Madre querida* is the master of the "cinematic bad taste" (229). In *La aventura del cine mexicano: En la Época de Oro y después*, Jorge Ayala Blanco criticizes the maternal roles played by Gracía for their lack of dignity.[12] For the Mexican journalist, Garcia's melodramas are masochistic, oedipal, unimportant and uncharacteristic of the genre.[13] He prefers, instead Gavaldón's *Una familia de tantas,* a film that he considers representative of the melodramatic genre and worth studying, since this director's melodramas are examples of the ingenuous middle-class desire to establish its idea of familial values. Charles Ramírez Berg relates Doña Lupe's maternal excess in *Cuando los hijos se van* to victimization. La señora Rosales "must be an innocent or an idiot. Either way, like most 'decent' Mexican women, Doña Lupe [Sara García] has no choice but to play dumb and accept her fate quietly" (1992, 24). The views of these Mexican film specialists exclude García's motherly roles from the symbolic (the History of Mexican Film); for De los Reyes, her roles are simplistic and reductive; for Mora, they are examples of bad taste; for Ayala Blanco, they are oedipal and masochistic; and for Ramírez Berg, they are a product of victimization. All these positions dismiss García's films because of their emphasis on what Kristeva calls the semiotic: the tears, the inexpressible maternal affect.

Feminist scholars have a more inclusive attitude regarding García's semiotic than their male counterparts. In "Tears and Desire: Women and Melodrama in the 'Old' Mexican Cinema" Ana María López (1994) takes an ambivalent position with regards to García's overt call to the semiotic. López includes the word "tears" in the title of her article, thus making García's maternal affect an element worth studying. By including the word "tears" in "Tears and Desire," she takes a position that opposes that of Ayala Blanco, for whom García's melodramas are not worthy of study. Despite including García's maternal affect within the history of Mexican cinema, López concurs with Ayala Blanco that these are "male oedipal dramas" (260). Although, the U.S.–based scholar recuperates García's tears, she nevertheless associates them with an illusion, a male dream of primary narcissism; not something that belongs to women.[14] In that sense, she also excludes the semiotic (the tears) from the symbolic (the history of Mexican cinema).

Mexican film scholar Julia Tuñón (1998) dedicates a section of her book *Mujeres de luz y sombra en el cine mexicano: La construcción de una imagen* to the roles played by Sara García. Unlike López, Tuñón considers García's roles to be male oedipal dramas. Nor do García's tears completely enter the symbolic. In a book dedicated to "two real women," Tuñón separates García's acting career from her star persona in order to emphasize that García's star persona is constructed. Tuñón quotes a newspaper article from 1947 by Marta Elba in which the journalist mentions that the actress is more attracted to making money than to cooking or sewing (179–180). By including Elba's comment, Tuñón differentiates the actress, who likes to make money, from the housewife, thus separating García's film tears from real life García. Sistach's appropriation of García's films in *Los pasos de Ana* contributes to feminism by recovering three decades of exclusion of the maternal from the history of Mexican cinema. While *Mecánica nacional* associates García's star persona with putrefaction and claustrophobia by making her die a car race on a hot summer day, in *Los pasos de Ana* maternal love is associated with joy.

Conclusion

In the three films selected, mother love goes full circle from the idealization of mother love in *Cuando los hijos se van* to a parody in *Mecánica nacional* and then to its re-emergence as feminist maternal affect in *Los pasos de Ana*. After comparing mother love in the 1940s, 1970s and late 1980s, it becomes clear that mother love is not always related to morality. There is a difference between classical mother love, a kind of affective tie in which morality plays an important role, and third-wave mother love, an affective tie that provides children's psychological support and nurturance but that is not geared toward teaching morality. Unlike Lupe, Ana is not a strong moral figure, and consequently, being close to Ana could not assure morality. Thus, 1940s and 1980s affective ties differ considerably.

Chapter 7 proposes a new reading of *Cuando los hijos se van* and of Sara García by taking into account the film's Catholic subtext. Bustillo Oro's Golden Age classic is another expression of the cult of the mourning mother; the Virgin's (García's) pain at her dying son (Raimundo) moves audiences at the church and inside cinemas. By examining García's classical performances of maternity from the perspective of *Mecánica nacional*, it is clear that Catholic culture shapes the representation of classical mother love in Mexico from its gestures to its framing to the understanding of the mother-son bond. Mexico's strong Catholic culture explains why classical mother love lasted longer in Mexico than in the United States. In the latter, less Catholic than Mexico, mother love is suspected of being oedipal as early as the 1920s. Men in Mexico can show love for their mothers without having to worry about incestual desire for fifty years longer than their U.S. counterparts. In Mexico, maternal affect is based on an asexual construct, because of which an oedipal interpretation of maternal love is not possible. As the analysis of *Mecánica nacional* illustrates, it is only when Catholicism loses influence that mother love becomes suspected of being oedipal. Third-wave narratives are interpreted as a counter-attack on the 1970s interpretation of mother love. Third-wave mother love is not a glorification of the nuclear family and thus a conservative return to family values. These narratives do not propose a recuperation of the paternal figure, but a recuperation of maternal affect in the absence of a central father figure.

Third-wave narratives also respond to the 1970s attack on mother love as oedipal. The love between mothers and children is presented as unrelated to the mother's desire for a partner. By clearly demarcating filial love from heterosexual love third-wave narratives make an important contribution to the understanding of maternal affect. At the same time, *Los pasos de Ana* resemantices the roles played by "The Mother of Mexico." García's morality and sacrifice are down played, and her capacity to love her children and enjoy their love are given pre-eminence. By using Kristeva's analysis of the maternal in "Stabat Mater," chapter 7 proposes that Sistach's recovery of Sara Garcia's maternal affect is in reality a way in which the semiotic enters the symbolic, in which maternal affect re-enters Mexican films in a positive fashion.

8

Making the Private Realm Political

Chapter 8 studies how the pain mothers feel is represented and how film narratives understand mothers' depression. In both Golden Age and third-wave films, mothers experience mental pain. For example, *Cuando los hijos se van* compares the pain a mother suffers to that of the Virgen Dolorosa (Virgin of Sorrows) and María Navaro's *Lola* to "Stabat Mater." Despite having mothers who experience mental pain, the two film narratives understand the pain in diametrically different ways. This chapter uses the way mothers' pain is represented to examine how film narratives establish the relationship between mothers and the societies in which they live.

The topic of this chapter was inspired by feminist scholarship on the depression of mothers. During the 1980s and 1990s, feminist psychologists and academics created theories that related the mental distress and psychic pain of mothers to the public realm, thus shifting the way mothers' problems are understood. Before the 1990s, Freudian interpretations linked a mother's melancholia (depression) to events and emotions taking place within the mother's family. After the 90s, third-wave feminist philosophers, like Judith Butler, Elisabeth Grosz, Teresa de Lauretis and Kelly Oliver, expanded the types of factors that could explain women's psychic distress (Oliver 2006, 201). For example, in "Psychic Space and Social Melancholy" and *The Colonization of Psychic Space* Oliver (2004, 2006) created the term "social melancholy" to refer to women's psychic distress originating in society's treatment of women.[1]

To contrast the way in which classical and third-wave narratives explain mothers' pain, the first part of the chapter examines *Cuando los hijos se van* and *Lola*. Oliver's ideas about the depression of mothers are used to distinguish between classical and third-wave depression. Thus the question: Is the pain of mothers in these films seen in relation to their biology and their families (melancholia) or is it tied to the society in which mothers live (social melancholy)?

Third-wave films created a dialogue not only with classical films, but also with other Mexican films of the 1980s. Film reviews in Mexican newspapers, scholarly articles and interviews with Novaro show that the depression felt by the protagonist in *Lola* caused a heated debate among film scholars and film critics, both at the time of its exhibition and afterward. Novaro explained that some feminists and conservative males in the audience responded negatively to Lola's depression; they thought that Lola should overcome her depression. The fundamental issue that emerges from this debate is: why is Lola's depression so upsetting for both feminist and conservative males?

In chapter 8, Lola's depression is understood as syntomatic of a change in Latin American film. At the feminist conference in Tijuana in 1990, Ruby Rich posited that the New Latin American Cinema (NLAC) had two phases. During the first phase of the NLAC, the 60s and 70s, the Latin America's political left considered taking an interest in the individual to be selfish and unworthy of respect. The political was social, not personal. This view, Rich claimed, shifted in the second phase. Starting in the 1980s, individual issues could be political. The chapter defines third-wave filmmaking in Mexico in relation to Rich's theory of Latin American cinema. Third-wave films about mothers, like *El secreto de Romelia*, *Lola* and *Los pasos de Ana*, approach their topic from the perspective of the subject but are concerned about the well-being of the collectivity of mothers. Making the private realm political is key to understanding why motherhood became a feminist issue in Mexico in the late 1980s and early 1990s. In her talk, Rich suggested that feminism needed to appropriate Latin American cinema, and this chapter follows her advice by looking at third-wave films as Latin American films.

The two phases of the NLAC that Rich differentiates between are used to compare two 1980s films. These films were inspired by the same court case, a mother accused of killing her four children, but they interpret mothers' mental pain differently. In *Elvira Luz Cruz* third-wave filmmaker Dana Rotberg linked Elvira Luz Cruz's mental state to the conditions in which she lived, to the poverty of the slums. A year later Felipe Cazals, a male filmmaker known for addressing class issues in his films, responded to Rotberg's film. *Los motivos de Luz* links Luz Cruz's mental state to her personal pathology and not to the poverty in which she lived. Could Cazals's and Rotberg's films be examples of the redefinition of the political that took place in the 1980s? Could Cazals be interpreting Luz Cruz's case through the lens of the Latin American left of the first phase when the private realm, including motherhood, was not political? Could Rotberg be making Luz Cruz's motherhood political? If the answer to this last question is yes, it has many implications. If what I call third-wave films make motherhood political, then these films can be seen as feminist. And if they are feminist, what is the definition of a feminist film? Could the negative response that some of the feminists gave to *Lola* be an indication that what is political for feminism changes after 1985? If that is so, then we need to rewrite the history of feminist filmmaking in Mexico. In addition, if third-wave films are part of the second phase of the NLAC, then the history of Latin American cinema needs to be rewritten.

Melancholia in Classical Films: Sara García's Heart Drips Blood

Cuando los hijos se van is perhaps the best example of García's melodramatic excess and also one of the most popular films in Mexico and Latin America.[2] In the film, Doña Lupe (Sara García) worries about whether her three sons and her daughter (most of them well into their twenties) will be at the dinner table for the family's dinner on Christmas Eve. *Cuando los hijos se van* introduces the Rosales family through a long shot of the house and its rose gardens. At this point, the voice-over explains a pun in Spanish. The house is *la casa de los Rosales* (the house of the Rosebush family), and also *la casa de los rosales* (the house with the rosebush garden). The voice-over's pun indicates the close connection between the family and its garden and, most importantly, between the Rosales's mother and her roses. When the camera gets a closer shot of the rosebushes, the voice-over says: "Always watered by the hand of the little mother ... and many times by her tears." The voice-over explains that Doña Lupe suffers tremendously. It hyperbolically dramatizes her emotions, stating that when her children are away, Lupe's heart drips blood. In many paintings and sculptures, the Mater Dolorosa's sorrow at losing her son is represented by knives stabbed into her heart; in a similar way, Lupe's pain at losing Raimundo is represented by the thorns on the roses in her garden, and by her tears.

The Stabat Mater or Mater Dolorosa is also important for the character of Lola. In one scene, Lola is too depressed to take care of Ana responsibly, and she takes the child to her mother's house. As Lola walks to Chelo's house at dawn, there is a long shot of her carrying Ana and a big bag of her daughter's clothes. Through this scene the soundtrack plays Vivaldi's "Stabat Mater." The camera follows the slow and melancholic pace of the soundtrack; it shows Lola walking from the beginning of the street to the end in one long uninterrupted shot. The blue color of the early morning light combined with Vivaldi's music heightens the sadness of the scene.

Lola is not the only depressed mother in third-wave films. There are many mothers who are stressed in third-wave films, ranging from depressed to suicidal. In Guita Schyfter's *Sucesos distantes* (*Distant Happenings*, 1995), Irene suffers from depression and insomnia and lives haunted by melancholic thoughts. In Eva López-Sánchez's *Dama de noche* (*Lady by Night*, 1993), a mother who prostitutes herself in order to live the life that she believes she deserves gets so depressed that she loses her capacity to act and, in despair, commits suicide. In Dana Rotberg's documentary *Elvira Luz Cruz*, the person featured in the documentary suffers from life in a deprived economic and emotional environment where she is violently abused. In Rotberg's *Ángel de fuego*, the protagonist burns herself alive to protest for not having been allowed to keep her child.

Depression in mothers is also represented in the literature of the same period. Beatriz Novaro (1996), the sister of the filmmaker and coscriptwriter of *Lola*, wrote a short novel, *Cecilia todavía* in which Cecilia, the protagonist, commits suicide. Cecilia does not know how to be a mother in a way that is meaningful to her. She is unable to change from being a young pregnant woman with feminist ideas to being a mother. After having had six abortions, pregnant Cecilia drowns herself in the ocean.

Though mothers suffer in both classical and third-wave films, their pain is interpreted differently and is used to make very different claims. Doña Lupe is a case of what Oliver terms melancholia; her suffering is related to the death of her son and the absence of her children. Doña Lupe's pain is linked to family dynamics, not to social issues. In *Cuando los hijos se van*, as well as in other Mexican films, a mother's ability to suffer is presented as a heroic deed. In *Salón México*, Beatriz, the sister of the protagonist, presents motherhood as a heroic act. Toward the end of the film, she is asked to talk about heroes for her final oral exam. In her speech, Beatriz says that "mothers are heroes because they have to fight to make their children the best ones."[3] In 1949, Mexico had entered World War II, and Beatriz, like the people in the United States described by Plant, see motherhood as heroic. By having children, mothers give the nation soldiers to defend their country.

In third-wave films by contrast, mothers' psychic distress is an accusation, a sign of protest and disagreement; these are not cases of melancholy but of social melancholy. Film reviews written following the premiere of *Lola*[4] quote the director as saying that at the beginning of the film, Lola is in a situation not very different from the many mothers dramatized in 1940s' maternal melodramas, but that she responds differently. When abandoned, mothers in classical melodrama cry and then heroically come to terms with their situation. In contrast, Lola becomes so depressed that she is incapacitated (Velázquez 1989).

Lola is a case of social melancholy. The sorrow of the mother who is separated from her child and the sorrow of the citizen who lives in a cracked city are inseparable. In the scene in which Lola takes Ana to her mothers with the soundtrack of the "Stabat Mater," as Lola walks in the background, the camera tilts upward to show the empty, destroyed buildings in the morning light. This scene connects social oppression and melancholia. Novaro, a previous Maoist militant, explained that at the time of making Lola she was "disillusioned with my country's government, especially the PRI, which I think should disappear" (Arredondo 2013, 148).

In *Lola* there is an explicit attack on the government's response to Mexico City's 1985 earthquakes. Two major earthquakes, measuring 8.0 on the Richter scale, shook Mexico City on September 19 and 20, 1985. Between seven thousand and ten thousand people died, and it is estimated that fifty thousand people lost their homes. After inspection, it became obvious that the Partido Revolucionario Institucional (PRI), the political party in power, had allowed contractors to use unsafe, low-quality materials.

The complaints against the PRI were not restricted to construction. In María del Carmen de Lara's (1986) documentary *No les pedimos un viaje a la luna* (*We Are Not Asking for a Trip to the Moon*), a group of seamstresses denounces their employers, accusing the employers of not paying the salaries owed to the seamstresses and not compensating them for the loss of their jobs. De Lara's film argues that because the government sided with the employers this was possible. Civic organizations were formed to deal with the catastrophe because the government failed to assist the victims.

Novaro showed her anger for the corrupt government in *Lola* by shooting the film in Tlalpan, one of Mexico City's working-class

Novaro directing (courtesy María Novaro).

neighborhoods where the effects of the 1985 earthquake were strongest.[5] She explained that she

> used a slogan painted on a wall that says "México sigue en pie" ("Mexico marches onward") ironically, as a gibe. It was the anger that I, like other Mexicans, felt because the government was unable to organize assistance after the 1985 earthquake and because it had disseminated lies regarding the true figures and the responsibility of the companies that had constructed the buildings. I angrily contrasted "México sigue en pie" with very strong images, and even had Lola walk with her daughter past a store where you could read: "Death to the PRI, electoral fraud" [Arredondo 2013, 148–149].

Lola's problems are an expression of Novaro's anger toward the irresponsibility and corruption of PRI. Novaro makes Lola walk in an area of destroyed buildings, empty lots, and graffiti incriminating the government for its inability to restore the city. The cityscape needs to be read as a historically specific space that testifies to the government's abandonment of its citizens.

Motherhood Made Political

Novaro's project for Lola's pain needs to be read in conjunction with Ruby Rich's history of Latin American cinema. In her presentation at Tijuana, Rich, a U.S.–based film scholar, proposed a shift: Latin American cinema as a whole had shifted, and the change had redefined what was considered political. Her presentation helps to understand how in 1990 motherhood became political.

In "Another View of the Latin American Cinema" Rich first contended that the NLAC could not be studied as a whole (Iglesias and Fregoso 1998, 127–140). This line of argument was directed to many in the audience who associated the NLAC exclusively with militant films, like Argentinian male filmmaker Fernando Solanas's *La hora de los hornos* (*The Hour of the Furnaces*, 1968). Rich proposed that the interests of the NLAC had shifted in the 1980s; in the 1960s and 1970s the NLAC was interested in a sociologically constructed reality, in the 1980s the personal lives of people became political. Using Solanas's films as examples, she argued that the 1980s films took the same subjects, Latin Americans, but treated these subjects differently. In the first phase of the NLAC, Solanas made agitation documentaries about Argentina's poor; during the second phase, he made *Tangos, el exilio de Gardel* (1985), a film about a famous Argentine singer in which emotion and nostalgia play an important role.[6] Another filmmaker whose films changed from exteriority to interiority, Rich continued, was Paul Leduc. In *Reed: Mexico insurgente* (1972), the director was interested in the social life and problems of the Mexican Revolution; thirteen years later in *Frida* (1985) he was interested in a Mexican painter's interior world: her emotions, her feelings, her sexuality. Rich insisted that the change toward interiority was voluntary, because Leduc's topic, the life of a Mexican woman painter, did not necessitate such approach. The director could have focused on social issues such as the painter's militancy in the Communist party or in other political aspects, such as her relationship with Trotsky (Iglesias and Fregoso 1998, 136). In the 1980s, Solanas's and Leduc's films, moved inward, toward more personal concerns.

Rich emphasized that the shift of the NLAC toward interiority was political. In the 1960s and 1970s, the Latin America's political left supported policies that benefited society; at the time, an interest on the individual was considered selfish and not worthy of respect. Because many of those attending the conference in Tijuana valued social issues not personal ones, Rich underscored that the shift in the NLAC should not be mistaken as selfish. To describe the consciousness of the 1980s, Rich coined the term "collective subjectivity" (Fregoso and Iglesias 1998, 133). The term combines the group and the individual by joining the words "collective" and "subjectivity." By "collective subjectivity" Rich means collectivity seen from an individual's perspective (135). By making the individual a particular instance of the collective, a person's emotional life becomes a site of struggle (135). In the case of Leduc's *Frida*, sexual identity becomes a political act (136). Rich also included examples from women directors in her analysis, such as that of Brazilian filmmaker Tisuka Yamasaki. Her film, *Patriamada* (1985), Rich explained, "insists upon the equality of private and public, man and woman, the sexual and the political. The planning of a baby and the planning of a government somehow became mutually metaphoric" (Iglesias and Fregoso 1997, 135). Yamasaki's film becomes of interest to feminism because in it the private becomes political.

Although most of the examples of films used by Rich were made by men, her term "collective subjectivity" was also meant to be applied to films made by women. Rich's presentation did not make this claim, in part because, as she clarified, the films of the younger generation of Mexicans had not reached New York.[7] However, the translation into Spanish of the title of Rich's talk suggests this idea. Rich titled her talk "Towards a Re-Appropriation of the New Latin American Cinema." Ilse Kornreich translated the name of Rich's talk in *Miradas de mujer* as "Hacia un reclamo feminista del Nuevo Cine Latinoamericano" ("Reclaiming the New Latin American Cinema for Feminism"); (Iglesias and Fregoso 1997, 126). If, as the title in Spanish suggest, feminists reclaim Latin American cinema, then the 1980s' shift toward seeing the world as a "collective subjectivity" also applies to feminist films.

If we follow the ideas proposed by Rich, Mexican feminist cinema has a pre- and post–1980s phase. The equivalent of *Reed: Mexico insurgente* and *La hora de los hornos* are Fernández Violante's films and the films made by Cine-Mujer. Between 1975 and 1985 feminists in Mexico viewed independent cinema as a medium to raise political consciousness about women's issues. Colectivo Cine-Mujer (Woman Film-Collective), strongly Marxist, gathered students from UNAM's film school, CUEC, and other feminist students from sociology and anthropology. These students worked together to make films in 16 mm about sexuality, woman's pleasure and rape.[8] These films aimed to depenalize abortion, to approach sexual workers critically and to examine domestic labor.

At Tijuana, a member of the collective, Mari Carmen de Lara, saw Cine-Mujer as a movement whose goals evolved. In her opinion, "the goal of Cine-Mujer changed at the pace of the feminist movement."[9] This change can be viewed through the phases described by Rich with regards to the NLAC. The first films, such as Rosa Marta Fernández's *Cosas de mujeres* (*Women Things*, 1978) and *Rompiendo el silencio* (*Breaking the Silence*, 1979), study a reality sociologically constructed and locate the oppression suffered by women within the broader context of class struggle.[10] De Lara proposed that after those initial films came a shift toward "more intimate films" (Iglesias and Fregoso 1998, 75).[11] The change toward intimacy is perhaps related to a different interpretation of women's issues. According to Elissa Rashkin (2001), *Es primera vez*, a documentary about a gathering of women's organizations that took place in Mexico City in October of 1980, "introduced the question of gender to social struggles previously understood solely in terms of class" (69).[12] The second phase of the collective, the change toward more intimate films, can be related to the introduction of gender as a category of analysis to approach women issues. The collective also made films about popular movements approached from a gender perspective. In the beginning and mid–1980s, these films overlap with films that approach women as individuals, which de Lara refers to as "more intimate films." So, although Cine-Mujer is representative of Marxist militant films that approach women as a sociologically constructed class, some of the collective's films were already shifting toward approaching its subjects from a gender perspective, which in the late 1980s will result in making motherhood political.

Several Mexican scholars have supported a view similar to that of Rich. Rashkin divides the history of women filmmakers in Mexico into three periods: trespassers (before 1960), student and feminist film (1961–1980), and revisions (1980 through the late 1990s). Rashkin uses the 1980s as a watershed for feminism, a time in which feminism revises its approach. In a similar way, Márgara Millán (1999) relates the making of feminist cinema to the cultural and political atmosphere of Mexico from the late 1960s to the mid–

1980s in *Derivas de un cine femenino* (111–123). For Millán, 1986 marks the turning point at which collectively made films with clearly political feminist views addressing social conditions give way to more subjective films, which for her reflect "a feminine experience" (Millán 1999, 123). For Millán, the films expressing a "feminine experience" (what I call third-wave films) are less political than the 1970s and early 1980s films from Cine-Mujer. However, if we look at the history of feminism from Rich's perspective, feminism's separation from Marxism does not mean that women films are less political; what it means is that gender is also used as a tool of analysis. We can say about third-wave films what Rich says about the second phase of the NLAC: while it questions interior issues, it is equally political. Thus, third-wave films are political; not in relation to a militancy within the left, but because they question issues of gender.

The shift toward "collective subjectivity" that took place in the mid-1980s is at times hard to grasp. For instance, third-wave filmmaker Marisa Sistach's (1988) *Conozco a las tres* (*I Know All Three*) can be seen as a dialogue with Cine-Mujer's call for awareness about rape. Sistach approaches rape from a different angle than the films from UNAM'S Colectivo. The social recognition of rape is one of the goals of Cine-Mujer; in contrast, in *Conozco a las tres*, social recognition is not enough. In Sistach's film, María, one of three friends, is raped. The other two friends try to comfort María without success. Ana reads her an article that her boyfriend wrote in the newspaper. The article, meant to be empathic, denounces the number of females raped every day and therefore makes María into a victim. Rather than feeling comforted, María feels distressed listening to the article, and her friends learn that the pain caused by rape doesn't go away when the raped person is acknowledged. By emphasizing María's feelings after being raped, Sistach´s film explores the personal dimension of rape. In contrast, Cine-Mujer emphasized the difficulty society had at accepting that rape took place. In *Conozco a las tres*, the private space of the home becomes political, as in *Patriamada*, the film discussed by Rich. María's home is the space associated with strong emotional feelings about being raped and about being made into a victim by the newspaper article. Thus, whereas Cine-Mujer emphasized the social dimension of rape, Sistach emphasizes the personal. Both positions are political, though in different ways.[13]

Rich's idea of a collective subjectivity is fundamental for *Motherhood in Mexican Cinema, 1941–1991*. If we agree with Rich's claim that the collective can be approached from an individual perspective and be political, then the feelings of an individual mother toward her social role as mother can also be seen as political. This means that the younger generation of filmmakers at the Tijuana conference took a feminist position in their portrayal of mothers.

Their post–1980s feminism is a feminism that looks inward. For this reason, they are referred to as third-wave filmmakers. Despite their refusal to be associated with feminism, their films are feminist, though not in the same way that second-wave films are feminist.[14] The term "collective subjectivity," which Rich coined to refer to films of the second phase (Fregoso and Iglesias 1998, 133), can be applied to *Lola*. Novaro approaches a post-earthquake situation, collective problems, from the perspective of an individual. Lola is a particularized instance of "collective subjectivity."[15]

When Lola walks by graffiti that directly incriminates the PRI for the damage to the buildings, the collective — represented by the broken buildings — is linked to the personal; the depression Lola feels is implied by Vivaldi's "Stabat Mater." Throughout the film, there is a visual pairing of the city and its citizens, a broken city and a broken mother. Novaro intentionally linked the personal to the collective. In her application for funding from the Instituto Mexicano de Cinematografía (IMCINE), Novaro wrote a synopsis of her argument that mentions the parallel between the city and its citizens: "Mexico City appears as a backdrop. Cracked after the 1985 seismic movement, the city resembles its inhabitants; hurt and full of life, strong and intimate, broken" (Latina 1989). Mexico City's poor neighborhoods are mirrored in Lola's broken life.

The economic crisis forces the poorest citizens into an informal economy. In this way, *Lola* accuses the government of abandoning its citizens. Unable to make ends meet, many Mexicans in the 1980s turned to street vending; as means of "self-employment" it helped many families to survive (Cross 1998). *Lola* refers to this informal economy by having the protagonist and her friends sell clothes in the street. Economic analysts have suggested that in postearthquake, economically deprived Mexico City, the government had an ambivalent policy, using street vendors alternatively as scapegoats for urban problems or as political allies (Cross 1998).

The synopsis of *Lola* that Novaro sent to IMCINE mentions the economic crisis: "Lola's friends: el Duende, Dora, Mudo, are this way [broken]. Street vendors take over the street and are driven away by undercover police. Street vendors come back to fight every day, trying to win their right to sell on the street" (Latina 1989). The synopsis disparages the government's position on street vending; street vending is described as a war in which vendors are urban guerrillas fighting for survival. Film critic Naief Yehya (1991) comments that *Lola* denounces the government's "double standard ... of street selling." On the one hand, the government allows street selling, but on the other, it raids vendors, turning street vending into a clandestine activity.

One of the reasons Lola is depressed relates to her job as a street vendor. Several times the film shows the police cracking down on "illegal" street sellers like Lola and confiscating their goods. In one of the scenes, as the police come down the street where Lola has her stand, Lola's friend, el Duende, runs down the street warning about the raid. The camera then cuts to a medium shot of Lola that sets up a contrast in speed. In the previous shot, el Duende was shown running as fast as he could; in contrast, Lola is shown motionless. Lola's friends have to hurriedly gather up her merchandise so the police will not confiscate it. Her immobility, her static body, connects abandonment to melancholy; she does not move because the government's raids immobilize and depress her. The protagonist's inability to act is a condemnation of her social reality. Living in a world without secure housing and being forced into an informal economy, Lola is depressed. A mother's depression is to point a finger to an irresponsible and corrupt government not to lay claims to a higher moral status. However, her social and economic environment is not the only reason why Lola is depressed.

Romantic Love: A Site of Struggle

Lola is depressed because her partner Omar neglects her emotionally. In *Lola*, romantic love is seen as a site for political struggle not a personal problem. *Lola* begins in a darkened room with six-year-old Ana imitating daddy's rock performances. The singing is interrupted by the sound of the phone ringing. At this point, someone turns the light on in the room, and it is apparent that it is Christmas Eve. There is a decorated Christmas tree and an elaborate dinner already set on the table. Lola has been intensely involved in preparing dinner. Lola and Ana, the ones singing, are waiting for Omar. During the phone conversation the audience learns that he won't be coming. Lola is upset and goes out to forget the disappointment she feels that Omar will not be there for Christmas. It is nighttime, and there is a long shot in slow motion of streets with colorful lights. The bright lights contrast with Lola's sadness, and the slow motion foreshadows Lola's depression in the scenes that follow.

The idea that Omar's abandonment creates a vacuum in Lola's life was not well received by some feminist critics and other feminist filmmakers. According to Novaro, "Some feminists were bothered by the fact that Lola's crisis is related to the emptiness that she feels when she finds herself without a partner" (Arredondo 2013, 151). For the feminist that Novaro describes, Lola's romanticism was a sign of compliance with established norms. She explained:

> A certain sector of feminist critique disagrees with the way *Lola* ends and thinks it should be different. It seems strange to me that this feminist criticism

is in agreement with a segment of the male audience that is bothered when Lola starts to cry and can't control herself. For a man, it would have been much easier to watch a movie in which the woman is abandoned but lifts herself up, works, and deals with things. If the woman lifts herself, up he bears no responsibility nor does he have to consider certain issues. However, when you let that woman be destroyed by some guy's selfishness, then the men get awfully irritated [Arredondo 2013, 153].

Novaro is aware that her portrayal of a mother was not well received by a sector of Mexican feminists and by male critics. These two groups hoped that the mother would heroically recover and overcome her circumstances. The director argues that her intention is to make the mother's suffering an accusation; she wants to show who is responsible for the mother's depression. For her, romanticism is a social problem.

The effects of Omar's neglect evolve during the film. Lola feels emotional pain for a second time when Omar, who is a singer, prepares for a year-long trip to Los Angeles. This time, *Lola* makes Lola's romanticism political. A medium shot of sad and absentminded Lola when Omar prepares to leave is followed by a flashback. Lola remembers Omar singing "Si tú te vas" (If you leave me) on stage.[16] The lyrics promise eternal love; they say that if she leaves him, the world will have no meaning and his heart will die. Downstage, Lola is part of the cheerful crowd attending the concert. The flash-

Depressed Lola in the bathroom (courtesy María Novarro).

back is to be understood as irony. Not only did Omar forget the promise of eternal love proclaimed in his song, he shows no sign of sadness. In fact, the flash-back is followed by Omar enjoying his preparation for a bright future in Los Angeles. This section argues that the emotional abandonment presented in *Lola* is political. Lola collapses because of her romantic feeling; romantic love is a sign of struggle, not of compliance.

Judith Butler's notion of the heterosexual matrix is helpful in understanding Novaro's critique and Lola's disappointment. In *Gender Trouble: Feminist and the Subversion of Identity* (1990) Butler questioned the notion of patriarchy, and in particular the feminist notion of a nonoppressive society that preceded patriarchy. According to Butler, the notion of a utopian prepatriarchal or even a postpatriarchal state is still compliant with patriarchy itself. She proposes instead the heterosexual matrix: seeing heterosexuality as the norm, and the use of homosexuality, a prohibited kind of sexuality, as a way to stabilize heterosexuality.

Butler describes a culture highly invested in heterosexuality, not unlike the one in which Lola lives. In the scene of Omar's departure, Novaro points to a widespread social phenomenon. Romantic songs like "Si tú te vas / mi corazón se morirá" and romanticism in general are tools through which the heterosexual matrix is conveyed. Lola's hunger for romantic songs when she travels—visually expressed by the red tape player she carries—and the scene at the concert show that Lola believes in society's norms. Lola is caught in social promises articulated in romantic songs; her emotional collapse is a denouncement of society's investment in the culture of romanticism and heterosexuality at the expense of women.

Lola's depression represents the social pain of women who live on the highly enforced culture of romanticism, not the protagonist's personal pain. Novaro referred to the social dimension of Lola's romantic feelings by saying: "I'm speaking about what I have observed in the lives of a great many women. Being abandoned creates a very serious emotional problem for us and I reflected on this in the movie, with much pain. Maybe it is possible one would want things to be otherwise" (Arredondo 2013, 151). Lola's problems are the problems of the collectivity of women to which Novaro belongs. She refers to this collectivity with "us."

Novaro's plan to show Lola's depression works. She first observed the social problem. She explained: "I simply told it as I've experienced it and seen it happen around me. I could have changed the story of Lola's depression, but I think that rather than mythologize that emotional emptiness, it's very important to reflect on it" (Arredondo 2013, 151). Novaro recommends reflecting on the pain, addressing it directly, and not ignoring it. She continued: "I don't think it works for us women to wish to be what we aren't, but rather, to look at what is happening to us and to transform ourselves from there" (Arredondo 2013, 151). So, rather than putting aside uncomfortable feelings, Novaro challenges the audience to face them.

Novaro's plan is apparent in the film. The idea that the culture at large encourages women to believe in romantic relationships reappears in a marginal but significant scene that takes place on the stairs leading to Lola's apartment. Chelo, Lola's mother, is ascending the stairs when she sees and hears a declaration of love. A middle-aged couple is embracing in the corner of the stair. The sound track catches the man's voice singing a love song about the moonlight and promising his partner an unforgettable night in a hotel. The scene parallels Lola's romantic views having sought love promised in songs. The scene expands Lola's situation to that of other Mexican women, pointing to a romantic deception that includes all classes, ethnicities, and ages. The promises Lola heard in Omar's songs are not exclusive to her; they are part of a culture in which promises of a constant supply of emotional support are made to women and then broken.

From beginning to end Lola is a depressed character. At the end of the film, she does recover enough to pick up her daughter and reinitiate their difficult life. However her comeback is not that of classical heroic mothers who overcome all odds. Lola's depression calls for a feminist reflection on women's engagement with the culture of romanticism. Lola's pain when Omar leaves serves as an accusation of the system that makes women believe in romantic love, the promise that a male partner will fulfill them emotionally. Lola's emotions are the site of a political struggle. With *Lola*, Novaro makes a third-wave feminist claim. Like Yamasaki in *Patriamada*, she makes the private, political.

The Attack on Novaro's Politization of Motherhood

Novaro's allegations—from her accusations of PRI to her questioning of romanticism — were highly contested. Some scholars and film critics wanted to keep a mother's suffering connected to women's biology or family background, where it had been before third-wave films. Oliver's separation of melancholy and social melancholy helps to distinguish Novaro's position from her critics. The term melancholia explains a woman's depression based on that woman's private life: her biology and/or family background.[17] The term social melancholy assumes that a mother is depressed because society forces women to identify with the abject, with what is considered polluted. This book uses the term "social melancholy" to see a mother's depression as a social problem. A mother is depressed because of the social milieu in which she lives. Her social environment includes different aspects of the culture in which she lives, like romanticism, and politics.

Some film critics accepted that the film narrative presents the protagonist's depression as a case of social melancholy. These critics' comments on the deterioration of the buildings often indicate their position. Those who liked seeing the destruction of the buildings featured in the film usually see the mother's depression as social melancholy. Their acceptance of the accusation the film makes of a corrupt government points to their recognition that the mother is affected by her environment (Velázquez 1989; Mam 1989).

Other film critics rejected the film's association between the mother and her environment. These critics commented that Novaro's portrayal of a decaying Mexico City was exaggerated (Albarrán 1989; Viñas 1989). For them, the urban environment cannot explain Lola's depression. Instead, these film critics linked Lola's depression to her personal, psychological problems, making her depression a case of melancholy. United States–based Argentinian film scholar David William Foster, well-known in the field of Latin American cinema for his championship of gay rights, interprets *Lola* as a case of melancholy. In *Mexico City in Contemporary Mexican Cinema*, Foster (2002) analyzes the representation of the city in several Mexican films, among them *Lola*.

Despite taking the urban environment in which Lola lives into account, Foster sees Lola as a case of melancholy. He begins his review with a small introduction about the large number of single women who are heads of households in Mexico City. Foster (2002) says that these women are "trapped in the lower depths of Mexico City's economic structure" (134) and that Novaro uses Lola to allude to the single mothers in Mexican society. Foster's description of the buildings in Lola's neighborhood is an example of the scholar's reinterpretation of maternal depression:

> Her apartment building is not a slum, but it is bare bones in the amenities it provides, and it serves as a point of reference for the surrounding neighborhood, characterized by unfinished buildings, buildings damaged by wear or perhaps by the recurring earthquakes of the city (these cheaply built and poorly maintained concrete structures are particularly susceptible to the constant seismological activity of the central Mexican valley) [Foster 2002, 140].

In Foster's (2002) interpretation, the cheaply built materials are not a result of PRI's alliance with the construction companies. The buildings are damaged because they are built with cheap materials. He does not refer to the idea that the political party in power had allowed contractors to use low-quality, unsafe materials nor that the government did not hold the companies accountable for using inadequate materials. Foster denies the film's implicit social claim by ignoring the political claim. Lola has no reasons for being discontent with the society in which she lives. Furthermore, in "Lola," Foster roots the protagonist's problems in her individual psyche; Lola's unresolved personal problems are the reason why she is in a bad economic situation. Foster mentions that Lola becomes a "vagrant mother ... because of her meaningless, yet dangerous rebellion against her mother" (139). This comment associates Lola's depression to family dynamics; it makes *Lola*'s social problem into a personal problem in order to discredit Lola's reasons. Her rebellion is meaningless and dangerous.

In addition, Foster (2002) sees Lola as an irresponsible lover and not as someone who lives in a society that promises women a romantic love life that is not delivered. He takes for granted that Omar does not have familial responsibilities to fulfill and accuses Lola of seducing other men without a good reason (139). Foster even suggests that Omar leaves because Lola does not take care of him. Other film critics like Jorge Ayala Blanco (1993) share this opinion (506–507). For them, Lola is responsible for her own depression, not the world around her.

Foster's rejection of Novaro's argument for social melancholia opens up questions. Foster's "Lola" indicates that some in the international intellectual community that the scholar represents did not accept Novaro's attempt to make motherhood political. Could the same be said about Mexican society? Is it possible that in the 1980s Mexicans also rejected the third-wave construction of motherhood as political? To answer this question the next section compares two films that interpret the depression of the same mother in two different ways.

Films About Elvira Luz Cruz

Dana Rotberg's documentary *Elvira Luz Cruz* and Felipe Cazals's *Los motivos de Luz* are interpretations of the life of Elvira Luz Cruz, a mother accused of strangling her four children in 1982. At twenty-six Luz Cruz was an illiterate, indigenous woman who lived in a neighborhood of shanty houses on the outskirts of Mexico City. Without clear evidence that proved whether she killed her children, she was sentenced to twenty-eight years in prison. Luz Cruz's case became the center of a public debate on the maternal: different groups gave different interpretations of her alleged crime.

A diverse group of people saw Luz Cruz's case as social melancholy. This group included Luz Cruz's neighbors from the poor community in which she lived, Bosques del Pedregal. They organized the Comité de Apoyo a Elvira Luz Cruz (the Defense Committee of Elvira Luz Cruz) to help her case. A group of young feminists who frequently visited the accused in jail also belong to this group. Among them was journalist Patricia Vega, who followed Luz Cruz's trial for one of Mexico's leading newspapers, *La Jornada* (see chapter 6 for more details). Vega denounced the unfair treatment Luz Cruz received by the judiciary. Dana Rotberg and Ana Díez, film students from CCC, were also part of this group. They made the medium-length documentary, *Elvira Luz Cruz, pena máxima*.[18]

Rotberg and Díez's Elvira Luz Cruz

Initially, Rotberg, influenced by the media, saw Luz Cruz as a Mexican Medea. After a year of research, however, Rotberg uncovered a story that "completely altered the preconception she had from the media" (Arredondo 2013, 195). Investigating the accused's background, the director found out that Luz Cruz had been a victim of domestic violence and of the legal system prior to the date of the crime. Not only had her partner, Nicolás Soto Cruz, beaten her into semiconsciousness; he used his status as an ex-policeman to imprison her. Rotberg also found out several irregularities had taken place with the evidence for the alleged filicide: no one had taken declarations for the policemen who found the bodies of the children. Instead, the declarations of Nicolás and his mother Eduarda were taken as the truth. Rotberg concluded that the impunity with which Nicolás acted casted doubts about the fairness of Mexico's legal system (Arredondo 2013, 196–98). The director's respect for Luz Cruz and her indignation with the Mexican legal system is illustrated by the film's title, *Elvira Luz Cruz, pena máxima*. The second part of the title, *Maximum Punishment*, suggests that the judiciary gave the maximum sentence unfairly, as was based on faulty evidence. In her research, Rotberg also discovered that Luz Cruz had lived in extreme poverty: the autopsy reports showed that her children had not eaten for four days (Arredondo 2013, 197).

Because of the evidence of domestic abuse, of faulty evidence and extreme poverty, Rotberg changed her approach. She no longer wanted to know if Luz Cruz had committed the crime. "In the process of investigating, filming, and editing" Rotberg explained, "I learned that the absolute objective truth does not exist; we will never know who murdered those children. I believe that Elvira did not kill them, but I will never know" (Arredondo 2012, 196). Instead of focusing on Luz Cruz's guilt, Rotberg's wanted to understand her life in Bosques del Pedregal: "What was important was to see this person in the context of very specific emotional, social, and economic conditions, because of which — whether or not she committed the murder — she is really the first victim of this story" (196).[19] Rotberg became interested in the social factors that surrounded Luz Cruz's life. These factors, the "very specific emotional, social, and economic conditions," explain the mother's case.

Rotberg and Díez's documentary describes the social and emotional environment in which the mother lived. The film combines snapshots of Bosques del Pedregal and interviews with the organizers of the Comité de Defensa Elvira Luz Cruz. Rotberg included interviews with the family members who had abused her: her partner, Nicolás, and his mother, Eduarda. Nicolás appears, strangely, singing romantic songs with his guitar. Although *Elvira Luz Cruz* does not question romantic feelings the way *Lola* does, Nicolás choice of self-representation: as a romantic man, attests to the presence of the same emotional world that surrounded *Lola,* although in Elvira Luz Cruz it is connected to abuse. The interviews with family members are paired with interviews with Luz Cruz's psychologist, Concepción Fernández, and her first defense lawyer, Mireya Soto.

Together, the interviews create two accounts: there are the family members who accuse Luz Cruz of killing the children, but their statements are discredited by the accounts of the neighbors, the psychologist, and the defense lawyer, who testify to her innocence and the abuse to which she was subjected. The neighbors describe her as a hard-working mother abused by her partner and his family. They argue that Nicolás had forced her to stop taking birth control pills, alleging that she took them so that there could be no consequences when she to had sex with other men. Her neighbors claim that Nicolás fathered three of her children but did not provide for them. From their testimony, one sees Nicolás as an irresponsible father who brought children into the world but neglected to care for them.[20]

The account of the neighbors makes clear that Luz Cruz was a victim. The day of the children's death, Nicolás was hitting Elvira when the oldest child (a child from a previous partner) came to her defense. Nicolás first knocked him down and killed him, and then hit Elvira into unconsciousness, probably thinking he had killed her, too.[21] The neighbors' testimony presented in *Elvira Luz Cruz* attests to a high level of domestic violence in the past and on the day of the incident; they were witnesses to a badly beaten Elvira when the police arrived. In the last part of the film, Luz Cruz's psychologist explains that after seeing Elvira once a week for a year, she could not find any memories that would come from having murdered the children. Intercut with the psychologist's account, the lawyer contends that Luz Cruz's detainment was faulty on three grounds: no one asked for a declaration from the policemen who found the bodies; Eduarda and Nicolás were not detained and their testimony went unquestioned; and Elvira, who could not read or write, was made to sign a prewritten declaration in which she pleaded guilty to having killed the children.[22]

In *Elvira Luz Cruz, pena máxima*, Luz Cruz's poverty and abusive treatment explain her depression. She is both a desperate mother trying to live with meager resources and then a victim of the Mexican legal system. She is an alienated subject within her own household, with a husband who subjects her to repeated beatings and objects to her use of birth control. The conclusions of Rotberg's documentary are clear: what is needed is the creation of an economic system in which low-income mothers can raise their children under decent conditions, the establishment of a better-trained police force free of corruption, and the enactment of effective laws against domestic violence. Rotberg sees Luz Cruz from the perspective of social melancholy. *Elvira Luz Cruz*'s approach to the protagonist's mental distress shares similarities with *Lola*'s. Like Novaro, Rotberg anchors Elvira's depression in the world that surrounds her, not in her biology or personal problems. Third-wave films make motherhood political by having the society that surrounds the mothers affect their lives.

THE GRIPPING PHANTASY OF A MONSTROUS MOTHER

Another group of Mexicans interpreted Luz Cruz's alleged filicide as a case of a mother's individual pathology. This group included the sensationalist press, Marta Luna's theater play *La fiera del Ajusco* (*The Wild Beast of Ajusco*, 1985) and Felipe Cazal's film *Los motivos de Luz*. All of them, in one way or another, suggest that Luz Cruz was ignorant (being an indigenous woman with no education) and mentally unbalanced. These reasons are used to explain why she killed her children.

The sensationalist press brought the case of Luz Cruz, who lived in Ajusco, one of Mexico City's poorest neighborhoods, to the front pages and called her "The Medea of Ajusco" and "The Wild Beast of Ajusco." Both epithets, "Medea" and "Wild Beast" assume that she is imbalanced; that she has a quasi-animalistic nature that makes her commit an inhuman act. A year after the crime, Marta Luna wrote the script for a play entitled *La razón de Elvira* (*Elvira's Motive*, 1983), which was presented in theaters in 1985 under the title *La fiera del Ajusco*. In Luna's paternalistic play, Luz Cruz appears as an unsympathetic maid who does not take advantage of the chances society provides. Among other things, Luz Cruz is presented as lazy and opportunistic; rather than doing her best, she is happy to do the minimum for her salary. As in the case of the sensationalist press, in Luna's play, Luz Cruz's personal traits—her unwillingness to excel as a maid, for example—are used to explain why she could not get more money to feed her four children. The relocation of a mother's pain, from the social, where Rotberg had located it, to the personal, where Luna places it, creates new responsibilities. In Luna's play, society does not have to change, Luz Cruz has to modify her behavior. Felipe Cazals's *Los motivos de Luz*, has similar assumptions as Luna's play does.

FELIPE CAZALS'S *LOS MOTIVOS DE LUZ*

Felipe Cazals is, and was in the 1980s, a very well-known Mexican filmmaker. In 1985, at the time of making *Los motivos de Luz*, he had created many television series and more than twenty films, and several of the third-wave filmmakers had worked with him as his assistants. Interestingly, Cazals was known for making films that criticize social inequality. Thus, we cannot say that society does not play an important role in his films. As part of the Latin American left, social justice is central to his films. Yet, in *Los motivos de Luz* poverty is not addressed as the reason a mother unable to feed her children for four days would feel emotional pain. *Los motivos de Luz* was made after Luz Cruz had been arrested, but before she was sentenced, with Rotberg as part of the crew. Cazals's narrative is structured around the question: is Luz, the protagonist, guilty of killing her four children?

Los motivos de Luz is narrated from the point of view of Luz's psychologist, Dr. Maricarmen Rebollar (Delia Casanova), and her lawyer (Marta Aura). In this fictional film based on a court case, the psychologist and the lawyer are complicit with the status quo. They put forward the argument that Luz Cruz is guilty. Luz is portrayed as a violent psychotic and an illiterate woman who believes in witches and apparitions. The lawyer and psychologist must determine whether Luz is sane. Parts of Luz's life are intercut with conversations of the psychologist and/or the lawyer. An example: apparitions that Luz saw are cross cut with a conversation between Dr. Maricarmen Rebollar and a friend. As the doctor is speaking with the friend, the audience is shown Luz's memories and her conversation with a priest. In another instance, the psychologist and lawyer have a conversation about Luz's anger and its potential threat to society. Intercut with their conversation are shots of Luz reacting violently in her cell.

One could argue that Cazals created a lawyer and a psychologist that differ considerably from the real ones and, consequently, that he distorts the truth in his film. The real psychologist, who asserted that she had found no memories in the accused of having killed the children, differs considerably from the Dr. Rebollar in *Los motivos de Luz*. Similarly, Mireya Soto, Luz Cruz's lawyer in real life denounced the irregularities of the legal process, unlike the lawyer Cazals created. However, rather than arguing that Cazals's film misrepresents reality, it is important to reflect on Cazals's use of the authority of the medical establishment to reach his goal.

Maternal depression, according to Kelly Oliver, has been misunderstood and misdiagnosed by the medical establishment. Oliver believes that the knowledge on which doctors and psychologists base their diagnostics has an interpretative component. Because psychologists are field specialists, Oliver argues, it is taken for granted that their diagnoses are true, and thus their conclusions go unchallenged. The interpretative component of the medical diagnostic is never challenged.[23] Oliver's critique directly applies to *Los motivos de Luz*.

In *Los motivos de Luz* the audience is lead to believe that the lawyer and psychologist can be trusted because they are based on facts. The film's narrative uses these professionals to give legitimacy to the film's argument. What they say appears as true because it is based on observation, shown as Luz's flashbacks intercut with their conversations. Yet, the flashbacks depicting the apparitions are a narrative inconsistency. If the film is narrated from the point of view of the psychologist, she could not have had direct access to the apparitions. In other words, since the flashbacks are part of Luz's memory, and the film is not told from her perspective, it is not logical to have direct access (the flashback) to her visions. This narrative impossibility attests to the film's attempt to use the legitimacy of the medical and legal establishment to make its point. The audience believes the psychologist because she is a professional and because her judgment is based on "evidence," the apparitions shown in flashbacks. If we look at *Los motivos de Luz* from Oliver's perspective, Cazals's film is faulty because it does not acknowledge that interpretation plays a role in Luz's diagnostic.

Interpretation plays a fundamental role in determining if Luz is a violent person. In one instance, she is shown screaming and banging her head against the cell bars at the sight of another inmate nursing her infant. Cazals's film connects Luz's violence to her personality and not to the circumstances that surround her. Luz reacts violently, *Los motivos de Luz* contends, because she is a violent person, not because the infant of the other inmate reminds her of her dead children. In a scene that follows, Luz is led away to a high-security cell. Isolating Luz in a cell for dangerous prisoners reinforces the idea that she has a violent nature. Rather than interpreting her response as a sign that she is in extreme pain over the death of her children, *Los motivos de Luz* presents her pain as a threat to society. A violent mother has to be closely monitored; her freedom has to be restricted. As the narrative develops, there are repeated examples of aggressive behavior that lead to the conclusion that the accused cannot be cured nor given a second chance. Nowhere in the specialists' interpretation is the idea that the protagonist's insanity could be related to her post-traumatic state: having lost her children and seeing another inmate with children shocks her. In *Los motivos de Luz* the psychologist and the lawyer are used to lead the audience to believe that Luz's violence is a fact without interpretation.

The violent mother, the film argues, represents a threat to society. This idea is expressed in *Los motivos de Luz* in an interaction between Luz and other mothers (who represent society at large). The film shows mobs of women inside and outside the prison demonstrating against Luz, condemning her for being a "bad mother." For the mothers protesting in *Los motivos de Luz*, Luz represents a monstrous mother. Society, thus, is not the cause of Luz's problem. Quite the contrary, in Cazals's film the violent mother is a problem for society. If we are to draw conclusions from Cazals's film, we might say that Luz is a deviant who has to be retrained through punishment in jail and therapy with a psychologist.

Society plays an important role in *Los motivos de Luz*, according to Mexican journalist Mauricio Montiel. He sees Cazals's film as a denunciation film, a film that denounces social inequalities.[24] Montiel contends that Cazals brilliantly portrays the unfair situation of people who live in slums. Denunciation and third-wave films conceive the relationship between mothers and the social very differently. While both types of film have society in mind, their positions on how poverty affects mothers are very different. For Cazals, poverty is a bad circumstance, unrelated to a mother's mental state.[25] Neither the poverty that surrounds Luz nor Nicolás's violence and irresponsibility are used to explain Luz's state. In contrast, Rotberg relates poverty very closely to the mother's mental state. After finding out that Luz Cruz's children had not eaten for four days, Rotberg said: "In the specific case of Elvira, if she did kill her children, it was a profoundly maternal act and an act of animal survival" (146). To Rotberg, Luz Cruz's poverty was so inhuman that it made sense to take the lives of her children so that they would not suffer. For Rotberg, Luz is not a threat to society, but a victim of it. As Foster reinterprets *Lola*, so does Cazals. *Elvira Luz Cruz, pena máxima* makes motherhood political. In contrast, Cazals's relocates the mother's problems to the personal. A mother's violence is a personal trait, not the product of the social system in which she lives.

Lola and *Los motivos de Luz* located the cause of a mother's depression in the social. Foster's review and Cazals' film responded by relocating mothers' mental pain to where it had been before third-wave films, in the personal. From the film scholar and the filmmaker's reactions we can conclude that third-wave ideas about mothers' depression as social melancholy were controversial.

Conclusion

Mothers suffer in classical films; they are depressed in third-wave films. Third-wave films respond to the representation of a mother's mental pain in classical cinema by highlighting the social environment in which mothers live. A comparison between Sara García's tears and Lola's depression illustrates the way mothers' heartache is found within the family in the 1940s, and within society in the third-wave films. Classical films find answers for the troubles mothers feel in the private lives of the mothers. In *Cuando los hijos se van* Lupe's heart drips blood because her children have left home. In third-wave films like *Lola* the troubles are located in society. Lupe does not suffer as a consequence of the shattered urban environment in which she lives; Lola does. Her heart "drips blood" because the social fabric is in ruins.

Third-wave filmmakers also respond to classical films by making mothers' suffering political. Mothers in both classical and third-wave films experience pain, but the way the films portray how the pain is manifested is very different. In classical films mothers heroically suffer pain, and this gives them high moral status. In third-wave films, pain is a sign of discontent and protest.

The depressed mothers of third-wave films are a response to classical films but, more importantly, they are an integral part of the New Latin American Cinema in its second phase. In regards to the interpretation of mothers' mental pain, third-wave films engage primarily in conversation not with the past, but with other films of the New Latin American Cinema. Lola's depression is used to call attention to the government's corruption in the post-earthquake conditions of 1985 and to society's investment in heterosexual love. And, in *Elvira Luz Cruz* a mother's pain at not being able to feed her children for four days, the irregularities that she suffered in her legal process and the precarious environment in which she lived are all used by Rotberg to attack the neoliberal government. The third-wave films studied have many points in common. *Lola* and *Elvira Luz Cruz* locate the causes of mothers' depression in the social, approach mothers as women and as individual citizens, and make motherhood political. Because they share these points, they are to be studied as part of a trend, not as isolated cases.

The responses that third-wave films elicited also share points in common. Foster's critique of *Lola* and Cazals's response to *Elvira Luz Cruz* shift the depression of mothers to the private sphere and dissociate mothers' pain from the political. For both, the personal traits of the mothers explain their depression. In Foster's reading of *Lola*, the protagonist's rebellion against her mother explains her depression, not a political reason. In Cazals's reinterpretation of Luz Cruz, her violent nature explains her mental imbalance, again this is not political. Despite being conscious of the role society plays on the individual, Cazals does not establish a cause-effect relationship between society and mothers' mental distress. According to his analysis, the poverty in which Luz Cruz lives does not affect her mental state.

The dialogue between Cazals and Rotberg can be understood as a discussion between the first and second phases of the NLAC. In the mid–1980s gender emerges as an analytical tool. By making motherhood political, third-wave films engage in a discussion that took place in the 1980s, a time in which Latin American cinema transitioned from the first phase to the second phase. Class is the preferred analytical approach of the first phase of the NLAC; gender and ethnicity, as well as sexuality, are characteristics of a second phase. Cazals uses class, the dominant approach of the 1960s and 1970s. Rotberg approaches Luz Cruz as a mother and not just as a poor citizen. Not being able to feed her children for four days could explain why a mother would consider killing her children as kindness.

The use of gender in the mid- and late 1980s as an analytical tool diverges from other analytical tools being used at the same time. Like sexuality and ethnicity, gender is an approach based on the individual and not the group. Foster rejects Novaro's gendered critique of the culture of romanticism and the effects that such culture has on mothers like Lola. There is still one question: Novaro mentioned that some feminists would have preferred to have seen Lola overcome her depression. What is the relationship of third-wave films to other feminist films? In the mid–1980s feminism evolved as did Latin American film. As Rich explained, before the 1980s, the political left—and feminists were part of the political left—viewed individual interests as selfish and unworthy of respect. With the emergence of third-wave films and the use of gender as an analytical tool, the private, motherhood, becomes political.

Conclusion

Motherhood in Mexican Cinema, 1941–1991 demonstrates that third-wave films redefine what it is to be a mother. Feminist films of the third-wave respond to the Ideal of Virgin Motherhood that conflates motherhood and womanhood and demands that women act like the Virgin by adopting a self-effacing personality and by having the core identity of a caretaker. These films question the qualities of "good mothers" (chapter 3); their agency (chapter 4); the hidden prohibition that mothers have an autonomous identity (chapter 5); and the narcissistic idealization of motherhood (chapter 6). In addition, third-wave films contest contemporaneous representations of mothers by positively valuing maternal affect (chapter 7); and by making mothers' depression cases of social melancholia and thus political (chapter 8).

Third-wave films respond to the ideal qualities a mother has to have. Classical films establish a positive association between self-effacing values and motherhood, encouraging mothers to act humbly. Doña Gracia's purity, self-effacement, and submission derive from the Franciscan's emphasis on humility. One would assume that Doña Gracia represents all the moral virtues a Christian person should have, yet she only has the moral virtues of a Christian woman; men have different virtues. By comparing third-wave films to classical films the misogyny prevalent in Christian thought becomes apparent. During the classical period, women's humility and submission are positively valued. In sharp contrast, third-wave films attach positive connotations to self-affirming qualities such as hope, fortitude and justice, which are Christian but are normally considered male qualities.

Third-wave films respond to mothers' agency. The bad women of classical cinema, such as the characters played by María Félix, are bad because they are agents. In contrast, third-wave films positively value agency; as an example, in *Danzón,* Julia is the master of "her own life." Possibly influenced by the entrance of women film graduates in the film industry, the agency of professional mothers in third-wave films is not seen as a contradiction to their role as caretakers. In *Los pasos de Ana*, Ana's job as an assistant director does not undermine the love she feels toward her children.

Third-wave films establish mothers' autonomous identities. In classical and third-wave films, women's identities have a spatial representation. In *Doña Bárbara*, the space of origins, Altamira, is conceived without fences, without women who have autonomous identities. Doña Bárbara's separate identity is represented by a fence; because of her actions as an independent woman and her "fencing," Doña Bárbara is banned from Altamira. In contrast, having an autonomous identity in the third-wave films is positively valued. In *Una isla rodeada de agua*, Edith is an island, a separate space, and her autonomous identity is related to pleasure; she can see the world in different colors. Classical and third-wave films take opposing positions in regards to the establishment of autonomous identities for women. While Doña Bárbara is discouraged to maintain her fence, Edith is encouraged to maintain her separate identity.

Third-wave films don't argue that mothers should give up their relationships to family members in order to develop an independent sense of self. Rather, feminist films of the 1980s present an autonomous identity and a relationship to others as compatible, as is the case of Edith and her mother. The metaphor that Novaro uses to refer to an autonomous identity, an island surrounded by water, conceives self-identity as an identity in relation to others. The island, the person with an autonomous identity, is always surrounded by water. In Edith's case, her mother, Lucía, associated with the ocean, always surrounds her daughter. Thus, third-wave films conceive of an autonomous identity as an identity that allows establishing relationships to family members.

Third-wave films respond to idealization. Classical films create narcissistic ideals; ideals that only the Virgin or dead women can reach. In *María Candelaria*, the protagonist has to die in order to be as "good" as the Virgin. Third-wave films put idealization to a different use. Idealization-at-a-distance, the idealization in films such as *Lola*, combines awareness that normative ideals are unachievable with an idealization of women themselves. Without idealization, defined as love and empathy, identification with imperfect mothers would be impossible. Luz Cruz's compelling battle to restore her self-image damaged by *Los motivos de Luz*, tellingly shows how idealization is fundamental for identification.

Third-wave films respond to the representation of maternal affect in classical and especially 1970s films. Mexico's strong Catholic culture explains why classical mother love lasted longer in Mexico than in the United States. In Mexico, maternal affect is based on an asexual construct, the Virgin, which makes an oedipal interpretation of maternal love difficult. It is only when Catholicism loses influence, as *Mecánica nacional* illustrates, that mother love is represented as asphyxiating and dangerous for male sexuality and associated with putrefaction. Third-wave films respond to the attack on maternal affect by dissociating mother love from morality and by positively valuing maternal affect. In *Lola*, *Ángel de fuego* and *Los pasos de Ana*, maternal affect is a joyful and precious tie that helps mothers and children. Sistach's recovery of mother love is strategic; mother love is a way to ease mothers' difficult existence.

New Conclusions

By studying third-wave films as a response to classical films, new conclusions about classical films emerge. Previous studies (Mora, Ramírez-Berg, Hershfield) drew an association between the "good mother" and the Virgin of Guadalupe. *Motherhood in Mexican Cinema, 1941–1991* demonstrates that the fundamental model of femininity in classical films is not the Virgin of Guadalupe, but the Virgin Mary. The role of Guadalupe, the patroness of Mexico, is associated with protection and national identity, not with the norms of femininity. Mary is the example of submissiveness, humility and mediation, fundamental characteristics of mothers, such as Doña Gracia in *Una familia de tantas*.

Motherhood in Mexican Cinema, 1941–1991 studies prohibitions for women in classical cinema unaccounted for. In "Tears and Desire," Ana López concluded that women in classical films had to face strict norms that regulate their sexuality. Chapters 4 and 5 demonstrate that the hidden but ever present prohibition mothers face in classical films is to become agents and acquire an autonomous identity. This analysis provides a new interpretation of classical cinema. In tracing the topography of the spaces classical actresses occupy, López explains that the "good mother" and the "bad woman" occupy the same central space. *Motherhood in Mexican Cinema, 1941–1991* argues that spaces appear differently when taking agency into account. Good mothers like Blanca, Doña Lupe and Doña Gracia occupy the central space of the home. In contrast, Doña Bárbara and Hortensia, the "bad women," live as far away from the center as possible. The *devora-hombres* (men-eater) lives in Los Llanos, a space far away from Mexico and from Caracas. The women who create an autonomous identity for themselves are the real transgressors of classical norms; they occupy the space further away from the center.

The changes third-wave films made to the representation of mothers are a contribution to feminism. In classical films, mothers are made to feel shame if they cannot reach the Ideal of Virgin Motherhood. In contrast, in third-wave films, mothers, such as Alma, refuse to internalize shame and thus keep away from alienation.

Third-wave films contribute to feminism by presenting the acquisition of a separate identity as a violent but necessary process. Classical and third-wave films associate the establishment of an autonomous identity for women with violence. Doña Bárbara's name suggests that she is barbarous, violent; similarly, female characters in Cortés's shorts kill the male characters. The difference is that classical films present the violence associated with having an autonomous identity as despicable, while third-wave films portray it as necessary. Cortés acknowledges that women have to commit a violent act in society to establish their own identities, to recuperate their own space. Space in third-wave films is redefined as psychic space, as a space in which women and mothers can psychologically and emotionally grow. The Buenromero sisters in *Las Buenromero*, Elia in *Un frágil retorno*, Fernanda in *Hotel Villa Goerne*, and the high-school girls of *El lugar del corazón* use violence to decolonize a space that should be theirs but is not. To open up women's psychic space in the church, in politics, in Mexican history, women have to kill men.

Third-wave films contribute to feminism by restoring the balance between the interest of children and the interest of mothers. Classical films create child-centered narratives; narratives in which the future and benefit of children, such as Beatriz in *Salón México*, are more important than those of their mothers. In Fernández's film, Mercedes has to die in order for Beatriz to marry into a better family. Third-wave films such as *Danzón*, restore the balance by taking into account the needs of mothers like Julia, who has to adapt to new phases in her life.

Third-wave films contribute to feminism by idealizing mothers at-a-distance. Feminism has questioned the way in which society idealizes mothers. The imperfect mothers portrayed in a positive light in third-wave films promote self-reflection; not about the idea that ideals are unreachable (which feminists already agree on), but about mothers' personal desire to see themselves as ideal. Third-wave films put this desire at a distance.

Third-wave films contribute to feminism by recovering the semiotic. From the 1970s to the 1990s, García's films, precisely because of her excessive maternal affect, were excluded from what was considered "good Mexican cinema." For De los Reyes, her roles are simplistic and reductive; for Mora, they are examples of bad taste; for Ayala Blanco, they are oedipal and masochistic; and for Ramírez Berg, they are a product of victimization. Sistach's recovery of Garcia's maternal affect is in reality a way in which the semiotic enters the symbolic, in which maternal affect re-enters the history of Mexican film.

Third-wave films contribute to feminism by showing women's problems within a social dimension, by making motherhood political. These films question 1980s' established ideas about the depression of mothers. Films like *Los motivos de Luz* relate mothers' depression to their biology and family history, while *Elvira Luz Cruz, pena máxima* relates mothers' depression to the social, political, cultural, economic and judicial environment in which mothers live.

For many scholars, the history of feminist filmmaking in Mexico ends in 1985 when the collective Cine-Mujer stopped producing films. Third-wave films, made in the late 1980s and early 1990s, are seen as films about women, not as feminist films. *Motherhood in Mexican Cinema, 1941–1991* demonstrates that motherhood in third-wave films is political, not in relation to militancy within the left, but in relation to women's issues. If motherhood in these films is political, these are feminist films.

Third-wave films also contribute to Latin American cinema. Social problems, Rich reminded the audience in Tijuana, can be approached from the perspective of the individual. In the 1980s, the NLAC approaches the problems of Latin American society as the problems of individuals differentiated by gender, sexuality and ethnicity. The third-wave films analyzed in this book are part of the second phase because they address the problems of mothers, as problems of citizens directly affected by laws, economic policies and cultural believes. *Lola* is an example of the shift toward interiority characteristic of the second phase. This film approaches the collective problems of a post-earthquake situation, from the perspective of an individual. The term "collective subjectivity," which Rich coined to refer to films of the second phase (Fregoso and Iglesias 1998: 133), applies to *Lola*. This mother's depression because of romantic ideals is a particularized instance of "collective subjectivity." These third-wave films about motherhood are an integral part of feminist filmmaking in Mexico and of the New Latin American Cinema.

Chapter Notes

Introduction

1. The notion of a second and third wave has also been used to talk about the shifts in feminism in general and in Mexican women's filmmaking in particular. In *Cinemachismo: Masculinities and Sexuality in Mexican Film*, Sergio de la Mora (2006) refers to María Novaro as a third-wave filmmaker (50). Drawing from Mora, we can presume that if Novaro is a third-wave filmmaker, Cine-Mujer, Landeta, and Fernández Violante are second-wave filmmakers. Thus, using Márgara Millán and Patricia Vega's chronology, which dates the end of the Collective's activity at around 1986–1987, the mid–1980s can be established as the end of second-wave feminism in Mexico.

2. Besides long feature films, the third-wave films examined also include short films made in film school such as Cortés's *Las Buenromero* (1979), *Un frágil retorno* (1980), *Hotel Villa Goerne* (1981), and *El lugar del corazón* (1984), Novaro's *Una isla rodeada de agua* (1985) and Sistach *Conozco a las tres* (1983).

3. "The Mexican films that I like, such as the films of Gavaldón or Galindo, especially the first, portray women in two ways, either as abnegated mothers or as prostitutes" (Millán 1999, 160; El cine mexicano que más me gusta, que puede ser el de Gavaldón o de Galindo, sobre todo el del primero, retrata a las mujeres de dos maneras, o como la madre abnegada o como la prostituta).

4. Unless otherwise noted, all translations are by the author. "Otro tipo de mujer que existe pero de la cual no había ninguna referencia cinematográfica" (Millán 1999, 142). Sistach told Millán that she wanted to bring to the screen women "who are not within the institution of the family and who obviously are not prostitutes" (Millán 1999, 160; que no están dentro de la institución familiar y que obviamente no son prostitutes).

5. The quotes from Arredondo 2013 can be consulted on line at http://digitalcommons.plattsburgh.edu/modernlanguages/1/. The book is cited by the page numbers printed on the manuscript. There is also a Spanish version of the interviews titled *Palabra de mujer: Historia oral de las directoras de cine mexicanas 1988–1994*.

6. A number of academics examined *Mildred Pierce*: Joyce Nelson (1977), Pam Cook (1978), Albert J. LaValley (1980), Andrea Walsh (1984), Janet Walker (1982), Linda Williams (1988), Pamela Robertson (1990), and Mary Beth Haralovich (1992). Another film that drew critical attention was *Imitation of Life*; Fischer edited a book of articles written about Sirk's film that bore the same title as the film. Feminist film critics were also interested in *Stella Dallas*; Ann E. Kaplan and Linda Williams published two separate articles about Vidor's film in 1990. In "Something Else Besides a Mother: Maternal Issues in Vidor's *Stella Dallas*," Linda Williams (2000) situates herself in opposition to Mulvey when she says that it is easier to claim that there is no room for pleasure in the classical films than to "discover within these existing modes glimpses of a more 'authentic' (the term itself in indeed problematic) female subjectivity" (483). Williams believes that to look for glimpses of subjectivity "is a more fruitful avenue of approach, not only as a means of identifying the pleasure there is for women spectators within the classical narrative cinema, but also as a means of developing new representational strategies that will more fully speak to women audiences" (483). For a comment on Kaplan's analysis of *Stella Dallas* see 68n19.

7. The other third-wave filmmakers studied

in this book received similar responses from feminist and male filmmakers and critics.

8. See chapter 1 for details.

9. O'Reilly was a founding member of the Association for Research on Mothering, an institution that publishes its own journal. She has created her own publishing house, Demeter Press, dedicated to issues of motherhood, and she participated in the organization of many national and international conferences around topics related to motherhood.

10. O'Reilly has written *Mothers & Sons: Feminism, Masculinity, and the Struggle to Raise Our Sons* (2001), *From Motherhood to Mothering: The Legacy of Adrienne Rich's Of Woman Born* (2004), *Toni Morrison and Motherhood: A Politics of the Heart* (2004), *Mother Outlaws: Theories and Practices of Empowered Mothering* (2004), and *Rocking the Cradle: Thoughts on Feminism, Motherhood, and the Possibility of Empowered Mothering* (2006). O'Reilly has also worked in collaboration with other authors. In *Mothers and Daughters: Connection, Empowerment, and Transformation* (2000), she worked with Andrea and Sharon Abbey, and in *Mothering, Law, Politics and Public Policy* (2004), she collaborated with Molly Ladd-Taylor. She also worked with a group of women, the Association for Research on Mothering, on *Mother Matters: Motherhood as Discourse and Practice: Essays from the Journal of the Association for Research on Mothering* (2004) and *Mothering and Feminism* (2006).

11. The Canadian scholar writes: "The term 'motherhood' refers to the patriarchal institution of motherhood which is male-defined and controlled, and is deeply oppressive to women, while the word 'mothering' refers to women's experiences of mothering which are female-defined and centered, and potentially empowering to women" (2005, 2).

12. "Acuérdate que, en las costumbres y en la vida judeo-cristiana, la única misión de la mujer era casarse para tener hijos; en la Iglesia Católica, la mujer está constituida como un vientre solamente" (Arredondo 2002, 201).

13. However, by refusing to take El Coyote in marriage she in turn is rejected from the community. *La negra Angustias* portrays a group of women who, wanting to "correct" the heroine's behavior, follow her, armed with stones and sticks. Asked in an interview why she made women the attackers of another woman, Landeta explained, "It was considered immoral that a young woman, from a good family, reject a marriage proposal" (Arredondo 2002, 201).

14. Forty years after her last classical film, Landeta directed *Nocturno a Rosario* (*Poem for Rosario*, 1991).

15. For an analysis of the relationship between third-wave films and the films of the Colectivo Cine-Mujer, see chapter 1.

16. The emphasis on the good and bad mothers based on sexuality carries over to the study of third-wave films. In *Identidades maternacionales en el cine de María Novaro*, Robles (2005) takes for granted that Novaro is reacting to the "good/bad" mother classical stereotype; "good" signifying the mother who keeps her purity.

Chapter 1

1. Years later, when Alfredo Joskowizc became CCC's director, he opened the school to other specialties. See interview with Joskowizc (Arredondo 2013, 41–9).

2. For CUEC's classes and early organization see 1974–1980 Centro de Estudios Universitarios. Mexico City: UNAM.

3. For example, Alfredo Joskowicz looked for alternatives to enter the commercial circuit. After having done *El cambio* (*The Change*, 1971), negotiations with the union took place. The director could pay a "displacement fee" to the union; a fee equivalent to the salary of the union director that was not hired. The union's authorization allowed him to show his film at Cannes in 1973, but the film still could not be sold for profit. In his interview Joskowicz explains that the copyright for *El cambio* belonged to the Universidad Nacional and that since the university was a nonprofit institution, the film could not be sold. Joskowicz's final remarks make quite clear that paying fees to the union in 1973 did not work; he said: "You can break from the norm but if you want commercial exhibition, you have to pay, you have to return to the norm" (Arredondo 2013, 46). Given that making 35 mm was out of the question, filmmakers opted to make their living working for educational television.

4. Patricia Martínez de Velasco, Matilde Landeta (*My Filmmaking, My Life*, 1992).

5. I would like to thank Nestor García Canclini for the conversation we had at the conference of the Privatization of Culture Project (New York University, 1998), in which he stressed the important parts that Juan José Bremer, UTEC, and Durán had played in maintaining a cultural policy in which the state played an active role in the arts.

6. For Rashkin (2001), "The proactive policies of IMCINE under Ignacio Durán had replaced the torpor of the 1980s with a vibrant cinema" (215). Maciel describes Durán as an able administrator, although he criticizes the legal reform and liquidation of COTSA that

were carried out under Durán's administration. According to Maciel (1999), "The state justifications were that the private sector would be more efficient in management and the sale would produce important revenues." In practice, however, "The profits from the sale of COTSA, like the great majority of the other state-owned companies, benefited only the elites and not the sectors intended" (215–216).

7. IMCINE was created in 1983, but did not play a very important role until five years later. At first, IMCINE was run by the Dirección General de Radio, Televisión y Cinematografía (RTC), which in turn belonged to the Department of the Interior. Since the RTC was also responsible for censorship, many film professionals felt that this structure was unnecessarily restrictive. In December 1988, at the very beginning of the *sexenio* of Carlos Salinas de Gortari (1988–1994), IMCINE was moved to the Department of Public Education. After IMCINE was moved, RTC remained in charge of the laws regulating the commercialization and public exhibition of films, including rentals and sales.

8. Patricia Torres refers to Cocina de Imágenes as the first meeting in which women filmmakers and critics came together to discuss their work in 1998 (Iglesias and Fregoso 76).

9. Enrique Feliciano: "Surge la 4ª directora de películas."

10. Patricia Vega's 1990 list appears in Iglesias and Fregoso (1998). Vega, "Una aproximación al cine trabajo de las directoras de cine en México" (91–102).

11. The majority of the histories focus on auteur directors who worked on 35 mm narrative film, leaving out videomakers and commercial filmmakers such as Iselda Vega and María Elena de Velasco. An example of this tendency is Patricia Vega's list of Mexican women filmmakers, which mentions Vega and Velasco as "atypical cases" (Iglesias and Fregoso 1998, 95). Jorge Ayala Blanco, whose essay on "La mirada femenina" dedicates as much space to popular as to auteur filmmakers, is an exception. His interest, however, is to study what he sees as extreme division between popular and elite forms of cinema in Mexico (1991a, 461–511). "La mirada femenina." *La disolvencia del cine mexicano entre lo popular y lo exquisito.* México, D.F., Barcelona, Buenos Aires, Grijalvo: 461–511.

12. There are also some studies that situate the Mexican directors within a Latin American frame, such as Trelles Plazaola's (1991) *Cine y mujer en América Latina.*

13. With the exception of Ayala Blanco's chapter, which deals only with contemporary cinema.

14. The conference was part of Mexico–United States Cruzando Fronteras (Crossing Borders).

15. The government bought an important studio (Estudios América) and created three production houses (Conacine, Conacite I and Conacite II). Several distribution companies were completely or partially nationalized: the international distribution house Películas Mexicanas and Azteca Films, which specialized in distributing in the United States, were completely nationalized, while the government became an important partner of Películas Nacionales. The state tried to buy Películas Nacionales outright but eventually settled for 10 percent of the company. The state also nationalized exhibition by buying Compañía Operadora de Teatros, a company that owned half of the country's movie theaters.

16. For a few years, there was a film school within the union, but due to internal conflict the school was closed.

17. In 1945 there was a split within the STPC. Following that split, two unions were created. STIC specialized in shorts and television and STPC in long feature films.

18. Unlike Landeta, who did not attend a film school, Fernández Violante went to CUEC, the film school at UNAM. However, at the time that she attended school, 1964 to 1969, Fernández Violante studied what we now call film studies, not film production. The film unions did not allow the teaching of film production or any other aspect of the professional part of filmmaking until the 1970s. For a detailed description of Fernández Violante's works and career, see Burton's "Marcela Fernández Violante (Mexico), inside the Mexican Film Industry: A Woman's Perspective."

19. "Las cosas van a cambiar, tienen que cambiar, tenemos que hacer que cambien, pero entonces hay que infiltrarse en los sindicatos.... ¿Por qué no está María Novaro? ¿Por qué no está Dana Rotberg? ¿Por qué no está Busi Cortés? ... ¿por qué no nos ayudan desde dentro a cambiar este rol en el que se hizo una parcialización de lo que la mujer y el hombre deben hacer en la creación cinematográfica?" (Iglesias and Fregoso 1998, 33).

20. "Dentro de esa enorme estructura, existen estudios y sindicatos que nos han estado aplastando durante un buen rato" (Iglesias and Fregoso 1998, 27).

21. There is one significant exception regarding unions. From 1985 to 1989, Dana Rotberg worked as a directing and production assistant for Felipe Cazals on a number of hour-long programs for Channel 13. However, she did not use her work on television as a plat-

form to experiment with the creation of characters as Cortés and Sistach did, but as a way to became acquainted with industrial cinema and the technicians of STPC. Rotberg's early work with union workers helped her to make an easier transition into the film industry. Whereas other directors saw unions as an obstacle to be overcome, Rotberg saw them as a force that could help her fight the excessive demands of the producers.

22. "Mis hijos han sido parte de las producciones siempre. Lo hice con los dos grandes y ahora también con Lucero. ¡Es una locura! porque de repente yo enloquezco, Lucero tiene hambre y llora y me quita atención. Todo eso te desgasta mucho, acabas más cansada en la noche. Pero ya he tomado la decisión de que lo importante es que no se sientan relegados por mi trabajo, que vean claramente qué hago y que participen en la medida en que quieran y que estén allí. Lucero, por ejemplo, aparece en una escena de la película. Se volvió fan de María Rojo.... Ella hacía los ensayos junto con María Rojo copiando sus acciones. Pero nunca se retrasa el trabajo porque soy la primera consciente de que el tiempo es oro."

23. In Spanish: *Cine de mujer, El cine de mujer hoy, Cultura popular y cine de mujer.*

24. Carlos Monsiváis and Márgara Millán debated the dangers (Monsiváis) and possibilities (Millán) of using the notion of a feminine aesthetic (Iglesias and Fregoso 1998, 192–193).

25. "Y que a uno le tocó la pastorela, que se tenía que disfrazar de angelito y que la mamá estaba en el rodaje, y no había quien le hiciera el disfraz y tuvo que ir de diablito, o ver de qué otra cosa lo disfrazaba su papá, porque yo no podía estar a la vez en la máquina de coser y al mismo tiempo dirigir una película" (Iglesias and Fregoso 1998, 33; And if one had to be in a Christmas play and the mother was shooting the film, and there was nobody to make his angel costume, and instead he had to go as a devil. Let's see what his dad could come up with, because I could not be at the sewing machine and at the same time directing a movie.).

26. "Cuando alguien dice: 'soy madre y tengo que ser directora,' que bueno que sea madre y que sea directora y que demuestre que la mujer, a pesar de ser madre, esposa, amante, madrina, sobrina y demás menesteres, puede profesionalmente abandonar por momentos esas tareas y ser capaz de entregarse y de volcarse en esto que se propuso, con todo el dolor que significa dejar hijos en casa" (When somebody says: "I am a mother and I have to be a director," I think how nice that she is a mother and a director and that she demonstrates that a woman, despite being a mother, a wife, a lover, a godmother, a nice and other obligations, can professionally abandon for a minute these obligations and be able to give all that she has to something she wants to do; with all the pain that it means to leave the children at home). Iglesias and Fregoso, 1998: 28.

27. "Una mujer preparada profesionalmente dentro y fuera de la universidad tiene que demostrar que puede hacerlo todo y que la familia pasa a segundo término, porque primero que nada se es creadora y después se es lo demás" (Iglesias and Fregoso 1998, 34).

28. Busi Cortés, who did not attend the conference, also rejected the title of feminist; she stated that her film was about women. Journalist Pablo Espinosa (1989) titled his interview with her: "Busi Cortés: Me choca el cine feminista; El mío es de mujeres." For a detailed account of each filmmakers' separation from feminism see "Del olvido al abandono" *Iberoamericana*, forthcoming.

29. There were other meetings during these years. At the 1997 meeting of the Latin American Studies Association in Guadalajara I organized a two-part panel entitled "Aproximaciones teóricas a la construcción de la imagen en el cine mexicano del último decenio" in which Cortés presented her history of Mexican women filmmaking referred to in this chapter.

30. The silence can be interpreted as a lack of interest on the part of the audience. Perhaps, the audience reaction means that by 2002 the making of films by women was understood as a diverse rather than unified practice, and thus the concept of a feminine aesthetic was no longer useful (Tuñon, "De la crónica al poema," in Torres 2004, 47).

31. Torres San Martín's position, however, is different from the one proposed in *Motherhood in Mexican Cinema 1941–1991*. Torres clarified that films made by women were not to be equated with feminist films (2004, 11–12). I believe that Torres San Martín meant that "feminist" was a term to be used for the militant films of Cine-Mujer in the 1970s and early 1980s. Torres uses the term "feminist" to refer to a smaller group of works. Like Torres San Martín, I do not consider all films by women feminist (*La India María's* for example is not feminist). However, unlike Torres San Martín, I do consider the younger generation of Mexican director feminists; for this reason I call them third-wave filmmakers.

32. Another important change was the move away from authorship; the speakers included women who were not filmmakers—such as scriptwriter Melanie Dimantes and producer Berta Navarro—but who had been involved in the process of making films.

33. Busi Cortés was an assistant to Alfredo Joskowicz and Felipe Cazals in the series *Historia de la educación* (*The History of Education*) in which they did twenty half-hour programs and Cortés participated in five of them.

34. Durán's idea was to build Mexico's cultural patrimony in film. Since, according to Durán, such patrimony did not exist, he worked to build up a video archive of Mexican culture that could be used by public television. "The objective was to gather a minimum amount of material that could be used by the public channels" (Arredondo 2013, 33).

35. Interestingly, UTEC's notion of culture combined an anthropological eye with the requirements of popular media. "México plural" said Durán, was about different ethnic groups. "We covered their way of life, being very respectful with the community, and making sure that it was the community members who told their story, almost with anthropological criteria. The challenge was to make it attractive to a viewer whose attention we had to steal from the soaps" (Arredondo 2013, 33). When interviewed in 2001, Durán felt that with his work at UTEC he had helped build Mexico's cultural patrimony, because today UTEC's series were available to the public in Mexico's libraries, and they are aired in Instituto Latinoamericano de Comunicación Educativa's television channels.

36. For example she directed the series *Los nuestros* (*Our Artist*) in which she presented the life of several Mexican artists: Rufino Tamayo, Vicente Rojo, Luis Cardoza y Aragón, Cavernario Galindo, and Héctor Mendoza.

37. Although working for educational TV was one of the best options, it also had its limits. Cortés explained that a group including the three scriptwriters, Alicia Molina, Pepe Buil, and Carmen Cortés, wanted to go a step further from the series and make a miniseries, a short television drama in a few episodes. They wanted to adapt Rosario Castellanos's *Balún Canán* for channel 13. The plan was to make seven episodes of fifty-five-plus minutes each, shot in various locations in Chiapas. Imevisión — the state-run television channel — bought the screenplays, but they ended up not producing the miniseries because they considered the budget too high. The miniseries' project shows the graduates' ambitions to move to forms of filmmaking closer to feature films that they had learned in film school. Television channels, even the educational ones, however, could not afford shooting on location or hiring actors for a short period of time; series, much longer in duration, were more profitable for actors (Arredondo 2013, 96–97).

38. Hiring somebody who did not belong to the union, however, doubled the pay, because the producer had to pay compensation to the union equal to the worker who wasn't hired plus the salary of the nonunion worker.

39. Rotberg complained about the conditions of assistant directors, saying that they were close to those of being a "slave"; although she was in the payroll, when money was short the first person that they stopped paying was her.

40. Sistach explained that she observed the traits that she depicts in Vidal — he drinks and wants to seduce Ana — in the lives of friends (Arredondo 2013, 125).

41. Another alternative for film graduates, although a less common and profitable one, was teaching in the film schools. During the eighties, Cortés taught classes at the CCC and the Universidad Iberoamericana, where she was the coordinator of film studies. Cortés helped to make the film schools a place where students had "hands on" experience in making films.

42. In contrast to Echeverría's *sexenio*, however, state involvement in film production was accomplished through privatization, not nationalization. For instance, in 1991, the distributor Películas Nacionales went bankrupt and was liquidated, and the theater chain COTSA followed a similar path.

43. The quality cinema of the late 1980s, however, differed in audience and budget from that of Echeverría's *sexenio*. The FFCC did not support experimental filmmaking for small audiences, but was interested in reaching a diverse audience. While the Echeverría administration had invested considerable amounts of money in its film productions, the FFCC only supported films whose budgets were equivalent to that of low-budget films.

44. According to Rashkin (2001), who cites Pérez Turrent's description of state policy during Salinas's *sexenio*, the state's "policy was not so much outright sponsorship as brokering of partnerships between a range of private investors and governmental agencies" (13).

45. At this time in Mexico, foreign film had to be subtitled, not dubbed.

46. See P. Vega 1991.

47. Tomás Pérez Turrent believed that *Los pasos de Ana* could not be easily exhibited commercially because of the quality of the final copy. Since the film had been blow up from a video master, the quality of the 35 mm final print was not on a par with other films being exhibited in commercial theaters in 1991 (1991a).

48. "Realmente la producción de la Televisión Española no fue un dinero extra, significó el punto de partida para que se hiciera la

película. No hubiera hecho Lola sin ellos, tenía el proyecto y nadie me había dado ningún apoyo, ni estaba en 'veremos,' ni nada" (Perales 1991, 39).

Chapter 2

1. Ayala Blanco's first edition was called *La aventura del cine mexicano* and dates from 1968. In 1985 he published *La aventura del cine mexicano 1931–1937*, and his latest edition is *La aventura del cine mexicano: En la Época de Oro y después* (1993).

2. Written in 1947, and published in Spanish in 1950 and in English in 1961, *The Labyrinth of Solitude* had one revision (1981 in Spanish and 1985 in English). In the year 2000 there was a commemorative edition and an international colloquium to celebrate the fiftieth year of its publication.

3. *Batalla en el cielo* (*Battle in Heaven*, 2005), a film by Carlos Reygadas, is another Mexican example in which the Virgin of Guadalupe plays a prominent role. As in *Tepeyac*, in *Batalla en el cielo*, the Virgin of Guadalupe plays the role of intercessor: she intercedes on Marcos's behalf with God. By the end of the film it is understood that Marcos is pardoned and admitted into the Catholic community.

4. Warner is not the only scholar who has wanted to bring a historical perspective to the study of the Virgin. In a chapter entitled "Timeless Paradox: Mother and Whore," Joanne Hersfield questions Paz's lack of historical perspective when using the Virgin of Guadalupe as a symbol of motherhood. Hershfield (1996, 12) examines the way in which the Virgin de Guadalupe is important to a majority of Mexicans.

5. Some Chicana artists have appropriated the cult of Guadalupe for their own purposes and discuss notions of mothering through the image of Guadalupe.

6. There are many other studies on Mary, although in them the gender-specific perspective is not so central. Important among them is Anne Baring and Jules Cashford's (1991) *The Myth of the Goddess*. In a chapter of their book, "Mary: the Return of the Goddess," these scholars use a Jungian approach and the notion of archetypes to defend the idea that the construct of the Virgin Mary is a later development of the Paleolithic Mother Goddess (547–608). For them, the cult of the Goddess introduces the notion of the feminine into the sacred.

7. Hersfield does not use the word "stereotype" in her study; she uses the words "symbol" and "image." However, two of her chapters "The Cabaretera" and the "Devoradora" (*bad woman*) are dedicated to studying what Mora calls stereotypes.

8. Silverman coined the term "cultural screen" based on Lacan's notion of the gaze. Following Lacan's seminar XI, "Of the gaze as petit object A," Silverman understands the gaze as a screen, as a place onto which we project things, and not as a mirror that simply reflects things. For a discussion of film studies' interpretation of Lacan's gaze, see Copjec 2000.

9. Meyer (1976) cites an interview in which García says: "From 1936 on, almost from the premiere of *Malditas sean las mujeres*, they began to call me 'the mother of national cinema'" (15–16; A partir de 1936, casi desde el estreno de la cinta *Malditas sean las mujeres*, me empezaron a llamar "la madre del cine nacional"). Similar information appears in Carl Mora (1985, 216).

10. Although García was famous for her motherly roles, she also played less known cabaretera and comical roles; see Muñoz (1998, 56).

11. Mauricio Peña, citing a text from Luis Terán, maintains that García was cast in her role of good mother and was obliged to be the "oficial mother" of the melodramas and comedies of the 1950s. "She could not get rid of the obligation to be the 'official mother' in abundant comedies and melodramas of the 50s" (2000, 53; No pudo separarse de la obligación de ser la "mamá oficial" de las comedias y melodramas que abundaron en el cine mexicano de los años 50).

12. According to Muñoz (1998), García's father, Isidoro García Ruíz died in 1904, and her mother, Felipa Hidalgo Rodríguez, the next year (12–14). Quite melodramatically, Teresa Carvajal (2000) sees García as an orphan whose only home was with the nuns. "Orphan from an early age, Sara García had in the school of La Paz Vizcaínas her only home" (36; Huérfana desde temprana edad, Sara García tuvo en el colegio de La Paz Vizcaínas su único hogar").

13. This information comes from Julia Tuñon (1998, 179), although other critics such as Julianne Burton also make reference to the extraction.

14. *Diccionario Porrúa*, 1995, 6th ed., 1069 (México City: D-K). See also more information about the director of the newspaper, Alducín, in *Revista de Revistas*, (1987, May 8:56).

15. "Sara was able to personify and give life to the Mexican mothers of that time [1940s] in that film (*Cuando los hijos se van*), which gave her a place among popular sensibilities. She was an innocent and tender mother able to cry in

one of the more convincing weeps of the films of that time" (Muñoz 1998, 40; A lo que Sara logró dar vida en esa cinta fue a la personificación de las madres mexicanas de esa época, la cual le ganó un lugar inamovible en la sensibilidad popular. Era una madre inocente, tierna, capaz de deshacerse en uno de los llantos más convincentes del cine de entonces).

16. The Virgin of Candelaria is a holiday celebrated in Mexico on February 2. The holiday references the biblical passage in which Mary takes Jesus to the temple to be blessed. One of the first instances of this image was found in the island of Tenerife and predates the Castillian conquest of the island. The first celebration in honor of this Virgin (February 2, 1497) coincided with the Castillian expansion and colonization of the Americas. The dark-skinned Virgin of Tenerife carried baby Jesus in one hand and a candle in the other, and for that reason she was called the Virgin of the Candle. In Mexico, the celebration of the Virgin of Candelaria is very important, in part because of the dark color of the Virgin and the pre–Hispanic importance of candles. Candles are still today one of the most valuable presents that are offered in celebrations, marking rites such as marriages or funerals. In many cities and villages all over Mexico, indigenous campesinos bring their images of baby Jesus to be blessed at temples dedicated to the Virgin of Candelaria. Xochimilco, a city located 30 kilometers outside Mexico City and the one refered to in *María Candelaria*, has an important celebration of Niñopan, which is an extension of the celebration of the Virgin of the Candelaria. Each year, the image of baby Jesus stays in the care of a family, who receives the title of *mayordomos*. As in many other indigenous celebrations, the mayordomos, who volunteer for the job, organize and pay for several days of festivities, including drink, food and candles for the whole community (there is a reference to this practice in the documentary *Xochimilco* (Eduardo Maldonado, 1987). Fernández, the director of *María Candelaria*, refers to the existing festivity; the blessing of baby Jesus and animals is portrayed in the film. Interestingly, however, the protagonist, who becomes the Virgin of the Candelaria, is not a mother and cannot fulfill the important function of presenting Jesus to the temple. The fact that María Candelaria is a bride, and not a mother, is another example of the lack of distinction between motherhood and womanhood in classical films.

17. Fernández's reference can be seen in relation to the church of Nuestra Señora de los Dolores, built in Xaltocan, a neighborhood of Xochimilco, in 1751. The church was first dedicated to baby Jesus (a symbol closely associated in Mexico with the Virgin of Candelaria), then to the Virgin of Candelaria, and afterward to La Virgin de los Dolores (Our Lady of Sorrows).

18. Fernández establishes in this scene a connection between Nuestra Señora de los Dolores and la Virgen de la Candelaria that is part of the folklore of Xochimilco. The church of Nuestra Señora de los Dolores, built in 1751, was first dedicated to la Virgen de la Candelaria and then to the Virgen de los Dolores.

19. The end of the meeting between María Candelaria and the Virgin already suggests differences between mediation and agency; María Candelaria can request things, but she cannot become an agent in making them happen. This difference is an essential component of the ideal that can be better understood by comparing María Candelaria to Rosaura (María Felix) in Fernández's *Río Escondido*. In *Mexican Cinema*, Joanne Hershfield (1996) points out that María Candelaria and Rosaura are aligned with the figure of the Virgin Mary (70) and that Rosaura stands in for the Virgin of Guadalupe (62). The scenes that Hershfield chooses are convincing in demonstrating that Rosaura is framed to bring out the similarities with the Virgin Mary. There is, however, a fundamental difference: Rosaura does not act Virgin-like. María Felix, the star famous for her roles as a "man-eater," plays a Virgin closer to the ideals of Liberation Theology than to those of the conservative Catholic Church. Hershfield describes Rosaura's deeds by saying: "According to the narrative of *Río Escondido*, Rosaura's short stay at Río Escondido destroys the oppressive, feudal Mexican hacienda system and restores the 'natural' balance between the Indians, the nation, and the Church" (71). Rosaura is a real agent, unlike María Candelaria, who obediently waits for her time to be helped. As Anne Baring and Jules Cashford (1991) put it, the character of the Virgin "is a model of loving obedience to something higher than herself" (550).

20. This assumption is not exclusively Mexican; in *From Reverence to Rape*, speaking about US films, Molly Haskell (1974) points out the double bind: "The persistent irony is that [a woman] is dependent for her well-being and 'fulfillment' on institutions — marriage, motherhood — that by translating the word 'woman' into 'wife' and 'mother,' end her independent identity" (159–160).

21. For a description of Kristeva's 1986 notion of abjection based on Douglas, see 173n17.

22. Other scholars, such as Judith Huggins

Balfe, who analyze the representations of the Virgin as a Queen in the eleventh to twelfth centuries, prove the same point.

23. Warner has a similar position to Kristeva. If the *Bible*, as Warner maintains, discriminates against women, and if the Franciscan notion of the Virgin as a Mother allowed women to gain a place in society, then we can conclude along with Warner that the construct of the Virgin as mother allows women to have a subordinate position within patriarchal society.

Chapter 3

1. "Lleva a tu hijo al monte y ofrécemelo en sacrificio. Mátalo con tus propias manos."
2. Voice in the tape recorder: "No lo hagas Abraham, has demostrado que tienes temor de Dios pues no te negaste a matar a tu hijo. Sacrifica al cordero que con eso él se conforma."
3. "¿Por qué Dios le pidió a Abraham que matara a su hijo?"
4. "Nada más lo estaba probando."
5. "Sí, pero lo iba a matar."
6. "Entonces le quería más que a su hijo."
7. "Con las penitencias que me puso me siento más limpia. Yo creo que ahora sí mi niño va a salir bonito."
8. Refugio: "Dios me habló de ti, me dijo que tu pecado fue muy grande." Alma: "Usted me dijo que con obediencia y fe eso se perdonaba."
9. Silverman (1996) uses the term "assimilation" when she examines the way in which people identify with other people who have different bodies than themselves. She explains: "But the spectator can only come into a politically productive relation to bodily otherness when he or she is encouraged to identify according to an exteriorizing, rather than interiorizing, logic — when the screen succeeds in soliciting the love he or she preserves for the ideal-ego, but no longer reflects back to him or her an image to be assimilated to the self" (86). For Silverman, to assimilate someone means to not respect the identity of the other person, the otherness of the other. Alma, in this case is the other. Audiences can respect her otherness, her desire to have a child that is the product of incest, or can deny it. If they respect it, they identify with her according to an exteriorizing logic. If they deny her desire, they are assimilating her to their own desires. In this case critics are using an interiorizing logic, denying Alma her otherness.
10. "Pequeña Alma" and "Desamparada Alma."
11. "Incestuoso y decrépito padre."
12. Incest is described in the script as a loving incest, meaning that Alma did not have anyone else to love her.
13. "Alma, la trapecista, escupe fuego del Circo Fantasía, es una niña cuyo amor es su padre, quien también sería el padre de su nieto si no muriera de un ataque por andar calenturoso."
14. Incest is "un acto de amor desesperado."
15. "Alma ... se enfrenta a una realidad incomprensible para ella. En su vientre lleva el producto de amor incestuoso que ha mantenido con su padre el payaso Renato (Alejandro Parodi), hombre enfermo que muere cuando ella más lo necesita."
16. "*Ángel de fuego* tiene como punto de partida un incesto que contradice las páginas rojas de los diarios; es un incesto que no nace de la violencia, sino que se asume como una conducta casi natural en un medio hostil en donde la tradicional idea de la familia pierde todas sus convenciones. Inframundo, circo de pobreza, redundancia si la hay, el ámbito en el que Alma (Evangelina Sosa) ha crecido le lleva de una manera casi normal a los brazos de su padre envejecido y enfermo, único lazo afectivo que la trapecista quiere perpetuar."
17. In "Ángel de fuego y otros asuntos," Pérez Turrent (1992) says: "Dana Rotberg does not give a look of understanding (¿piety?), hers is a look of astonishment towards a world whose understanding scapes her because it is too complex, and at the same time she is fascinated by this world for its unsuspected possibilities" (Dana Rotberg no lanza una mirada comprensiva [¿piadosa?], la suya es una mirada de asombro a un mundo que se le escapa por su complejidad y al mismo tiempo la fascina por sus insospechadas capacidades).
18. In "Ángel exterminador" Perez Turrent (1993) describes the change as follows: ([Alma's] learning experience begins with incest, an incest of love, wanted, accepted, assumed, and which leads not to the acquisition of knowledge ... but to the loss of innocence and the birth of anger). "El aprendizaje se inicia con el incesto, un incesto de amor, querido, aceptado, asumido y que desemboca no en la obtención de la sabiduría ... sino en la pérdida de la inocencia y el nacimiento de la ira."
19. In "The Case of the Missing Mother" Kaplan tackles an interesting point: mothers have been studied from the point of view of daughters. Kaplan (2000) argues that while patriarchy and psychoanalysis have ignored the mother all along, feminists have pretty much done the same thing. For that reason, she tries to look at the way in which Stella Dallas in the film of the same name is pushed aside by the

narrative. At the beginning of the film, the spectator can see Stella's desire, and she has a subject position that Kaplan describes as being able to make the narrative advance. Kaplan claims that the film makes the spectator learn that the mother's desire has to be annihilated, transformed into a desire for the good of the child. This is what takes place in the final scene of the film, when Stella is made into an on-screen spectator by having to watch rather than be part of her daughter's wedding.

20. According to Novaro it is a "troba yucateca adanzonada."

Chapter 4

1. Written in 1947 and first published in Spanish in 1950 and in English in 1961, *The Labyrinth* had one revision (1981 in Spanish and 1985 in English). In the year 2000 there was a commemorative edition and an international colloquium to celebrate the 50th year of its publication. Paz was awarded the Nobel Prize in 1990.

2. Most importantly see Norma Alarcón (1981). Alarcón also disagreed with Paz's interpretation of Malintzin's role as a traitor see her 1989 publication. See also Moraga (1986).

3. Warner, however, calls our attention to the fact that the emphasis on the feminine virtues establishes a double standard; she writes: "The woman in the home can be seen as the keeper of her husband's conscience, the vicarious Christian who is humble and obedient — and chaste — enough for two" (188).

4. *Danzón*, 71. "La verdad no sabe qué es lo que le da temor, pero como que no se atreve a salir así" (Beatriz and María Novaro's published script *Danzón*, 1994, 71).

5. In her second feature film, *Anoche soñé contigo* (*I Dreamed of You Last Night*, 1991), Sistach collaborated with Buil to adapt Alfonso Reyes's story "La venganza creadora." The movie reflects on the pleasure and the sexuality of adolescents and shows the erotic awakening of Toto, the protagonist, and Quique, his neighbor and friend. Initially, Toto and Quique spy on Quique's female servant from the roof. Later, Azucena, Toto's 30-year-old cousin, comes to stay for the first time with him and Irma, his mother. Azucena, who wants to be a chorus girl in a musical, becomes the object of Toto's sexual obsession. Sistach's camera follows Toto in his obsession for Azucena.

6. Freud rarely used the word desire, and if he did, it was in relation to the fulfillment of unconscious wishes (Laplanche and Pontalis, 481–3).

7. Melanie Klein proposes another interpretation of women's behavior. Working with object-relation theory, she emphasizes the relation between object and subject; she is interested in the way in which the subject constitutes his or her objects, as well as the way in which the objects shape the actions of the subject (Laplanche and Pontalis, 278).

8. In an attempt to understand women's identificatory processes, Doane turns to film magazines contemporaneous with the 1940s films that she studies. In these magazines, women are considered the biggest consumers of women's films and of products related to these films, and it is assumed that the films are made for them.

9. In afterthoughts on "Visual Pleasure and Narrative Cinema," Mulvey (1975) discusses the possibility of having a female spectator who identifies with a male hero.

10. Doane's conclusion that female spectators cannot desire because they identify too closely with the images projected on the screen has been questioned by many scholars.

11. Third-wave filmmakers are not the only directors to use classical scenarios. Arturo Ripstein, for example, remade Boytler's *La mujer del Puerto* in 1991. Ripstein focused on the incestuous relationship between the protagonists. In the classical films the protagonists only discover that they are brother and sister at the end of the film. In Ripstein's *La mujer del puerto* Nicolás, "El Marro," and Perla, brother and sister, are well aware of their familial ties. Unlike the classical film, in Ripstein´s *La mujer del Puerto*, incest does not lead to tragedy. At the end of Ripstein's film, the female protagonist does not commit suicide; she establishes a family with Nicolás.

12. For an explanation of Freud's position on object relations and narcissism see p. 99.

13. However, as *Señora tentación* shows, social values of the classical period encourage women to mimic what Freud calls narcissism.

Chapter 5

1. Since Doña Bárbara's open desire is so obvious in this scene, I do not agree with López's emphasis on Felix's lack of desire. López says that María Felix "could not embody female desire, for she was an ambivalent icon, as unknowable, cold and pitiless as the mother figure was full of abnegation and tears" (156). Doña Bárbara's desire is her own active desire. She is the subject rather than the object of desire.

2. Some feminists have left Freud's association of women and narcissism unquestioned.

In "Visual Pleasure and Narrative Cinema," Laura Mulvey (1975) contends that women cannot have external objects, whether inside or outside the screen. To support her argument, Mulvey uses Freud's (1915) "Instincts and Their Vicissitudes," in which Freud proposes that there is an auto-erotic stage, which consists of "oneself looking at a sexual organ" that leads to another stage, "oneself looking at an extraneous object (also called active scopophilia)" (131). According to Mulvey's reading of Freud, the classical psychoanalyst relates this auto-eroticism to narcissism: "The preliminary stage of the scopophilic instinct, in which the subject's own body is the object of scopophilia, must be classed under narcissism, and that we must describe it as a narcissistic formation" (132). Freud sees narcissism as an obstacle to the development of the active scopophilic instinct. "The active scopophilic instinct develops from this, by leaving narcissism behind" (131). For Mulvey, the person associated with narcissism has no object relations; the narcissist only has a relationship of identification with his or her image. Mulvey's association of women with narcissism was developed later by Mary Ann Doane and adapted to the specific context of watching films. Doane considers that men and women identify differently with the images projected in the screen. Following Freud's idea that daughters have difficulty in separating from their mothers (a sign that they do not grow outside the Oedipus complex), Doane sees the female spectator as a consumer who cannot separate herself from the images projected in the screen. However, in "Love, Guilt and Reparation," for instance, Melanie Klein (1975) contends that a narcissistic stage of development does not exist, since babies, independent of their gender, have the breast as an object (1).

3. *Doña Bárbara* is based on the novel of the same title written by Venezuelan Rómulo Gallegos in 1929.

4. While going through Novaro's photographic archives, I came across several photographs related to the scene in the photography studio. Other members of the film crew, including Novaro and photographer María Cristina Camus, also posed in front of the island backdrop, juxtaposing their bodies with the island. The photographs are part of Novaro's private collection.

5. Cortés said: "I don't understand why I was so misogynist toward the men in my exercises at the CCC" (Arredondo 2013, 91).

6. Cortés explained to me that this idea appears in the novel *La mañana está gris*.

7. In 1929, when Gallegos wrote the novel, he saw Páez, a local caudillo from the area of western Venezuela called Los Llanos (the same one in which *Doña Bárbara* is set), as barbaric. Páez's help had been fundamental for gaining the independence from Spain, but his unruliness was problematic for Bolivar's process of national unification.

Chapter 6

1. For Silverman (1996), "Idealization means the increase in an object's value which occurs when it is elevated to the level of the impossible non-object of desire" (40).

2. From the sixteenth century on, the popular cult and the Vatican battled over the Mater Dolorosa or Lady of Sorrows. In 1506, the Vatican refused to accept the cult of the Lady of Sorrows. Popular fervor was very strong, most importantly among the Servites, a monastic order that claimed that the Virgin had revealed her Seven Sorrows to their seven founder saints in a vision in the oratory near Florence. In the seventeenth century, Pope Paul V allowed the cult to develop. The sorrows of the Virgin were set at seven: "the prophecy of Simeon, the flight into Egypt, the loss of Jesus in the temple, the meeting with Jesus on the road to Calvary, the Crucifixion, the Deposition, and the Entombment" (Warner 1976, 218). The pain of the Virgin has, since then, been represented by a breast pierced by seven swords.

3. The association of the protagonist with light is reinforced by the protagonist's name; Mexicans know that the name María Candelaria refers to a local Virgin whose literal name is a candle, a *candela*, a stick of light.

4. A painter had asked Lorenzo Rafael if he could paint María Candelaria's portrait. Lorenzo Rafael's initial refusal changed to agreement once he was in jail and had more time to talk with the painter, who had argued his case. A very shy María Candelaria went to the painter's studio, but finding out that she was to be painted naked she ran away; for that reason, the painter had to ask another woman to pose in her place. When people from María Candelaria's community saw the finished portrait, they mistakenly assumed that she had posed naked. After a long persecution scene, the outraged campesinos stoned María Candelaria to death below Lorenzo Rafael's jail cell.

5. Silverman (1996) separates herself from Doane and Mulvey in her view of the relation between women and their images. Silverman refuses to situate the "feminine" domain in a pre-symbolic space from which women never fully emerge or to which they easily regress from the symbolic order. Silverman situates

femininity in the social and in acts such as wearing red high-heel shoes (47).

6. In his 1990 review of Lola, Paul Lenti already called Lola an imperfect mother: "Lola explora nuevos territorios profundizando en el frágil mundo de una mujer moderna imperfecta, quién tiene que mantenerse a sí misma y a su hija en la ausencia de la figura tradicional de la familia, el padre."

7. "Es molesto verla tan desaliñada."

8. Ana's uniform is also an indirect reference to Lola's work. Lola has to sew cheap clothes at home to sell in the street, so she does not have the time or energy to adjust the hem of Ana's school uniform.

9. Silverman (1996) proposes an alternative system of identification that she derives from Lacan's concept of sublimation. Unlike narcissistic love, "sublimation works to the credit of the object" (74). Silverman views sublimation and narcissistic love as different when she states: "The all-important undertaking with respect to the domain of images is to idealize at a distance from the self ... the goal is to confer ideality upon an image which cannot be even delusorily mapped onto one's sensational body" (45). Narcissistic love is an idealization created from the parameters of the self, while sublimation allows idealizing the other from his or her own parameters. Silverman, more concerned with ways to idealize the "other," does not propose a direct alternative to narcissistic idealization. Yet, one can infer this alternative from her work. Silverman remarks, "The all-important undertaking with respect to the domain of images is to idealize at a distance from the self" (45). From this sentence comes the term idealization-at-a-distance. Silverman uses the term "identification-at-a-distance" to refer to the distance between the ideal imago and the self. While narcissistic love makes the self one with the ideal imago, identification-at-a-distance promotes critical distance by making one self-aware, realizing that ideals cannot be achieved personally.

10. The dilemma is to choose between being a mother [meaning: giving to others, such as children] or self-realization, enjoying yourself. "El dilema es decidir ser madre o realizarse personalmente, disfrutarse ella sola" (Murúa 1989).

11. Luz Cruz was initially sentenced to twenty-three years, as shown in a clip in Dana Rotberg's *Elvira Luz Cruz*. It is difficult to understand why after her lawyer, Mireya Soto, defended her, her sentence was increased to twenty-eight years.

12. Through her lawyers (first Mireya Soto and afterward Efraín Ramírez), Cruz sued Cazals for defamation in an attempt to stop the showing of the film while her trial was still pending.

13. According to Patricia Vega, "Elvira Luz Cruz has started, with the help of her lawyers, to sue — although it has not been resolved yet — Cazals' film for being based on her life and for distorting facts related to her life." (ELC ha promovido mediante sus abogados un juicio — aún sin resolver — contra la cinta por estar basada y distorsionar hechos relacionados con su vida).

14. "No me satisfizo en nada el hecho de conocer que se había filmando una película de la tragedia que yo había vivido" (Vega 1996, 25).

15. More than a decade after she published the columns, a compilation of Vega's articles appeared in *A gritos y sombrerazos* (*Throwing Down the Gauntlet with a Howl*, 1996). The section "Elvira Luz Cruz, sus motivos" (23–45) begins with a summary of the lawsuit and is followed by a reproduction of Vega's newspaper articles in chronological order.

16. The title of Vega's section, "Elvira Luz Cruz, sus motivos" ("Elvira Luz Cruz, Her Reasons"), is a poke at Cazal's *Luz's Reasons*. It implies that the reasons of Luz in Cazal's film are not the same ones that Elvira Luz Cruz, the real person, had.

Chapter 7

1. Unlike Warner, who believes that psychoanalytic approaches have oversimplified the role of the Virgin (xxiv).

2. The same idea can be inferred by reading Warner's study. According to her account, men conduct highly violent, emotional discussions outside the orthodoxy about different aspects of Mary (238–249).

3. During the eleventh through fourteenth centuries, the Passion played an important role in France, Spain, Italy, England, and the Netherlands because real death was widespread (Warner 1976, 210). High mortality was in part the result of crusades wars to retain control of the places associated with Jesus's birth, death and resurrection during the eleventh to thirteenth centuries. Many casualties were also the result of natural disasters. In the fourteenth century, Europe lost a fifth of its population during the Black Death. At a time in which the number of deaths made Europe's population decrease, the Stations of the Cross became a direct referent to the real threat to life. To allow those who could not afford to travel to the Holy Places an opportunity to experience the passion, the Stations of the Cross were reproduced

in many European cities. This reenactment of Christ at the Cross was a way to disseminate religious thought: "The Stations of the Cross are a cycle of meditations that operated as satellite television of some great international event does now: it reported the drama of Christ's suffering at first hand" (Warner 1976: 211). In the chapter on "Faith and Knowledge" in *Acts of Religion*, Derrida (2002) understands the dissemination of Catholic culture, what he terms Latinity, in much the same way. For him, religion would not be what it is today if it were not for the media. Derrida writes: "Religion today allies itself with tele-technoscience, to which it reacts with all its forces. It is, *on the one hand*, globalization; it produces, weds, exploits the capital and knowledge of tele-mediatization" (82).

4. Kristeva puts the notion of the Stabat Mater into perspective by reminding us that the sufferings of the Virgin are a projection of human emotions. The Virgin, a nonhuman, did not have to worry about the death of her son because she knew that he was immortal.

5. The lyrics of the song in Spanish are "Por esos siete puñales que tiene clavados la Virgen María, María madre del redentor. Madre, por un beso tuyo diera yo la vida. Madre, no hay otra alegría. Quien pudiera como entonces, arrullado entre tus brazos. Madre, sólo un beso tuyo es la única ilusión. Madre, diera yo mi vida por tenerte cerca de mi corazón."

6. For a more general study of *Mecánica nacional*, see David Foster's (2002) *Mexico City in Contemporary Mexican Cinema* (57–66).

7. The fundamental difference between classical and third-wave films is the organization within the family, the power structure that prevails. In the same interview with the author, Sistach explains: "Ana also fully assumes motherhood and, of course, desires to have a husband and to form a nuclear family ... Ana gets divorced, breaks with familial security, works, and has sexual relations with several men" (Arredondo 2013, 129–30). Even if Ana did have a husband, as she desires, this would not be a contradiction, because the husband will not play the role of Pepe in *Cuando los hijos se van*. Third-wave films are not organized around a father figure, as films of the Golden Age are; Ana's search for a man is a search for a sexual partner and a companion, not a search for a father to impose order in her household.

8. The Escuela Internacional de Cine y Televisión (International Film and Television School) in San Antonio de los Baños, Cuba, directed by Gabriel García Márquez, offers scholarships to directors to work on their screenplays.

9. The article was first published in 1977 as "Heretique de l'amour" in *Tel Quel*, 74 (Winter 1977, pp. 30–49). It was reprinted in 1983 with the title "Stabat Mater" in *Histoires d'amour* (1983, Paris: Deneoël). At least two translations of the article appeared in 1986: "Stabat Mater" was part of Susan R. Scheiman's *The Female Body in Western Culture* and Toril Moi's *The Kristeva Reader*.

10. Kristeva's notion of the semiotic is similar to what Melanie Klein and other British Object Relation theorists call the pre-oedipal stage, and to what in Lacanian terms would be a pre-mirror stage.

11. De los Reyes adds: A mother like in an art-nouveau post-card, sweet, self-less, self-sacrificing, tremulous, melodramatic, and on top of all that, a sentimental cheater, asexual, shuddering with pain, withered, ready to hide the unpleasant (another fundamental pillar of the morality of appearance proposed by our cinema). "Una madre tarjeta postal Art Noveau; tierna, abnegada, sufridora, trémula, melodramática y por supuesto y además fundamentalmente chantajista sentimental, asexual, estremecida por las penas; mustia, dispuesta a disimular (otro pilar fundamental de nuestra moral de la apariencia siempre propuesta por nuestro cine)" (110–111).

12. Ayala Blanco says refering to Fernando Soler (who often plays the role of father in classical melodramas) that his roles have more dignity than the motherly roles played by García: "Con bastante más dignidad cinematográfica que Sara García al simbolizar a la madre mexicana" (51).

13. Ayala Blanco (1993) explains: "The glorious masochism of Sara García ... [is an] emblem of the 'white heads' and of the 10th of May, Oedipus complex day, is not where the genre of melodrama peaks. Despite its qualities of common and typical melodrama, the characteristic of being inoffensive and psychological are only one element. It only represents a trend. "El masoquismo glorioso de Sara García ... emblema de las 'cabecitas blancas' y del 10 de mayo, día del complejo de Edipo nacional, no es una culminación genérica. A pesar de sus cualidades de melodrama común y típico, inofensivo y psicoanalizable, es sólo un elemento. Sirve para marcar una pauta" (43).

14. López's (1994) position, although feminist, does not include a recuperation of García. She explains, "Mothers may have a guaranteed place in the home as pillars of strength, tolerance, and self-abnegation—in other words, as

oedipal illusions—but outside the home they are prey to the male desires that the Mexican home and family disavow (261).

Chapter 8

1. The interpretation of mothers' pain is also informed by feminist historical analysis. In *Mom*, Plant (2010) maintains that after World War I mothers are viewed as heroic because of the pain they endured. The physical pain of mothers at childbirth, as well as the psychological pain of mothers who lost their sons in the war, justified their elevated moral status. As an example, the United States Congress created the Gold Start Mothers' Program (1930–1933) so that mothers of soldiers who died in World War I and were buried in Europe could visit their sons' graves. Plant's study suggests that the idea of mother as war-hero emerged at a time when the country needed soldiers to fight abroad. The pain of childbirth before the 1940s gave status to mothers, who often died from complications during labor (118–127). However, as new methods for easing pain during childbirth were developed, and as deaths from childbirth decreased, mothers' pain was no longer seen as a reason for mothers' high moral status (127–145). Alisa Klaus's area studies article, "Depopulation and Race Suicide: Maternalism and Pronatalist Ideologies in France and United States," demonstrates that the welfare of mothers became a national problem only when population decreased. Klaus established a relationship between the dramatic fall of France's birth rate after World War I and the state's invested interest in mothers, manifested through pronatalist policies.

2. The comment comes from Ramírez Berg, who considers the film representative of the "classic transparent text" (17). He has an excellent gender and socio-historical analysis of the film on pages 17–28.

3. "Las madres son héroes porque luchan para hacer que sus hijos sean los mejores."

4. *Lola* was released in November 1989 at Mexico City's Muestra Internacional de Cine (XXII International Film Festival in Mexico City), a showcase of international films that includes the best Mexican films.

5. Novaro indirectly alludes to this relationship when she says: "I'm interested not only in the particular story of Lola and her child; Lola is also the means by which I can reflect more deeply on women, motherhood, and Mexico City" (Arredondo 2013, 150).

6. Rich did not use the word "phase" to refer to the shift; I take this word from Paul A. Schroeder Rodríguez (2011, 15) who proposes a similar shift.

7. Rich did mention in her presentation the work of some of the older Latin American women filmmakers, including Maria Luisa Bemberg's films, and Matilde Landeta's *La negra Angustias*.

8. Rashkin (2001, 68) dates the creation of Cine-Mujer to 1975. See also Millán 1999, 96–7.

9. "La propuesta del cine de mujer fue avanzando a medida que se iba modificando el movimiento feminista" (Iglesias and Fregoso 1998, 75).

10. For a description and analysis of these films see Rashkin (2001, 69).

11. My translation of "Un cine más intimista" and "Posteriormente se abarcaron temas más relacionados con movimientos populares, centrándonos en una temática femenina."

12. Some third-wave filmmakers participated in feminist independent cinema efforts. A group of feminists from the Colectivo asked for María Novaro to participate in the Collective; they wanted her help because she was familiar with poor neighborhoods were they wanted to work. Novaro participated in the documentaries *Es primera vez* (*It's the First Time*, 1981) by Beatriz Mira, about a meeting of farming women and women from urban neighborhoods, and *Vida de Ángel* (*Angel's Life*, 1992) by Ángeles Necoechea, about domestic work.

13. The two meetings of Mexican filmmakers also shared another trait that Rich mentioned: the effort toward inclusion. Rich attributes this shift inward that takes place in the 1980s to political reasons. It is a time when "democracies have superseded military rule in Argentina, Brazil and Uruguay" (Iglesias and Fregoso 1990, 133). The organizers of the Tijuana Encuentro tried to democratize the field. The inclusion of women who worked in video was important at a time when scholarship and criticism of Mexican cinema emphasized auteur narrative films made in 35 mm. The Encuentro also included sessions about directors such as María Elena de Velasco (La India María), who had worked in popular genres, but whose work had not been given much attention by critics or academics. The impulse to democratize the field was led by Matilde Landeta who argued that "the only thing that we should consider is that we are all women who produce images." At Guadalajara in 2002, the push toward democratization manifested differently: the people invited included women involved in other areas of film and media production, such as screenwriters and producers.

14. I want to thank Patricia Vega who encouraged me to follow this line of thinking when we met in 2012.

15. In "'Otro Modo de Ser Humano y Libre': La mirada feminista de Busi Cortés en el Nuevo Cine Mexicano," Ilana Luna argues, following Rich, that Busi Cortés's *El secreto de Romelia* makes the private political. According to Luna, Cortés makes the story of feminist Mexican writer Rosario Castellanos, *El viudo Román*, political. When Cortés adapts Castellanos's novel, she establishes a relationship between the story of the family and Mexico's political history (Luna 2011, 216).

16. Juan Luís Guerra's song "Si tu te vas" http://www.lyrics007.com/Juan%20Luis%20G uerra%20Lyrics/Si%20Tu%20Te%20Vas%20L yrics.html, downloaded 9/23/2013.

17. Oliver's (2002) first interpretation of maternal depression appeared in "Psychic Space and Social Melancholy." In this article, Oliver expands Julia Kristeva's notions of abjection and psychic space, taking these ideas from the level of the individual, where Kristeva applied them, to the social. Kristeva's interpretation of depression was based on the notion of abjection, which was derived from Mary Douglas. In *Purity and Danger: An Analysis of Concepts of Pollution and Taboo*, Douglas (1966) studied pollution and taboo in several cultures in order to understand how concepts of defilement arise. She came to the conclusion that rules regulating what is dirty or untouchable (i.e., what is considered polluted or taboo) do not come from an attempt to avoid disease but from an effort to reorder the environment, to make it conform to an idea (2001, 2). For Douglas, then, defilement is about mental boundaries that societies set up. Kristeva incorporates Douglas's idea of defilement into her study of patriarchy, proposing that within patriarchal society, the female body is abjected. Oliver takes Kristeva's notion a step further by suggesting that society forces women to identify their bodies with the abject. For Oliver (2002), the culture at large devalues maternity by reducing it to repellant animality (50); sexism, for example, "reduces its targets to unthinking animal bodies driven by natural instincts rather than by rational thought process" (62).

In *The Colonization of Psychic Space* (2004), Oliver situates her position vis-a-vis other scholars working in the field. Besides extending the psychoanalytic framework to include the social, she modifies the concepts that underlie classical psychoanalysis. The Freudian psychoanalytic term "melancholia" assumes that maternal depression is caused by a woman's biology or family background; in contrast, Oliver's proposed term, "social melancholy," shifts the weight of responsibility to society. It is society's abjection of mothers that is at the root of maternal depression. Oliver expands her analysis of depression to include the social, and what is even more important, she also changes its meaning. For her, maternal depression is a mental illness that results from the way society treats mothers.

18. Both were students at Mexico City's film school, the CCC. For the final project in her documentary class, Rotberg chose to feature Luz Cruz's case, and Díez helped her. Students were given six cans of positive film to do their exercises. Since six cans were not enough for a 46-minute film, Díez contributed her six cans and worked as Rotberg's assistant.

19. Rotberg gave a similar response to Martha Coda in 1985. When Coda asked: "Why doesn't your film attempt to explain the case of Elvira Luz Cruz?," Rotberg answered that she did not know. Instead she gave a description of what had interested her: "The documentary talks about the lacks, the absences, the failures of the Mexican juridical process."

20. From the interviews conducted by Díez and Rotberg and included in the film, the audience also deduces that Eduarda and Nicolás are accomplices in the cover up of the killing of the children. When giving her own account of the crime, Eduarda stated that she went to Elvira's house looking for a guitar, and it was there that she saw Elvira strangling the youngest daughter and discovered the murdered children. She then called her son who brought the police.

21. Afterward, Eduarda and Nicolás were in Elvira's house for thirty minutes without any sound; the neighbors believe that this is when they strangled the other children.

22. As the trial was reviewed, more irregularities surfaced: when Luz Cruz was asked if she could recognize the bodies of the children as her own, her affirmative answer was taken to mean that she had killed them (G. García 1986).

23. In *Mom* Plant makes a similar stand regarding the way doctors in the 1940s used a Freudian understanding of sexuality to make maternal love threatening and unhealthy soldiers (86–117).

24. Cazals has a reputation in Mexico for being a filmmaker who made social denunciation films. In a review of *Ángel de fuego*, Mauricio Montiel suggests that *Ángel de fuego* takes a disengaged look at social compromise and adds: "The compromise of the spectator with what is being shown on the screen decreases [as time go by]; it is at this point that social denouncement—so masterfully done by

Cazals in *Los motivos de Luz*—fails." For Montiel, Cazals is a master of social denunciation, a fact widely recognized in Mexico. *Los motivos de Luz* is included in the list of the best 100 Mexican films made by the Mexican Film Institute (IMCINE). Despite making social denunciation films, he does not use a social basis to explain Luz's case.

25. Cazals was much criticized for asserting Luz Cruz's guilt while her case was still being appealed. In 1985, her lawyers requested that the Dirección General de Cinematography (the institution in charge of censoring films) stop *Los motivos*' exhibition, arguing that the film distorted reality.

Works Cited

Abbey, Sharon and Andrea O'Reilly. 1998. *Redefining Motherhood: Changing Identities and Patterns*. Toronto: Second Story Press.

Alarcón, Norma. 1981. "Chicana's Feminist Literature: A Re-Vision through Malintzin; or, Malintzin: Putting the Flesh Back on the Object." In *This Bridge Called My Back: Writings by Radical Women of Color*, edited by Cherríe Moraga and Gloria Anzaldúa, 182–90. Watertown, MA: Persephone.

——. 1989. "Tradutora, Traditora: A Paradigmatic Figure of Chicana Feminism." *Cultural Critique* 13:57–87.

Albarrán, Jairo Calixto. 1989. "Lola (mas no la trailera)." *Excélsior*, November 26, 4.

Alcoriza, Luis. 2002. *Mecánica nacional*. VHS, 100 min. Northridge, CA: Laguna Films.

Almond, Barbara. 2010. *The Monster Within: The Hidden Side of Motherhood* [in English]. Berkeley: University of California Press.

ANSA. 1994. "No soy una directora feminista." *El Nacional*, August 21, Sección espectáculos 40.

Arredondo, Isabel. 2001. *Palabra de mujer: Historia oral de las directoras de cine mexicanas 1988–1994*. Madrid: Iberoamericana & Universidad Autónoma de Aguas Calientes.

——. 2002. "Tenía bríos y, aún vieja, los sigo teniendo: Reflexiones y entrevista a Matilde Landeta." *Mexican Studies/Estudios Mexicanos* 18(1):189–204.

——. 2012. *In Our Own Image: An Oral History of Mexican Female Filmmakers 1988–1994*. http://digitalcommons.plattsburgh.edu/foreignlanguages/1/

Ayala Blanco, Jorge. 1991a. "La mirada femenina." In *La disolvencia del cine mexicano entre lo popular y lo exquisito*, 461–511. México DF, Barcelona, Buenos Aires: Grijalvo.

——. 1991b. "Novaro y los goces de la feminidad insóplida." *El Financiero*, July 3, 56.

——. 1993. *La aventura del cine mexicano: En la Época de Oro y después*. Mexico DF: Editorial Grijalbo.

Bald, Margaret. 1991. "The Feminist Vision of Maria Novaro." *Towards Freedom*, October–November, 22.

Baring, Anne, and Cashford, Jules. 1991. *The Myth of the Goddess*. London: Viking Arkan.

Barriga Chávez, Ezequiel. 1989. "Lola." *Excélsior*, November 30, 59-A.

Bautista, Gabriela. 1992. "Ángel de fuego." *La Jornada Semanal* 159 (June 28):8–9.

Benerstein, Robert. 1992. "Mexican Comedy *Danzón* Offers Feminist Message with Light Touch." *Rocky Mountain News*, November 6.

Bowlby, John. 1995. *Maternal Care and Mental Health*. Northvale, N.J.: J. Aronson.

Burton, Julianne. 1986. "Marcela Fernández Violante (Mexico), Inside the Mexican Film Industry: A Woman's Perspective." In *Cinema and Social Change in Latin America: Conversations with Filmmakers*, 195–207. Austin: University of Texas Press.

Burton-Carvajal, Julianne. 1997. "Mexican Melodramas of Patriarchy: Specificity of a Transcultural Form." In *Framing Latin American Cinema: Contemporary Critical Perspectives*, edited by Ann Marie Stock, 186–234. Minneapolis: University of Minnesota Press.

Bustillo Oro, Juan. 2008. *Cuando los hijos se van*. DVD, 138 min. Santa Monica, CA: Lions Gate Entertainment.

Butler, Alison. 2002. "Introduction: From Counter Cinema to Minor Cinema." In *Women's Cinema: The Contested Screen*, 1–25. London: Wallflower.

Butler, Judith. 1990. *Gender Trouble: Feminism and the Subversion of Identity*. New York: Routledge.

Candelaria, Cordelia. 1980. "La Malinche, Feminist Prototype." *Frontiers: A Journal of Women Studies* 5(2):1–6.

Carrera, Mauricio. 1991. "*Danzón*, himno a la cachondería." *El Nacional*, January 5.
Carvajal, Teresa. 2000. "Vizcaínas." *Somos Uno*, January, 36–42.
Cazals, Felipe. 1986, *Los Motivos de Luz*. VHS, 100 min. Huntington Park, CA: Film-Mex Productions.
Celin, Fernando. 1991. "¡Hey Familia!, Danzón Dedicado a..." *El Semanario de Novedades*, July 21, 7.
Celín, Fernando. 1989. "Lola." *El Semanario*, December 3.
Coda, Martha. 1985. "Dana Rotberg: *Elvira Luz Cruz, pena máxima*, historia que se repite a diario." *unomásuno*, June 29.
Copjec, Joan. 2000. *The Ortopsychic Subject: Film Theory and the Reception of Lacan*. Oxford [England] and New York: Oxford University Press.
Cortés, Busi. 1979. *Las Buenromero (The Buenromero Sisters)*. 16 mm, 29 min. Mexico City: Centro de Capacitación Cinematográfica.
———. 1980. *Un frágil retorno (A Fragile Return)*. 16 mm, 20 min. Centro de Capacitación Cinematográfica.
———. 1981. *Hotel Villa Goerne*. 16 mm, 50 min. Centro de Capacitación Cinematográfica.
———.1983–84 "Las rumberitas" ("The Little Rumba Dancers"), "Alfonsina," "Amor de radio" ("Radio Love"), "La mujer de Nicolás" ("Nicolás's Woman"), "Fuera máscaras" ("Masks Off") and "La niña robada" ("The Abducted Girl"), *De la vida de las mujeres (On Women's Lives)*, television series edited by Ignacio Durán: Unidad de Televisión Educativa y Cultural.
———. 1984. *El lugar del corazón (The Heart's Place)*. 16 mm, 30 min. Centro de Capacitación Cinematográfica, Universidad Iberoamericana.
———. 1988. *El secreto de Romelia (Romelia's Secret)*. VHS, 100 min. Mexico City: Fondo de Fomento a la Calidad Cinematográfica, Centro de Capacitación Cinematográfica, Consejo de Radio y Televisión de Tlaxcala, Universidad de Guadalajara and Conacite II.
Cross, John C. 1998. *Informal Politics: Street Vendors and the State in Mexico City*. Stanford, CA: Stanford University Press.
De Lauretis, Teresa. 1989. "Rethinking Women's Cinema: Aesthetics and Feminist Theory." In *Multiple Voices in Feminist Film Criticism*. 140–161. Minneapolis: University of Minnesota Press.
———. 1993. "Sexual Indifference Lesbian Represtation." In *The Gay and Lesbian Studies Reader*, 141–158. New York and London: Routledge.

De la Vega, Eduardo. 1985. "Primera Década del CCC." *El Nacional*, October 6, Revista mexicana de cultura 16.
———. 1991. "Entrevista con Dana Rotberg I." In *Manuscript from CIEC*. Guadalajara, Jalisco. Mexico.
———. 1991. "Entrevista con Dana Rotberg II y III." In *Manuscript from de CIEC*. Guadalajara, Jalisco, Mexico.
De los Reyes, Aurelio. 1977. "Madre sólo hay una: la del cine mexicano." In *80 años de cine en México Mexico*, 109–112. Mexico City: UNAM, Difusión Cultural.
Derrida, Jacques. 2002. *Acts of religion* [in English]. New York: Routledge.
Dever, Susan. 2003. *Celluloid Nationalism and Other Melodramas*. Albany: State University of New York Press.
Diaz Morales, José Silva David, and Susana Sevilla Ninón Guizar. 2000. *Señora Tentación*. VHS, 90 min. Northride, CA: Laguna Films; Madera, CA: Madera CineVideo.
Diez, Rolo. 1991. "*Lola*." *El Universal*, February 26, Sección cultural 2.
Doane, Mary Ann. 1987. *The Desire to Desire: The Woman's Film of the 1940s*. Bloomington: Indiana University Press.
———. 1991. "Film and the Masquerade: Theorizing the Female Spectator." In *Femmes Fatales: Feminism, Film Theory and Psychoanalysis*, 17–32. New York: Routledge.
Douglas, Mary. 1966. *Purity and Danger; an Analysis of Concepts of Pollution and Taboo*. New York: Praeger.
EFE. 1991. "Que el machismo de nuestros productores anula perspectivas a mujeres cienastas." *El Heraldo*, February 23, 1D, 6D.
Espinasa, José María. 1991. "Neorrealismos." *La Jornada Semanal*, March 10, 46.
Fanon, Frantz. 1965. *The wretched of the earth*. New York: Grove.
———. 1967. *Black Skin, White Masks*. New York: Grove.
Feliciano, Enrique. 1989. "Surge la 4ª directora de películas." *ESTO*, January 11, 15.
Fernández, Emilio. 2004. *María Candelaria (Xochimilco)*. DVD, 97 min. Mexico City: AlterFilms, Televisa.
Fischer, Lucy. 1996. *Cinematernity: Film, Motherhood and Genre*. Princeton, NJ: Princeton University Press.
Foster, David William. 2002. *Mexico City in Contemporary Mexican Cinema*. Austin: University of Texas Press.
Freud, Sigmund. 1914. "On Narcissism: An Introduction." In *The Standard Edition of the Complete Psychological Works of Sigmund Freud*, 73–102. London: Hogarth Press and Institute of Psychoanalysis.
———. 1915. "Instincts and Their Vicissitudes."

In *The Standard Edition of the Complete Psychological Works of Sigmund Freud*, 109–40. London: Hogarth Press and Institute of Psychoanalysis.

———. 1921. "Group Psychology and the Analysis of the Ego." In *The Standard Edition of the Complete Psychological Works of Sigmund Freud*, 88–145. London: Hogarth Press and Institute of Psychoanalysis.

Fuentes, Fernando de. 1987. *Doña Barbara*. VHS, 138 min. Fresno, CA: Condor Video.

Galindo, Alejandro. 1996. *Una familia de tantas*. VHS, 133 min. Harlingen, TX: Archivo Fílmico Agrasánchez.

Gallegos, Rómulo. 1964. *Doña Bárbara*. Buenos Aires: Espasa-Calpe Argentina.

García Canclini, Nestor. 1991. *Públicos de arte y política cultural: Un estudio del II Festival de la Ciudad de México*. Edited by Nestor García Canclini. Mexico City: Universidad Autónoma Metropolitana.

García, Gustavo. 1986. "Anatomía de un asesinato." *unomásuno*, January 26.

García Riera, Emilio. 1969. *Historia documental del cine mexicano*. México DF: Era.

García Tsao, Leonardo. 1991. "Buscando desganadamente a Carmelo." *El Nacional*, July 11, Sección cultural 13.

Gracida, Ysabel. 1993. "*Ángel de fuego*." *El Universal*, March 4, Sección cultural 3.

Grovas, y Cia. 1941. "Cuando los hijos se van." *Excelsior*. July 31.

Guerrero, Juan. 1990. "Maryse Sistach: *Los pasos de Ana*." *El Nacional*, July 16, Sección espectáculos 21.

Haskell, Molly. 1974. *From Reverence to Rape* [in English]. New York: Holt, Rinehart and Winston.

Hernández, Rubén. 1989. "El cine femenino toma su lugar." *El Nacional*, March 14.

Hershfield, Joanne. 1996. *Mexican Cinema/Mexican Woman, 1940–1950*. Tucson: University of Arizona Press.

Hershfield, Joanne, and David R. Maciel. 1999. "Women and Gender Representation in the Contemporary Cinema of Mexico." In *Mexico's Cinema: A Century of Film and Filmmakers*, 37–48. Wilmington, DE: Scholarly Resources.

Hershfield, Joanne Leslie. 1993. "The Representation of Woman in Mexican Cinema, 1943–50."

Iglesias Prieto, Norma, and Rosa Linda Fregoso, eds. 1998. *Miradas de mujer: encuentro de cineastas y videoastas mexicanas y chicanas*. Tijuana, BC, México: Colegio de la Frontera Norte; Davis: Chicana/Latina Research Center, University of California, Davis.

Johnson Celorio, Rodrigo. 1989. "María Novaro demuestra con *Lola* la calidad." *El economista*, November 22, 29.

Kaplan, E. Ann. 2000. "The Case of the Missing Mother: Maternal Issues in Vidor's *Stella Dallas*." In *Feminism and Film*, edited by E. Ann Kaplan. New York: Oxford University Press.

King, John. 1990. *Magical Reels: A History of Cinema in Latin America*. London: New York.

Klein, Melanie. 1975. *Love, Guilt, and Reparation & Other Works, 1921–1945*. New York: Delacorte Press/S. Lawrence.

Klein, Melanie, and Juliet Mitchell. 1987. *The Selected Melanie Klein*. New York: Free Press.

Kristeva, Julia. 1980. *Motherhood According to Giovanni Bellini*. New York: Columbia University Press.

———. 1986. "Stabat Mater." In *The Kristeva Reader*, edited by Toril Moi, 160–186. Harvard: Columbia University Press.

———. 1987. *Tales of Love*. New York: Columbia University Press.

Ladd-Taylor, Molly and Andrea O'Reilly. 2004. "Mothering, Law, Politics and Public Policy." *Journal of the Association for Research on Mothering*. Vol. 6, no. 1. Toronto: Association for Research on Mothering.

Laplanche, Jean, and J. B. Pontalis. 1974. *The Language of Psycho-analysis*. New York, Norton.

Latina. 1989. "*Lola* (Synopsis)." Mexico City: Latina.

Leal, Alejandro. 1992. "María Novaro es descarada feminista y antimachista." *El Universal*, October 4.

Lenti, Paul. 1990. "*Lola*." *Variety [Mexico]*, January 17.

Lewis, Helen Block. 1987. "Shame and Narcissistic Personality." In *The Many Faces of Shame*. Ed. Donald L. Nathanson. New York: Guilford Press. 93–132.

López, Ana M. 1994. "Tears and Desire: Women and Melodrama in the 'Old' Mexican Cinema." In *Multiple Voices in Feminist Film Criticism*, 254–279. Minneapolis: University of Minnesota Press.

López Aranda, Susana. 1993. "*Ángel de fuego*." *Dicine*, May 19, 51.

Maciel, David R. 1999. "Cinema and the State in Contemporary Mexico, 1970–1999." In *Mexico's Cinema: A Century of Film and Filmmakers*, 193–97. Wilmington, DE: Scholarly Resources.

Mam, Yehudit. 1989. "La semana en la muestra." *La Jornada Semanal*, December 10, 6.

Martínez de Velasco, Patricia. 1993. *My Filmmaking, My Life*. New York: Women Make Movies.

Maslin, Janest. 1992. "*Danzón* Steps to Feminist Beat." *Entertainer*, October 16.

Maslin, Janet. 1992. "A Melodious Variation on Feminist Awareness." *New York Times*, September 25.

Melche, Julia Elena. 1992. "*Ángel de fuego*." *La Jornada*, May 31, Sección cultura 37.

Meyer, Eugenia, Alba Fulgeira, and Ximena Sepúlveda. 1976. "Sara García." In *Cuadernos de la Cineteca Nacional: Testimonios para la historia del cine mexicano*, vol. 8, 2:11–26a.

Millán, Márgara. 1999. *Derivas de un cine femenino*. Mexico City: Porrúa.

Millán Moncayo, Margarita. 1995. "Género y representación: Tres mujeres directoras de cine en México." Thesis in Sociology. Mexico City: Universidad Nacional Autónoma de México.

Millet, Patricia. 1994. *Exposición y análisis de la problemática actual en la industria cinematográfica*. Mexico City: Instalaciones en Productividad.

Montiel, Mauricio. 1992. "*Ángel de fuego*, de Dana Rotberg." *El Occidental*, March 30, Sección D 1, 14.

Mora, Carl J. 1985. "Feminine Images in Mexican Cinema: The Family Melodrama; Sara García, 'The Mother of Mexico'; and the Prostitute." In *Studies in Latin American Popular Culture*, 4: 228–35.

Mora, Sergio de la. 2006. *Cinemachismo: Masculinities and Sexuality in Mexican Film*. Austin: University of Texas Press.

Moraga, Cherríe. 1986. "From a Long Line of Vendidas: Chicanas and Feminism." In *Feminist Studies/Critical Studies*, edited by Teresa de Lauretis, 173–190. Bloomington: Indiana University Press.

Mulvey, Laura. 1975. "Visual Pleasure and Narrative Cinema." In *Film Theory and Criticism*, edited by Leo Braudy and Marshall Cohen, 833–44. New York and Oxford: Oxford University Press.

Muñoz, Fernando. 1998. "Sara García." *Clío*, vol. 12–14.

Murúa, Sara. 1989. "Lola, la reivindicación femenina en filme mexicano." *El Nacional*, November 24, Sección espectáculos 5.

Novaro, Beatriz. 1996. *Cecilia todavía*. México DF: El Atajo.

Novaro, Beatriz, and María Novaro. 1994. *Danzón*. Mexico City: Ediciones el Milagro.

Novaro, Beatriz, and María Novaro. 1994. *Danzón* (script). Mexico City: Ediciones el Milagro.

Novaro, María. 1984. *Una isla rodeada de agua* (*An Island Surrounded by Water*). 16 mm, 28 min. Mexico City: Centro Universitario de Estudios Cinematográficas.

———. 1987. *Azul celeste* (*Sky Blue*). 35 mm, 28 min. Mexico City: Dirección de Actividades Cinematográficas UNAM.

———. 1989. *Lola*. VHS, 92 min. Mexico City: Macondo Cine-Video, Televisión Española, Conacite II, Cooperativa José Revuelta.

———. 1991. *Danzón*. VHS, 96 min. Mexico City: Macondo Cine-Video, IMCINE, Televisión Española, FFCC, Tabasco Films, State government of Veracruz.

Oliver, Kelly. 2002. "Psychic Space and Social Melancholy." In *Between the Psyche and the Social: Psychoanalytic Social Theory*. Lanham, MD: Rowman & Littlefield.

———. 2004. *The Colonization of Psychic Space: A Psychoanalytic Social Theory of Oppression*. Minneapolis: University of Minnesota Press.

O'Reilly, Andrea. 2007. *Maternal Theory: Essential Readings*. Toronto: Demeter Press.

———. 2006. *Mothering and Feminism*. Toronto: Association for Research on Mothering.

———. 2006. *Rocking the Cradle: Thoughts on Feminism, Motherhood and the Possibility of Empowered Mothering*. Toronto: Demeter Press.

———. 2004. *From Motherhood to Mothering: The Legacy of Adrienne Rich's Of Woman Born*. Albany: State University of New York Press.

———. 2004. *Toni Morrison and Motherhood: A Politics of the Heart*. Albany: State University of New York Press.

———. 2001. *Mothers and Sons: Feminism, Masculinity and the Struggle to Raise Our Sons*. New York: Routledge.

——— and Sharon Abbey. 2000. *Mothers and Daughters: Connection, Empowerment and Transformation*. Lanham, MD: Rowman & Littlefield.

Ortega Mendoza, Jesús. 1993. "*Ángel de fuego*." *El Universal*, February 24, Sección universo joven 3.

Ottinger, Ulrike. 1979. *Bildnis einer Trinkerin Aller jamais retour*. VHS, 108 min. New York: Women Make Movies.

Paz, Octavio. 1961. *The Labyrinth of Solitude: Life and Thought in Mexico*. Translated and edited by Lysander Kemp. New York, London: Grove Press.

Peña, Mauricio. 2000. "Sara García." *Somos Uno*. Mexico City: Editorial Eres, Vol. 191.

Peón, Ramón. 1996. *No basta ser madre*. VHS, 107 min. Harlingen, TX: Agrasánchez Film Archives.

Perales, Conchita. 1991. "Nuevos caminos para filmar: Entrevista con María Novaro." Textual (*El Nacional*) III:36, 37, 38 and 39.

Pérez Turrent, Tomás. 1991a. "Ana, divorciada y con dos hijos, vive la duda." *El Universal*, March 14, 1, 2.

———. 1991b. "*Lola*: retrato femenino de una estudiante del CUEC." *El Universal*, February 10.

_____. 1992. "*Ángel de fuego* y otros asuntos." *Dicine* 46 (July): 5, 6, 7.

_____. 1993. "*Ángel exterminador.*" *Siempre!*, March 17, 16.

Piña Jarillo, Verónica. 1991. "Intimidades de Dana Rotberg." *El Nacional*, September 29, Sección espectáculos 9.

Plant, Rebeca Jo. 2010. *Plant, Rebecca Jo. 2010. Mom: The Transformation of Motherhood in Modern America*. Chicago: University of Chicago Press.

"Profunda visión feminista a *El jardín del Edén.*" 1993. *Novedades*, September 5, Sección espectáculos 14.

Projansky, Sarah. 2001. *Watching Rape: Film and Television in Postfeminist Culture*. New York: New York University Press.

Quiroz Arroyo, Macarena. 1992. "No pretendo mostrar una temática feminista en mis películas, dice la realizadora Dana Rotberg." *Excélsior*, November 19.

Ramírez Berg, Charles. 1992. *Cinema of Solitude: a Critical Study of Mexican Film, 1967–1983*. Austin: University of Texas Press.

Ramos, José Manuel. 1998. *Tepeyac*. VHS, 47 min. Rio de Janeiro: Ministério da Cultura, FUNARTE, Decine /CT.

Ramos Navas, Saúl. 1993. "El público mexicano está apto para ver *Ángel de fuego*: Lilia Aragón." *El Universal*, February 28, 15, 22.

Rashkin, Elissa. 2001. *Women Filmmakers in Mexico: The Country of Which We Dream*. Austin: University of Texas Press.

Robles, Óscar. 2005. *Identidades maternacionales en el cine de María Novaro*. New York: Peter Lang.

Rotberg, Dana. 1989. *Intimidad* (*Intimacy*). VHS, 100 min. Mexico City: Producciones Metrópolis.

_____. 1991. *Ángel de fuego* (*Angel of Fire*). DVD, 90 min. Mexico City: IMCINE, Producciones Metrópolis, FFCC, Otra Productora Más.

Rotberg, Dana, and Ana Díez.1985. *Elvira Luz Cruz: Pena máxima*. 16 mm, 46 min. Mexico City: Centro de Capacitación Cinematográfica.

Schroeder, Paul. 2011. "La fase neo-barroca del Nuevo Cine Latinoamericano." *Revista de Crítica Literaria Latinoamericana* 73:15–35.

Schyfter, Guita. 1995. *Sucesos distantes* (*Distant Events*). VHS, 99 min. Mexico City: IMCINE, Arte Nuevo, Cooperativa Conexión, Universidad de Guadalajara, Fondo de Fomento para la Cultura y las Artes.

"Sera. D. Amalia S. de Cárdenas, quien presidirá hoy en la mañana la fiesta de Excelsior en el teatro Alameda." 1937. *Excelsior*, 1.

Silva, David. 1990. *La gallina clueca*. VHS, 124 min. Madera, CA: Madera CineVideo.

Silverman, Kaja. 1996. *The Threshold of the Visible World*. New York: Routledge.

Sistach, Marisa. 1985. "Gilberto Owen, el recuerdo olvidado." Television series. Edited by Ignacio Durán. Mexico City: Unidad de Televisión Educativa y Cultural.

_____. 1988. *Conozco a las tres* (I know all three). New York: Women Make Movies.

"Soy madre en primer lugar, otros son padres en quinto, afirma María Novaro." 1991. *Siglo 21*, November 12.

Todorov, Tzvetan. 1984. *The Conquest of America: The Question of the Other*. New York: Harper & Row.

Torres San Martín, Patricia, ed. 2004. *Mujeres y cine en América Latina*. Guadalajara, Jalisco: Universidad de Guadalajara.

Trelles Plazaola, Luis. 1991. *Cine y mujer en América Latina: directoras de largo-metrajes de ficción*. Río Piedras: Editorial de la Universidad de Puerto Rico.

Tuñón, Julia. 1998. *Mujeres de luz y sombra en el cine mexicano: La construcción de una imagen (1939–1952)*. Mexico DF: Colegio de México, Instituto Mexicano de Cinematografía.

Turim, Maureen Cheryn. 1989. *Flashbacks in Film: Memory and History*. New York: Routledge.

Vega, Patricia. 1989. "En *Lola*, quiero desmitificar la maternidad: María Novaro." *La Jornada*, January 11, Sección cultural 19.

_____. 1989. "*Lola.*" *La Jornada*, November 24, Sección cultura 41.

_____. 1990. "El filme *Lola* una propuesta emocional ante la depresión." *La Jornada*, April 11, Sección cultural 27.

_____. 1990. "En la escuela no se aprende a hacer cine: Dana Rotberg." *La Jornada*, February 7, Sección cultural 29.

_____. 1991. "Concluye en Guadalajara la VI Muestra de Cine Mexicano." *La Jornada*, March 13, Sección cultura 41.

_____. 1996. *A gritos y sombrerazos*. Mexico City: Consejo Nacional para la Cultura y las Artes.

Velázquez, Carolina. 1989. "La idea de la película *Lola* es mostrar los lados oscuros de la maternidad, indica su directora María Novaro." *El Financiero*, November 24, Sección cultural 83.

Vera, José. 1991. "Júbilo en la premier de *Intimidad.*" *El Nacional*, March 12, Sección espectáculos 5.

Vidor, King. [1937] 2000. *Stella Dallas*. Santa Monica, CA: MGM Home Entertainment.

Viñas, Moisés. 1989. "*Lola.*" *El Universal*, November 26, Sección espectáculos 1, 5.

_____. 1991. "*Lola.*" *El Universal*, February 21, Sección espectáculos 1, 6.

Virgen, Lucy. 1991. "Lola de María Novaro." *El Informador*, June 9.

Warner, Marina. 1976. *Alone of All Her Sex: The Myth and Cult of the Virgin Mary.* New York: Knopf.

Williams, Linda. 2000. "Something Else Besides a Mother: Maternal Issues in Vidor's *Stella Dallas.*" In *Feminism and Film,* edited by E. Ann Kaplan, 479–504. New York: Oxford University Press.

Yehya, Naief. 1991. "*Lola:* ¿México sigue en pie?" *unomásuno,* March 9.

———. 1993. "*Ángel de fuego.*" *unomásuno,* March 27, Suplemento Sábado.

Works Consulted

ÁNGEL DE FUEGO

AFP. 1992. "Dana Rotberg presentó en el festival de cine de la Ciudad de Biarritz su Filme Intimidad." *Excélsior,* September 25, Sección espectáculos 3.

———. 1992. "El día feliz de Dana Rotberg." *El Universal,* May 10, Sección espectáculos 12.

———. 1992. "Más elogios a la mexicana *Ángel de fuego.*" *El Universal,* May 10, Sección espectáculos 12.

———. 1993. "Premio en Marsella Para *Ángel de fuego,* de Dana Rotberg." *Excélsior,* September 20, Sección espectáculos 2.

———. 1994. "Dana Rotberg, en la línea de fuego." *El Nacional,* May 17, Sección espectáculos 39.

———. 1994. "Filmará Dana Rotberg *La Guerra de los Cristeros.*" *Excélsior,* May 17, Sección espectáculos 1, 13.

"*Ángel de fuego.*" 1993. *El Nacional,* February 28, Sección carteleras 3.

ANSA. 1992. "*Ángel de fuego* logró impresionar." *El Universal,* May 9, Sección espectáculos 1, 4.

———. 1992. "Los directores de mi generación hemos aprendido que no se puede hacer mal cine." *Excélsior,* May 11.

AP. 1992. "*Ángel de fuego* inauguró la quincena de los realizadores." *El Universal,* May 10, Sección espectáculos 18, 12.

Ayala Blanco, Jorge. 1989. "María Novaro y la dificultad de ser a la deriva." *El Financiero,* November 22, Sección cultural 82.

Barriga, Ezequiel. 1993. "*Ángel de fuego.*" *Excélsior,* March 22, Sección espectáculos 9.

Bautista, Gabriela. 1992. "*Ángel de fuego.*" *La Jornada Semanal* 159 (June 28):8–9.

Camargo, Ricardo. 1991. "Comenzó el rodaje de *Ángel de fuego.*" *El Nacional,* October 22, Sección espectáculos 5.

Cato, Susana. 1993. "Intimidad." *Proceso,* October 11, 57, 59.

"La cinta *Ángel de fuego* habla de muchos tabúes, Dice Lilia Aragón." 1993. *Excésior,* February 26, 1, 11.

Coda, Martha. 1985. "Dana Rotberg: *Elvira Luz Cruz, pena máxima,* historia que se repite a diario." *unomásuno,* June 29.

"Dana Rotberg: El cine como pasión." 1993. *El Nacional,* February 28, Sección espectáculos 12.

"*Danzón* (anuncio publicitario)." 1992. *Los Angeles Times,* October 16, F12.

EFE. "1992. *Ángel de fuego,* de Dana Rotberg, participa en el Festival Cinematográfico de Jerusalén." *Excélsior,* July 9.

———. 1992. "Buen recibimiento de la crítica internacional para *Ángel de fuego.*" *Excélsior,* May 11, 1, 15.

"Evangelina Sosa Estelariza el Filme *Ángel de fuego* de Dana Rotberg." 1991. *Excélsior,* November 4.

"Evangelina Sosa, Lilia Aragón, Meche Pascual, Alejandro Parodi y Salvador Sánchez, felices por su labor en *Ángel de fuego.*" 1992. *Excélsior,* February 23.

Gallegos, José Luis. 1991. "Alejandro Parodi: Positiva transformación de la Cinematografía Nacional." *Excélsior,* October 24.

———. 1991. "Dana Rotberg filmará la cinta *El Ángel de fuego.*" *Excélsior,* June 22, 1, 10.

———. 1992. "*Ángel de fuego* es una cinta ciento por ciento Mexicana, Dice Dana Rotberg." *Excélsior,* January 18, Sección espectáculos 5.

———. 1992. "*Ángel de fuego* es una obra importante en el cine Mexicano contemporáneo." *Excélsior,* April 24, 9.

———. 1992. "Dana Rotberg recibió el premio musa del cine y una placa que le otorgó la crítica extranjera por *Ángel de fuego.*" *Excélsior,* April 4, 5, 10.

———. 1992. "Gusta y Convence Evangelina Sosa en su Actuación, en la Cinta *Ángel de fuego.*" *Excélsior,* April 8, Sección espectáculos 2.

———. 1994. "Me interesa plasmar en mis películas la problemática social, Dice Dana Rotberg." *Excélsior,* June 6.

García, Gustavo. 1986. "Anatomía de un asesinato." *unomásuno,* January 26.

———. 1986. "Las fieras andan sueltas." *unomásuno,* February 4, Suplemento Sábado.

Garfias Ramírez, Bety. 1994. "Arturo Fabre e Irene Gorenko un matrimonio muy especial." *El Universal,* March 31, Sección espectáculos 1, 2.

Gracida, Ysabel. 1993. "*Ángel de fuego.*" *El Universal,* March 4, Sección cultural 3.

Hernández, Juan. 1991. "*Ángel del fuego* busca recuperar la identidad perdida del cine mexicano: Dana Rotenberg." *unomásuno,* October 22.

Hussein Ramírez, Juan. 1992. "Ángel de fuego." El Nacional, May 30, 1992, Sección espectáculos 7.

"Intimidad (cartelera)." 1993. El Nacional, October 6, Sección carteleras 2.

"Lilia Aragón en el Papel Principal de la cinta Ángel de fuego; Dirige Dana Rotberg." 1991. Excélsior, September 4.

"Lola, de María Novaro nació en el Sundance Institute de Robert Redford." 1993. El Universal, January 24, Sección espectáculos 18, 5, 7.

López Aranda, Susana. 1992. "Dana Rotberg, entre la realidad y la imaginación." Dicine 46 (July):8–9.

———. 1993. "Ángel de fuego." Dicine 51 (May 19).

Marin Conde, Eduardo. 1992. "El Incesto Cinematográfico." Esto, April 1.

Martínez Diez, Luis Ángel. 1990. "María Novaro y el buen cine mexicano." El Sol de México, July 15, Sección cultura 1.

Melche, Julia Elena. 1993. "Ángel de fuego." La Jornada, May 31, 1992, Sección cultura 37.

———. 1993. "Intimidad." La Jornada Semanal, October 24, 8–9.

"Los Mexicanos." 1992. Variedades, October 15, 5.

Moheno, Gustavo. 1992. "Ángel de fuego recorrerá el mundo." El Occidental, June 22, 1, 11.

Montiel, Mauricio. 1992. "Ángel de fuego, de Dana Rotberg." El Occidental, March 30, Sección D 1, 14.

Morelos, Torres. 1994. "Ángel de fuego." Siempre!, February 16, 66.

"The movie: Danzon." 1992. Los Angeles Times, November 20, E10.

"Mujeres Cineastas es el III Festival de Buenos Aires." 1990. El Universal, April 10, Sección cultural 3.

Murrieta, Rosario. 1991. "Son los jóvenes los hacen el 'nuevo cine' mexicano." Novedades, November 10.

Ortega Mendoza, Jesús. 1993. "Ángel de fuego." El Universal, February 24, Sección universo joven 3.

Peguero, Raquel. 1993. "Cancela Rotberg los trabajos para filmar Otilia Rauda." La Jornada, March 15, Sección cultura 52.

Pérez, Ernesto. 1992. "México en Cannes con Dana Rotberg." El Universal, May 11, Sección espectáculos 6.

Pérez Turrent, Tomás. 1992. "Ángel de fuego y El bulto." El Universal, March 31, Sección espectáculos 1, 4.

———. 1992. "Ángel de fuego y otros asuntos." Dicine 46 (July):5, 6, 7.

———. 1992. "El espíritu de Buñuel domina Ángel de fuego." El Universal, May 11, Sección espectáculos 1, 4.

———. 1993. "Ángel de fuego." El Universal, February 21, Sección espectáculos 22, 8.

———. 1993. "Ángel exterminador." Siempre!, March 17, 16.

Piña Jarillo, Verónica. 1991. "Intimidades de Dana Rotberg." El Nacional, September 29, Sección espectáculos 9.

Pineda Muñoz, Miguel Angel. 1992. "El guionismo fílmico, actividad menospreciada." El Nacional, August 19, Sección espectáculos 5.

"Por Elvira Luz Cruz, premian a Dana Rotberg y Ana Diez." 1986. La Jornada, November 3, Sección cultural 23.

"Premian en Nueva York a las Películas Mexicanas Ángel de fuego y Miroslava como las mejores del Festival Latino." 1993. Excélsior, August 31.

"La presencia de la mujer en el cine." 1991. El Nacional, March 12.

Quiroz Arroyo, Macarena. 1991. "No limita la libertad de expresión en las películas, por el hecho de que el estado participe en la producción." Excélsior, October 22.

———. 1992. "Inaugurará la Película Mexicana Ángel de fuego, la Quincena de Realizadores." Excélsior, April 30, 13, 15.

———. 1992. "No pretendo mostrar una temática feminista en mis películas, Dice la Realizadora Dana Rotberg." Excélsior, November 19.

Ramos Navas, Saúl. 1991. "Ángel de fuego retrata el drama de una adolescente." El Universal, October 22, 2, 14.

———. 1991. "Dana Rotberg regresa con Ángel de fuego. El Universal, December 28.

———. 1992. "Dos jóvenes judías viven en México y...." El Universal, July 28, Sección espectáculos 1, 4.

———. 1993. "Miroslava y Ángel de fuego, películas estelares en Nueva York." El Universal, August 30, 3, 16.

———. 1993. "El público mexicano está apto para ver Ángel de fuego: Lilia Aragón." El Universal, February 28, 15, 22.

Rivera, Héctor. "1992. Dana Rotberg hizo Ángel de fuego con el sistema que considera ideal: el de coproducción de IMCINE." Proceso, April 20.

Rodríguez Flores, Juan. 1992. "Llegó el Danzón." La Opinión, October 16, 1F.

———. 1992. "Me gusta explorar el espíritu fe August 9, 1E, 4E.

Salazar Hernández, Alejandro. 1991. "'Detractora del feminismo,' para Dana Rotberg no hay cine femenino o masculino, sólo bueno o malo." El Heraldo, March 12, 1-D, 6-D.

"El secreto de Romelia participará en el Festival Anual de la Mujer en el Cine." 1989. Excélsior, October 16.

"Los secretos y desaires de Busi Cortés." 1991. *El Nacional*, March 3, Sección espectáculos 9.
Serdio, Luis Roberto. 1992. "Dana Rotberg: el placer de hacer cine." *El Nacional*, April 26, Sección espectáculos 12.
Taibo I, Paco Ignacio. 1992. "*Ángel de fuego*." *El Universal*, March 31, Sección universo joven 1.
Torres, Maruja. 1993. "Franco, padre simbólico de una época cruel." *El Nacional*, September 22.
Vázquez Villalobos. 1993. "Qué, Quién, Cómo, Dónde...." *El Heraldo de México*, September 10, Sección espectáculos 1 D.
Vega, Miguel de la. 1995. "María Novaro: 'No me da lo mismo hacer cualquier película por encargo, quiero hacer mis propias historias y quiero hacerlo en México.'" *Proceso*, September 25, 66.
Velázquez Yebra, Patricia. 1991. "La mujer, presencia constante en el cine mexicano." *El Universal*, March 12, 1, 4.
Vidal, Nuria. 1992. "El cine mejicano renace de sus cenizas." *El Observador*, April 20, 48.
Viñas, Moisés. 1993. "*Ángel de fuego*." *El Universal*, February 28, 1, 3.
Wilmington, Micheal. 1992. "Exhilaration, Charm and Grace in Musical-Romance *Danzón*." *Los Angeles Times*, October 16, F8.
Yehya, Naief. 1993. "*Ángel de fuego*." *unomásuno*, March 27, Suplemento Sábado.

Danzón

"A María Rojo, el premio *Hugo de Plata*." 1992. *El Nacional*, June 30, Sección espectáculos 5.
AFP. 1991. "Cannes aplaude al film *Danzón* de María Novaro." *Cine Mundial*, May 13, Sección farándula 4.
_____. 1991. "Cannes todo completo; mejor espacio a *Danzón* que a "La mujer del puerto." *El Heraldo de México*, May 9.
_____. 1991. "La cinta *Danzón*, ganadora de la mano de bronce como el mejor largometraje del Festival Latino de NY." *Excélsior*, August 25, 3, 5.
_____. 1991. "*Danzón*, de México, salva el honor del cine latino en Cannes." *La Afición*, May 12, Sección espectáculos 26.
_____. 1991. "*Danzón* dedicado." *2º de Ovaciones*, May 10, 10.
_____. 1991. "*Danzón*, excelente cinta mexicana en el festival francés." *La Afición*, May 13, 30.
_____. 1991. "*Danzón*, presente en Cannes sin concursar." *Cine Mundial*, May 11, Sección Cine 11.
_____. 1991. "El filme *Danzón* presente en el Festival Fílmico de Cannes." *La Prensa*, May 11, Sección espectáculos 42.
_____. 1991. "Inaugurará Gabriel García Márquez Muestra de Cine Latinoamericano." June 13.
_____. 1991. "México, presente en la Quicena de realizadores con *Danzón*." *Novedades*, May 11, Sección espectáculos 13.
_____. 1991. "La película *Danzón* coloca a México entre los 13 grandes." *El Universal*, May 11, Sección espectáculos 1.
_____. 1991. "La película *Danzón*, de María Novaro, recibida con nutridos aplausos en Cannes." *El Día*, May 13, Sección espectáculos 17.
_____. 1991. "Siguen los elogios para *Danzón*." *El Día*, May 12, Sección espectáculos 19.
_____. 1991. "Venden disco compacto con la banda original del filme mexicano *Danzón*, en París." *Excélsior*, December 21.
Anderson, John. 1992. "Last Waltz South of the Border." *Newsday*, September 25.
ANSA. 1991. "Caluroso aplauso para el filme mexicano *Danzón*." *El Occidental*, May 16.
_____. 1991. "*DANZON* conquistó por el color, música e historia." *Ovaciones*, May 13, 10.
_____. 1991. "Extraordinaria ovación en Cannes para el filme mexicano *Danzón*, de María Novaro." *Excélsior*, May 13, 1, 5.
_____. 1991. "Ripstein y Novaro los únicos latinoamericanos." *El Universal*, May 9.
_____. 1992. "El filme *Danzón* de María Novaro, tiene buenas críticas en su exhibición, en Roma." *Excélsior*, July 18, 1, 5.
_____. 1992. "El filme mexicano *Danzón*, dirigido por María Novaro, será distribuido en Estados Unidos por la empresa Sony Classics." *Excélsior*, July 30, 1, 5.
_____. 1994. "Exhibirán la cinta *Danzón*, en Santiago, Chile." *Excélsior*, July 10.
ANSA/AFP. 1991. "Ovación en Cannes a María Novaro por *Danzón*." *unomásuno*, May 13, Sección cultura 22.
AP. 1991. "Premian al filme *Danzón* en el XV Festival Latino de Nueva York." *La Jornada*, August 25, Sección cultura 25.
Arankowsky, Alberto, and Lortia, Patricia. 1991. "*Danzón* dedicado a las marías de mi corazón." *Epoca*, July 22, 76, 77.
Armstrong, David. 1991. "*Danzón*." *San Francisco Examiner*, April 30, C-1.
Arroyo, Macarena Quiroz. 1991. "Importante que el Cine Nacional Recobre Presencia Internacional: Carmen Salinas." *Excélsior*, May 8, 1, 7.
Aviña, Rafael. 1991. "*Danzón*." *unomásuno*, July 3.
Ayala Blanco, Jorge. 1991. "Novaro y los goces de la feminidad insóplida." *El Financiero*, July 3, 56.
Azpeitia Gómez, Hugo. 1992. "*Danzón* dedi-

cado a María Novaro." *El Sol en la Cultura*, February 16, 3.
Bald, Margaret. 1991. "The Feminist Vision of Maria Novaro." *Toward Freedom*, October-November, 22.
Barriga Chavez, Ezequiel. 1991. "*Danzón* I." *Excelsior*, July 31.
———. 1991. "*Danzón* II." *Excélsior*, August 1.
Bautista, Gabriela. 1991. "Un danzón para María." *La Jornada Semanal*, July 14, 4.
Benerstein, Robert. 1992. "Mexican Comedy *Danzon* Offers Feminist Message with Light Touch." *Rocky Mountain News*, November 6.
Billson, Anne. 1993. "*Danzón*." *Slowgay Telegraph*, January 10.
"Blanca Guerra filma en el Puerto de Veracruz la película *Danzón*." 1990. *Excélsior*, August 26, 1, 11.
Blowen, Michael. 1992. "Upbeat Note from Mexico." *The Boston Globe*, November 9.
Bonfil, Carlos. 1991. "*Danzón*." *La Jornada*, July 3, Sección cultural 39.
———. 1993. "*El jardín del Edén*." *La Jornada*, October 15, 1995, Sección cultural 28.
Brown, Groff. "*Danzón*." *The Times*, January 7.
Bustos, Víctor. 1991. "María Novaro: De *Lola* a *Danzón*." *Dicine*, July, 10–11.
Camara, Madeleine. 1991. "Al ritmo del danzón." *El Universal*, November 1, 2.
Camarena, Amelia. 1991. "*Danzón* a la conquista del mundo." *Esto*, June 13, 6.
Camargo, Ricardo. 1990. "Intensa actividad cinematográfica." *El Nacional*, September 20, 20.
Carr, Jay. 1992. "*Danzon*: Feminism Meets Femininity." *Boston Globe*, November 6.
Carrasco, Jorge. 1991. "*Danzón* dedicado a las feministas." *Tiempo*, August 2, 10.
Carrera, Mauricio. 1991. "Conversación con María Novaro y Leticia Huijara (segunda y última parte)." *El Nacional*, March 1, Sección espectáculos 20.
———. 1991. "*Danzón*, himno a la cachondería." *El Nacional*, January 5.
Casillas de Alba, Martín. 1991. "Voy a ver *Danzón* hasta que me canse." *El Economista*, June 27.
Cato, Susana. 1991. "*Danzón* dedicado a ..." *Proceso*, June 24, 56, 57, 58.
Celín, Fernando. 1991. "¡Hey Familia!, *Danzón* dedicado a...." *El Semanario de Novedades*, July 21, 7.
———. 1995. "Comparta nuestros sueños." *Novedades*, November 5, El Semanario 7.
"Comenzará el lunes próximo, en el Estado de Veracruz, el rodaje de la cinta *Danzón*, con María Rojo." 1990. *Excélsior*, August 4, Sección espectáculos 2.
"Crece cada día la participación de la mujer, en los distintos ambitos del mundo del cine." 1991. *Excélsior*, June 23, Sección espectáculos 11.
Crucet, Vivian. 1992. "*Danzón*: Una de las mejores películas del Festival renueva la fe en el cine mexican." *Diario las Americas*, February 14, 3B.
Cuéllar, Oscar L. 1991. "*Danzón*." *Siempre*, July 31.
"*Danzón*." 1991. *Siglo 21*, December 28.
"*Danzón* (Anuncio publicitario)." 1992. *Los Angeles Times*, October 16, F12.
"*Danzón* cierra con broche de oro el ciclo 'Hoy en el cine mexicano.'" 1991. *El Universal*, June 27, 5, 16.
"*Danzón*, de María Novaro, será exhibida en el Festival de Cannes." 1991. *La Jornada*, April 23, Sección cultural 33.
"*Danzón* o el vehículo de Julia para vivir sin complicaciones." 1991. *El Occidental*, July 15.
Davenport, Hugo. 1993. "*Danzón*." *Daily Telegraph*, January 7.
"Después de 17 años el cine mexicano regresa al Festival de Cannes con *Danzón*." 1991. *Excélsior*, April 20, 1, 10.
"Dio inicio el Festival de Cannes." 1991. *El Día*, May 10, 19.
Domingo, Alberto. 1991. "¡Heey, familia...!" *Proceso*, July 24.
EFE. 1992. "Premian a la película mexicana *Danzón*, en el Festival Cinematográfico de Montevideo." *Excélsior*, April 25, 1, 13.
EM. 1992. "Un *Danzón* del Caribe." *El Mensajero*, April 15, C3.
Espinosa, Jorge Luis. 1991. "Apena que México pierda su fisonomía cultural: María Novaro." *unomásuno*, June 20, Sección ciencia, cultura y espectáculos 26.
"Exitosa exhibición comercial de la película mexicana *Danzón*, en Estocolmo, Suecia." 1992. *Excélsior*, June 9, 1, 5.
"Filman en el Puerto de Veracruz la película *Danzón*." 1990. *Excélsior*, August 10, Sección espectáculos 2.
"El filme, *Danzón*, de María Novaro se proyectará en diez festivales." 1991. *Excélsior*, July 19, Sección espectáculos 5.
Fusco, Coco. 1991. "Dance and Remembrance." *The Village Voice*, August 27.
Gallegos, José Luis. 1990. "El Gobierno de Veracruz Inicia la Producción de Filmes, con *Danzón*." *Excélsior*, August 6, Sección espectáculos 5.
———. 1991. "María Novaro informa que exhibirán en cines de París, el filme *Danzón*." *Excélsior*, December 17, Sección espectáculos 1, 9.
———. 1992. "Leticia Perdigón, José Alonso y Soccorro Bonilla, en la cinta *Anoche Soñé Contigo*." *Excélsior*, January 10, Sección espectáculos 3, 10.

García, Javier. 1991. "Once Festivales Esperan el filme *Danzón*." *El Occidental*, August 6, 6, 7.
García Liñán, Salvador. 1991. "*Danzón* o la defensa del talento." *El Financiero*, July 3, Sección industria 23.
García Martínez, Luz. 1991. "El sublime danzón de una vida." *El Búho*, August 18, 1, 6.
García Romero, Francisco. 1991. "*Danzón*." *El Occidental*, September 8.
García Tsao, Leonardo. 1991. "Buscando desganadamente a Carmelo." *El Nacional*, July 11, Sección cultural 13.
_____. 1991. "*Danzón*, de María Novaro, ovacionada en Cannes." *El Nacional*, May 13.
Golden, Tim. 1992. "*Danzón* Glides to a Soft Mexican Rhythm." *The New York Times*, October 11, 24H.
González Mello, Flavio. 1991. "*Danzón*, un cálido retrato de la idiosincrasia jarocha." *El Economista*, June 27, 38.
Gracida, Ysabel. 1991. "*Danzón* dedicado a...." *El Universal*, July 8, Sección cultural 1.
Guthmann, Edward. "Festival Finds a Charmer." 1992. *San Francisco Chronicle*, April 30.
"Ha recaudado mil millones de pesos la película *Danzón*." 1991. *Excélsior*, August 6, Sección espectáculos 3.
"Hay *Danzón* en Veracruz." 1990. *El Nacional*, August 9, Sección espectáculos 11.
Hernández Villegas, Ernesto. 1991. "*Danzón* demuestra que tenemos alguna calidad...." *El Universal*, June 21, 1, 12.
Howe, Desson. 1992. "*Danzon*." *Washington Post*, November 6.
Keough, Peter. 1992. "*Danzón*." *Boston Phoenix*, November 6.
Leal, Alejandro. 1992. "María Novaro es descarada feminista y antimachista." *El Universal*, October 4.
Lenti, Paul. 1991. "*Danzon*." *Variety*, April 29.
León, Mariví. 1992. "Tres películas mexicanas aplaudidas en el Festival." *El Universal*, February 20, Sección cultural 2.
Malcolm, Derek. 1993. "*Danzón*." *The Guardian*, January 7.
Mam, Yehudit. 1991. "*Danzón*." *La Jornada Semanal*, August 4, 7, 8.
Mangin, Daniel. 1992. "Fresh Vision." *Bay Area Reporter*, October 15, 40–41.
"María Novaro." 1991. *expansión*, December 25, 76.
"María Novaro inició la edición del largometraje titulado *Danzón*." 1990. *Excélsior*, September 29, 1, 11.
Martínez, Alegría. 1991. "Tienen constante movimiento interno los personajes de *Danzón*: Tito Vasconcelos." *unomásuno*, June 20, Sección ciencia, cultura y espectáculos 26.
Matsumoto, Jon. 1992. "Light *Danzon*." *Village View*, October 16–22.
Mejía, Eduardo. 1994. "Xavier Villaurrutia Danzoneando." *El Financiero*, May 20, Sección cultural 47.
Mendoza de Lira, Alejandra. 1990. "María Rojo es una señora que baila danzón, allá en Veracruz." *El Universal*, August 8, 8.
Menell, Jeff. 1992. "*Danzon*." *The Hollywood Reporter*, September, 19–32.
"Los Mexicanos." 1992. *Variedades*, October 15, 5.
Michel, Daniela. 1992. "Entrevista con María Novaro." *Milenio*, May–June, 12–16.
Minero, Alberto. 1991. "Comienza el Festival de Cine Latino." *el diario*, 16 August, 21, 23.
Montero, José Antonio. 1991. "*Danzón*." *El Financiero*, July 4, Sección cultural 60.
"The movie: *Danzon*." 1992. *Los Angeles Times*, November 20, E10.
Muñoz, Luis. 1990. "La tía Tiburcia tiene una casa de huéspedes." *El Universal*, August 10, 2, 12.
Murrieta, Rosario. 1992. "Becas de la Fundación Rockefeller a María Novaro y Sara Minter." *Novedades*, March 29.
_____. 1992. "María Novaro, de *Danzón* pasa ahora a *Fronteras*." *Novedades*, June 7.
Notimex. 1991. "El filme *Danzón*, de María Novaro, representará a AL en Cannes." *La Jornada*, May 11, Seción cultura 32.
_____. 1992. "*Danzón*, una fábula dulce y encantadora fantasía." *El Nacional*, June 23, Sección espectáculos 5.
_____. 1992. "México, en el Festival de Cine de Miami." *unomásuno*, February 8, Sección ciencia, cultura y espectáculos 28.
Novaro, María. 1992. Carta al director: "María Novaro amplia sus declaraciones sobre el Festival de Cannes." *Proceso*, May 25.
Ortega Mendoza, Jesús. 1991. "*Danzón*." *El Universal*, July 3, Sección universo joven 3.
"Para bailar a otro ritmo." 1992. *Siglo 21*, January 3.
"Penultimatum." 1992. *La Jornada*, May 16, Sección cultura 24.
Pérez Turrent, Tomás. 1991. "De *La Mujer del Puerto* y *Danzón*." *Novedades*, July 28, El Semanario 12.
_____. 1991. "En cuatro funciones, hoy, *Danzón* de María Novaro." *El Universal*, May 12, 1, 10.
_____. 1991. "Un éxito de México es ahora el filme *Danzón*." *El Universal*, May 13, Sección espectáculos 1, 6.
_____. 1991. "*Le Monde* y *Liberación* celebran el éxito mexicano de María Novaro." *El Universal*, May 15, 1, 2.
_____. 1991. "Ver buen cine mexicano ¡sólo en el extranjero!." *El Universal*, May 14, Sección espectáculos 1, 2.
"Personajes de *Danzón*: Tito Vasconcelos." 1991. *unomásuno*, June 20.

"Premian a María Rojo en el Festival Fílmico de Chicago." 1991. *El Nacional*, November 8, 7.

Quiroz Arroyo, Macarena. 1990. "A través de la película *Danzón* descubrí la Magia de Este Ritmo Musical: María Rojo." *Excélsior*, September 18, Sección espectáculos 1, 5.

———. 1990. "Concluyó el Rodaje de la película Danzón con María Rojo y Blanca Guerra." *Excélsior*, September 21, 1, 15.

———. 1991. "Asistir con *Danzón* al Festival de Cannes, es para María Novaro un Sueño Hecho Realidad." *Excélsior*, April 22, Sección espectáculos 1, 9.

———. 1991. "Proyectarán en Cannes la cinta *Danzón*, de María Novaro." *Excélsior*, May 7, 1, 5.

———. 1992. "Inaugurará la película mexicana *Ángel de fuego*, la quincena de realizadores." *Excélsior*, April 30, 13, 15.

———. 1992. "No pretendo mostrar una temática feminista en mis películas, dice la realizadora Dana Rotberg." *Excélsior*, November 19.

———. 1994. "Contribuyó la cinta *Danzón*, de María Novaro, a Revivir el Gusto de los Veracruzanos por Este Baile." *Excélsior*, April 17, Sección espectáculos 19.

———. 1995. "María Novaro: Mi tema es México." *El Nacional*, October 8, Sección espectáculos 38.

Ramírez, Luis Enrique. 1991. "En las películas mexicanas, los diálogos no son creíbles." *El Financiero*, June 28, 50.

———. 1991. "Perjudicar a *Danzón* es perjudicarme a mí: María Novaro." *El Financiero*, June 27, Sección cultural 58.

Ramos Navas, Saúl. 1992. "María Rojo, premiada por el Festival de Cine de Chicago con el *Hugo de plata*." *El Universal*, July 3, Sección espectáculos 1, 6.

"Recibe promoción internacional Blanca Guerra por la película *Danzón*." 1991. *Excélsior*, May 27, 1, 4.

Reyes, Juan José. 1991. "Del buen cine mexicano." *El Nacional*, August 1, Sección cultura 12.

Ríos Alfaro, Lorena. 1997. "Las mujeres tenemos el peso de Santa en nuestras vidas." *Unomásuno*, February 22.

Rivera, Luz María. 1991. "*Danzón* y sus Mitos." *El Occidental*, October 18.

Rodríguez Flores, Juan. 1992. "Llego el *Danzón*." *La Opinión*, October 16, 1F.

———. 1992. "Me gusta explorar el espíritu femenino a través de mis películas." *La opinión*, August 9, 1E, 4E.

Rubio, Lilia. 1991. "*Danzón*." *La Jornada*, July 30, Sección cultura 33.

Serdán, Amado Talabera. 1991. "Desesperadamente buscando a Julia." *Tiempo Libre*, November 14, 1D, 6D.

Serdio, Luis Roberto. 1992. "Dana Rotberg: El placer de hacer cine." *El Nacional*, April 26, Sección espectáculos 12.

Smith, Russell. 1992. "*Danzon*." *The Dallas Morning News*, November 6.

Stevenson, William. 1991. "*Danzón* Tops Honors at Latino Film Fest." *Varitety*, September 2.

Su, Margo. 1991. "Las Marías y su *Danzón*." *La Jornada*, June 13, Sección cultural 33.

Taibo I, Paco Ignacio. 1991. "El encanto del danzón." *El Universal*, July 9, Sección cultural 1.

Tallmer, Jerry. 1992. "*Danzon*: Steps in search of love." *New York Post*, September 25.

Tetzpa Zayaz, Jaime. 1990. "La mujer en el cine." *El Nacional*, April 22, Sección espectáculos 16.

Thomas, Kevin. 1992. "Lighthearted 'Club' Due at Silent Movie." *Los Angeles Times*, November 20, F-9.

———. 1992. "A New Generation of Filmmaker from Mexico Dances into the Scene." *Los Angeles Times*, October 16, F10.

Torres, Esmeralda. 1991. "*Danzón*." *Diario de Juárez*, November 15, Sección espectáculos 1-E, 2-E, 3-E.

Torres San Martín, Patricia. 1993. "El cine mexicano y sus cineastas: María Novaro." *Siglo 21*, July 11, Suplemento 4, 5.

"Tres mujeres para un *Danzón*: Carmen y las dos marías." 1990. *El Universal*, August 10, Sección espectáculos 3.

Ulmer, James. 1992. "Novaro Helping Lead Mexican Film Comeback." *Hollywood Reporter*, August 11.

UPI. 1992. "Obtuvo *Danzón* premio a la mejor película en el Festival Uruguay." *Excélsior*, May 5, Sección espectáculos 3.

Vance, Kelly. 1992. "Dances with Zebras." *Express*, October 23, 30.

Vega, Patricia. 1991. "Entrevista con María Novaro." *La Jornada Semanal*, August 25, 27–30.

Velázquez, Carolina. 1990. "Comienzan a rodar *Danzón*, otro largometraje Novaro." *La Jornada*, August 18, Sección cultura 28.

———. 1991. "Meneadito, en Europa se bailó *Danzón*." *Doble Jornada*, July 1, 5, 6.

———. 1991. "Teléfono descompuesto." *Doble Jornada*, July 1, 6.

Velázquez Yebra, Patricia. 1991. "La mujer, presencia constante en el cine mexicano." *El Universal*, March 12, 1, 4.

Vera, José. 1990. "*Danzón* dedicado ... a María Rojo y Héctor Bonilla." *El Nacional*, July 28, 24.

———. 1990. "*Lola* viajará todo el año." *El Nacional*, April 9, 13.

———. 1990. "María Novaro: La mujer en el cine mexicano." *El Nacional*, June 4, 21.

———. 1991. "*Danzón*, a Europa, Canadá y

Japón." *El Nacional*, June 7, Sección espectáculos 5.
Viñas, Moisés. 1991. "*Danzón*: La primavera veracruzana de una telefonista y su Carmelo." *El Universal*, June 30, Sección espectáculos 1, 14.
Wilmington, Michael. 1992. "Exhilaration, Charm and Grace in Musical-Romance *Danzón*." *Los Angeles Times*, October 16, F8.
Woldenberg, José. 1991. "*Danzón*." *La Jornada*, July 6, Sección País 5.
Zalko, Nardo. 1991. "Los cubanos bailaron al ritmo de *Danzón*." *El Nacional*, December 8, Sección espectáculos 5.

Lola

AFP. 1991. "*Lola*, de María Novaro, en el Festival de Ostia." *Excélsior*, May 3, Sección espectáculos 7.
Albarrán, Jairo Calixto. 1989. "Lola (mas no la trailera)." *Excélsior*, November 26, 4.
Amado, Ana María. 1990. "Realizadoras del Cine Mexicano." *Fempress*, June, 8.
ANSA. 1991. "Caluroso aplauso para el filme mexicano *Danzón*." *El Occidental*, May 16.
_____. 1991. "Los ganadores del Oso." *El Nacional*, February 27.
AP. 1990. "El filme *Lola*, de María Novaro, en el Festival de Biarritz." *Excélsior*, September 25.
Arredondo, Arturo. 1995. "*El Jardín del Edén*, es la mejor cinta de Novaro." *Novedades*, October 1, Sección espectáculos 16.
Aviña, Rafael. 1995. "*Los Pasos de Ana*, de Maryse Sistach." *unomásuno*, June 10, 13.
Ayala Blanco, Jorge. 1989. "María Novaro y la dificultad de ser a la deriva." *El Financiero*, November 22, Sección cultural 82.
Bald, Margaret. 1991. "The Feminist Vision of Maria Novaro." *Toward Freedom*, October-November, 22.
Barbachano Ponce, Miguel. 1989. "Reflexiones sobre nueve películas." *Excélsior*, November 26.
Barriga Chávez, Ezequiel. 1989. "*Lola*." *Excélsior*, November 30, 59-A.
_____. 1991. "*Lola*." *Excélsior*, February 13, Sección espectáculos 2.
Bonfil, Carlos. 1991. "*Danzón*." *La Jornada*, July 3, Sección cultural 39.
_____. 1991. "*Lola*." *La Jornada*, February 21, Sección cultura 41.
_____.1995. "*El jardín del Edén*." *La Jornada*, October 15, Sección cultural 28.
Bustos, Víctor. 1991. "María Novaro: De *Lola* a *Danzón*." *Dicine*, July, 10–11.
Carrera, Mauricio. 1991. "Conversación con María Novaro y Leticia Huijara (segunda y última parte)." *El Nacional*, March 1, Sección espectáculos 20.
Cato, Susana. 1989. "Y el vituperio de los críticos *Lola* y *Goitia* entre el elogio." *Proceso*, December 4, 48–50.
Celín, Fernando. 1989. "*Lola*." *El Semanario*, December 3.
Coria, José Felipe. 1989. "*Lola*." *unomásuno*, November 24.
Cuéllar, Óscar L. 1991. "*Lola*." *Siempre*, March 13.
"*Danzón* o el Vehículo de Julia para vivir sin complicaciones." 1991. *El Occidental*, July 15.
Diez, Rolo. 1991. "*Lola*." *El Universal*, February 26, Sección cultural 2.
_____. 1991. "Otorgan en Berlín el *Oso de oro* al filme *La casa de la sonrisa* de Ferreri." *La Jornada*, February 27, Sección cultural 37.
Espinasa, José María. 1991. "Neorrealismos." *La Jornada Semanal*, March 10, 46.
Espinosa, Jorge Luis. 1991. "Apena que México pierda su fisonomía cultural: María Novaro." *unomásuno*, June 20, Sección ciencia, cultura y espectáculos 26.
Espinosa, Pablo. 1989. "Busi Cortés: Me choca el cine feminista; el mío es de mujeres." *La Jornada*, March 12.
Feliciano, Enrique. 1989. "Surge la 4ª directora de películas." *ESTO*, January 11, 15.
García, Gustavo. 1989. "La nueva (L)ola." *unomásuno*, December 2, 13.
García Cruz, Rubén. 1990. "Las realizadoras ganamos terreno en la cinematografía mexicana." *El Nacional*, September 9, Sección espectáculos 15.
García Romero, Francisco. 1991. "*Lola*." *El Occidental*, June 9.
García Tsao, Leonardo. 1991. "Buscando desganadamente a Carmelo." *El Nacional*, July 11, Sección cultural 13.
_____. 1991. "Retrato de una madre chilanga." *El Nacional*, February 7.
Golden, Tim. 1992. "*Danzón* Glides to a Soft Mexican Rhythm." *New York Times*, October 11, 24H.
Instituto Nacional de Cinematografía. 1990. "*Lola* (Ficha de técnica en el concurso La Mujer y El Cine)." Buenos Aires: Instituto Nacional de Cinematografía.
Johnson Celorio, Rodrigo. 1989. "María Novaro demuestra con *Lola* la calidad." *El economista*, November 22, 29.
Lara, Hugo. 1991. "*El secreto de Romelia*." *Dicine*, May, 9, 10.
Latina. "*Lola* (Ficha técnica)." Latina.
Latina SA, 1989. "Lola" [promotional pamphlet in English], 1–4. Mexico City: Macondo Cine-Video.
Leal, Alejandro. 1992. "María Novaro es descarada feminista y antimachista." *El Universal*, October 4.

Lenti, Paul. 1990. "*Lola*." *Variety*, January 17.
"*Lola*." 1989. *ESTO*, November 24, Sección carteleras.
"*Lola*." 1989. *Gramma*, December 11, 5.
"*Lola* ... breve película sobre el amor." 1989. *El Día*, November 24, Sección espectáculos 21.
"*Lola*, de María Novaro nació en el Sundance Institute de Robert Redford." 1993. *El Universal*, January 24, Sección espectáculos 18, 5, 7.
"*Lola*: Retrato de mujeres con paisaje." 1991. *Siempre*, March 13.
Mallo, N. N. 1990. "*El secreto de Romelia* ganó el premio ACE." *Esto*, March 27.
Mam, Yehudit. 1989. "La semana en la muestra." *La Jornada Semanal*, December 10, 6.
"María Novaro debuta como directora en *Lola*." 1988. *El Occidental*, September 18.
"María Novaro inició la edición del largometraje titulado *Danzón*." 1990. *Excélsior*, September 29, 1, 11.
Martínez, Carmen. 1991. "Premios a *Lola*, de María Novaro." *El Occidental*, March 21.
Martínez Diez, Luis Ángel. 1990. "María Novaro y el buen cine mexicano." *El Sol de México*, July 15, Sección cultura 1.
Mendoza, Eduardo. 1990. "Baños, asesinatos y mujeres en la V Muestra de Cine Nacional." *El Universal*, March 31.
"Los Mexicanos." 1992. *Variedades*, October 15, 5.
Michel, Daniela. 1992. "Entrevista con María Novaro." *Milenio*, May–June 1992, 12–16.
"Mujeres Cineastas es el III Festival de Buenos Aires." 1990. *El Universal*, April 10, Sección cultural 3.
Murúa, Sara. 1989. "*Lola*, la reivindicación femenina en filme mexicano." *El Nacional*, November 24, Sección espectáculos 5.
NOTIMEX. 1991. "El filme *Danzón*, de María Novaro, representará a AL en Cannes." *La Jornada*, May 11, Seción cultura 32.
"La película mexicana *Lola*, en la Sección Oficial del Festival Internacional de Filmes Hecho por Mujeres." 1990. *Excélsior*, June 13.
Pérez Turrent, Tomás. 1991. "*Lola*: Retrato femenino de una estudiante del CUEC." *El Universal*, February 10.
Pixel, Juan. 1989. "*Lola* (México)." *ESTO*, November 25, 17, 22.
Ramírez, Luis Enrique. 1991. "Perjudicar a *Danzón* es Perjudicarme a mí: María Novaro." *El Financiero*, June 27, Sección cultural 58.
Ramírez Aguilar, Walter. 1991. "El nuevo cine mexicano." *El Nacional*, June 10, Sección cultura 15.
Rodríguez, Rodrigo. 1992. "Leticia Huijara, una chava *bien* intensa." *El Nacional*, June 21.
Rodríguez Pineda, Arturo. 1989. "El snobismo de la Muestra Internacional de Cine." *Excélsior*, November 26, Sección el búho 4.
Ruiz, Blanca. 1990. "María Novaro: *Lola* en el corazón." *Mira*, July 11, 34–36.
Salinas Salinas, Adela. 1991. "*Lola* un cine con ojos de mujer." *Despegue*, March 14, 18–21.
"*El secreto de Romelia* y *Lola* participarán en el Festival de Cine en Buenos Aires." 1990. *El Nacional*, April 10, 31.
Thomas, Kevin. 1992. "Lighthearted 'Club' Due at Silent Movie." *Los Angeles Times*, November 20, F-9.
———. 1992. "A New Generation of Filmmaker from Mexico Dances into the Scene." *Los Angeles Times*, October 16, F10.
Torres San Martín, Patricia. 1993. "El cine mexicano y sus cineastas: María Novaro." *Siglo 21*, July 11, Suplemento 4, 5.
Vega, Patricia. 1989. "En *Lola*, quiero desmitificar la maternidad: María Novaro." *La Jornada*, January 11, Sección cultural 19.
———. 1989. "*Lola*." *La Jornada*, November 24, Sección cultura 41.
———. 1990. "Comienzan a rodar *Danzón*, otro largometraje de Novaro." *La Jornada*, August 18, Sección cultura 28.
———. 1990. "En la escuela no se aprende a hacer cine: Dana Rotberg." *La Jornada*, February 7, Sección cultural 29.
———. 1990. "El filme *Lola* una propuesta emocional ante la depresión." *La Jornada*, April 11, Sección cultural 27.
———. 1991. "Concluye en Guadalajara la VI Muestra de Cine Mexicano." *La Jornada*, March 13, Sección cultura 41.
———. 1992. "La disolvencia del cine mexicano." *La Jornada*, January 4, Sección cultura 25.
Velázquez, Carolina. 1989. "La idea de la película *Lola* es mostrar los lados oscuros de la maternidad, indica su Directora María Novaro." *El Financiero*, November 24, Sección cultural 83.
Vera, José. 1990. "Apoyo a nuestro cine en Europa." *El Nacional*, April 6, Sección espectáculos 17, 18.
———. 1990. "*Lola* viajará todo el año." *El Nacional*, April 9, 13.
———. 1990. "María Novaro: La mujer en el cine mexicano." *El Nacional*, June 4, 21.
———. 1991. "*Danzón*, a Europa, Canadá y Japón." *El Nacional*, June 7, Sección espectáculos 5.
Viñas, Moisés. 1982. "El síndrome 68." *unomásuno*, July 30, 25.
———. 1991. "*Lola*." *El Universal*, February 21, Sección espectáculos 1, 6.
Viñas, Moises. 1989. "*Lola*." *El Universal*, November 26, Sección espectáculos 1,5.

Virgen, Lucy. 1991. "*Lola* de María Novaro." *El Informador*, June 9.
Woldenberg, José. 1991. "*Danzón.*" *La Jornada*, July 6, Sección País 5.
_____. 1991. "*Lola.*" *La Jornada*, March 2, 17.
Yehya, Naief. 1991. "*Lola*: ¿México sigue en pie?" *unomásuno*, March 9.

LOS PASOS DE ANA

Aviña, Rafael. 1995. "*Los Pasos de Ana*, de Maryse Sistach." *unomásuno*, June 10, 13.
Espinasa, José María. 1990. "Correspondencias." *La Jornada Semanal*, April 15, 44.
Gallegos, José Luis. 1991. "Los cineastas José Buil y Marisa Sistach trabajarán juntos en el IV Concurso de Cine." *Excélsior*, April 9, Sección espectáculos 5.
_____. 1991. "*Los Pasos de Ana*, una película que habla de la virtud de la mujer para sacar adelante a los hijos." *Excélsior*, March 18, 2, 9.
_____. 1994. "Habla Marisa Sistach de su cinta *Los Pasos de Ana.*" *Excélsior*, December 10.
Guerrero, Juan. 1990. "Maryse Sistach: *Los pasos de Ana.*" *El Nacional*, July 16, Sección espectáculos 21.
Ortega Mendoza, Jesús. 1993. "*Los pasos de Ana.*" *El Universal*, March 13, Sección universo joven 3.
Pérez Turrent, Tomás. 1991. "Ana, divorciada y con dos hijos, vive la duda." *El Universal*, March 14, 1, 2.
_____. 1993. "*Los pasos de Ana.*" *El Universal*, March 7, Sección espectáculos 1, 18.
_____. 1994. "*Los pasos de Ana.*" *El Universal*, February 2, 1, 3.
Salazar, Alejandro. 1994. "Los pasos de Marisa Sistach." *El Nacional*, April 17.
Salazar Hernández, Alejandro. 1991. "Júbilo de nuevos cineastas al exhibir lo que les costó sangre filmar." *El Heraldo de México*, March 13, 1-D, 3-D.
Torres San Martín, Patricia. 1992. "Marisa Sistach, cineasta." *Siglo 21*, March 22, Sección suplemento 9.
Vega, Patricia. 1991. "Concluye en Guadalajara la VI Muestra de Cine Mexicano." *La Jornada*, March 13, Sección cultura 41.
Viñas, Moisés. 1993. "*Los pasos de Ana.*" *El Universal*, March 30, 1, 10.

EL SECRETO DE ROMELIA

Aguilar Camín, Héctor. 1989. "Un cine mexicano posible y deseable." *unomásuno*, March 16, 27.
AP. 1992. "*Ángel de fuego* inauguró la quincena de los realizadores." *El Universal*, May 10, Sección espectáculos 18, 12.

Arredondo, Arturo. 1988. "*El secreto de Romelia.*" *La Jornada*, December 4, Sección cultura 26.
Barriga Chávez, Ezequiel. 1988. "*El secreto de Romelia.*" *Excélsior*, December 6.
_____. "*El secreto de Romelia.*" 1989. *Excélsior*, October 6.
Casas de la Peña, Alfonso. 1989. "*El secreto de Romelia* o hay un fantasma en mi melodrama." *El Occidental*, March 10, 12, 2.
"Cuatro nominaciones a *El secreto de Romelia*, en NY." 1990. *La Jornada*, March 13, Sección cultural 28.
"Diana Bracho aplaude que haya más participación de la mujer." 1989. *El Occidental*, March 11, 2, 17.
DPA. 1990. "*El secreto de Romelia* ganó el premio Opera Prima, en el Festival de San Juan, Puerto Rico." *Excélsior*, October 24, Sección espectáculos 3.
Espinasa, José María. 1989. "*El secreto de Romelia* (II y último)." *La Jornada Semanal*, October 8, 48.
_____. 1989. "*El secreto de Romelia* (I)." *La Jornada Semanal*, October 1.
Espinosa, Pablo. 1989. "Busi Cortés: Me choca el cine feminista; el mío es de mujeres." *La Jornada*, March 12.
"Exhibirán en la Unión Soviética la cinta *El secreto de Romelia.*" 1989. *Excelsior*, July 7.
Gallegos, José Luis. 1988. "El Centro de Producción Cinematográfica produce largometrajes en el formato de 35 milímetros." *Excélsior*, August 5.
_____. 1988. "La cineasta Busi Cortés habla sobre *El secreto de Romelia.*" *Excélsior*, August 4.
_____. 1989. "Busi Cortés habla sobre la mujer cineasta, en México." *Excélsior*, March 15.
_____. 1990. "Busi Cortés está feliz, de que su película, *El secreto de Romelia*, fuera premiada." *Excélsior*, October 25, Sección espectáculos 1, 11.
_____. 1990. "Exhibirán en Israel la película *El Viudo Román* de la Realizadora Busi Cortés." *Excélsior*, April 9, Sección espectáculos 14.
_____. 1990. "Ha ganado la Mujer Importantes Espacios en el Medios de Comunicación, afirma Busi Cortés." *Excélsior*, May 20, Sección espectáculos 6.
García, Gustavo. 1989. "Échale la culpa a Cárdenas." *unomásuno*, March 11.
_____. 1989. "No llames corazón lo que tu tienes." *unomásuno*, February 26.
González Escobar, Martha G. 1989. "Un cambio de mirada." *El Occidental*, 15 March, 2, 8.
Hernández, Rubén. 1989. "El cine femenino toma su lugar." *El Nacional*, March 14.
Hernández Tamayo, Víctor. 1988. "Filman en

Tlaxcala cinta basada en obra de Rosario Castellanos." *La Jornada*, September 1, 17.
Krauze, Ethel. 1988. "*El secreto de Romelia*." *Excélsior*, December 15, 2.
Lara, Hugo. 1991. "*El secreto de Romelia*." *Dicine*, May, 9, 10.
Mallo. 1990. "*El secreto de Romelia* ganó el premio ACE." *Esto*, March 27.
Marín Conde, Eduardo. 1988. "*El secreto de Romelia*." *El Nacional*, December 4.
"Lo mejor de lo peor." 1988. *Novedades*, December 9.
Peña, Mauricio. 1988. "*El secreto de Romelia*." *El Heraldo de México*, December 4.
Pérez Turrent, Tomás. 1989. "Confusiones y fantasma en *El secreto de Romelia*." *El Universal*, September 24, Sección espectáculos 1, 4.
_____. 1989. "*El secreto de Romelia*." *El Universal*, February 19, 1, 9.
_____. 1989. "*El secreto de Romelia*." *El Universal*, September 26, Sección espectáculos 1, 3.
"La presencia de estrellas, esencial para la supervivencia de nuestra industria fílmica en 1988." 1989. *El Heraldo de México*, January 24, 1-D, 2-D.
Quiroz Arroyo, Macarena. 1989. "Interés de productores en apoyar a nuevos realizadores." *Excélsior*, October 17.
Ríos Alfaro, Lorena. 1996. "La industria del cine ya no existe como tal, algunos individuos levantamos sueños propios." *unomásuno*, March 23, 19.
Salazar Hernández, Alejandro. 1992. "Los problemas de Romelia." *El Nacional*, February 12, Sección espectáculos 5.
"*El secreto de Romelia*." 1988. *Esto*, December 4
"*El secreto de Romelia* participará en el Festival Anual de la Mujer en el Cine." 1989. *Excélsior*, October 16.
"*El secreto de Romelia* y *Lola* participarán en el Festival de Cine en Buenos Aires." 1990. *El Nacional*, April 10, 31.
"Los secretos y desaires de Busi Cortés." 1991. *El Nacional*, March 3, Sección espectáculos 9.
Solares Heredia, Martín. 1991. "Frustraciones medianas, a ritmo de frenesí debutante." *El Financiero*, March 13.
Vega, Patricia. 1988. "*El secreto de Romelia*, filme basado en obra de Castellanos." *La Jornada*, November 22, Sección cultural 27.
Ventura Ramírez, Nancy. 1988. "El secreto de Romelia." *El Nacional*, December 4, 14.
Vera, José. 1990. "Filmes de directoras mexicanas, al extranjero." *El Nacional*, June 9, Sección carteleras 27.
Viñas, Moisés. 1988. "*El secreto de Romelia*." *El Universal*, December 6, 1, 2.
_____. 1989. "Lola." *El Universal*, November 26, Sección espectáculos 1, 5.
_____. 1991. "*Anoche soñé contigo*." *El Nacional*, November 25, 1, 6.

Index

Numbers in ***bold italics*** indicate pages with photographs.

abjection 46, 202*n*17
Alcoriza, Luis 4, 145
Alisa Klaus 201*n*1
Almond, Barbara 62, 65–66
Alone of All Her Sex see Warner, Marina
Ángel de fuego 1, 27, ***52–54***, ***55–57***, 59–63, 72, 151, ***153***, 163, 185, 202*n*24
anger 56, 63–64, 164–165, 179, 179
Anoche soñé contigo 197*n*5
Armendáriz, Pedro 28
Ascension 123
Assumption 37
attachment theory 65, 72
Ayala Blanco, Jorge 8, 31, 75, 156–157, 187, 191*n*11

bad women (malas mujeres) 8, 102–103, 106–107, 184, 186
Beltrán, Cándida 16
Bildnis einer Trinkerin (*Ticket of No Return*) 124–126
Block Lewis, Helen 63
blood 154, 162
Bowlby, John 65
Las Buenromero 96, 112, 115, 119, 186, 189*n*2
Buil, Pepe 193*n*39
Burton-Carvajal, Julianne 7, 137, 191*n*18
Butler, Judith 7, 160, 169

Cáceres, Olga 25
Cananea 6
Candelaria, Virgen de la (Virgin of Light) 123, 125, 194–195*n*15, 195*n*17, 198*n*4
Catholicism 144–145, 149–150, 152, 155, 158–159
Cazals, Felipe 4, 12, 25, 132–135, 161, 175, 178, 191*n*21, 192–193*n*35
CCC *see* Centro de Capacitación Cinematográfica
Centro de Capacitación Cinematográfica 13, 25, 28, 110, 113, 176, 193*n*43, 198*n*5

Centro Universitario de Estudios Cinematográficos 13, 14, 191*n*18
Cine-Mujer (colective) 167, 189*n*1
Cocina de imágenes 16
collective subjectivity 166, 168–169, 187
colonization 112–113, 115
CONACULTA *see* Consejo Nacional para la Cultura y las Artes
Conozco a las tres 1–2, 26, 151, 168
Consejo Nacional para la Cultura y las Artes 15
Constantiner, León 27
cooperatives 29
coproduction 15, 29
Cortés, Busi 1, 10, ***14***, 16, 18, 25, 28, 112–116, 186, 192*n*29, 192–193*n*35, 193*n*39, 26, 193*n*43
Cortés, Carmen 193*n*39
Cuando los hijos se van 1, 11, **40**, 43, 137–***140***, 141–145, 150–151, 154, 157–158, 160, 162, 182
CUEC *see* Centro Universitario de Estudios Cinematográficos

Danzón 1–***3***, 21, 49, 68–73, 82, ***83***–84, 86, ***87***–89
De la vida de las mujeres 24
De todos modos Juan te llamas 6
De la Madrid, Miguel 26
De la Mora, Sergio 189*n*1
De Lauretis, Teresa 160
De los Reyes, Aurelio 156–157
depression 160, 163
Derba, Mimi 16
desire 99
Dever, Susan 2
Díaz Morales, José 10
Díez Díaz, Ana 176
Doane, Mary Ann 86, 89, 94, 197*n*10, 197*n*2, 198*n*6
Dolores, Virgin of (Our Lady of Sorrows) 44–46; history 198*n*3, 143–144, 160

219

Doña Bárbara 10, 97–99, **100**, 101–107, 116–119, 184
Douglas, Mary 202*n*17
Durán, Ignacio 15, 24

Echeverría, Luis 13, 15, 18
Elvira Luz Cruz 1, 4, 12, 161, 163, 175–178
Encuentro de Mujeres Cineastas y Videoastas Latinas 16
Estudios Churubusco 28

Una familia de tantas 1, 10, 43, 49–**52**, 72, 97, 103, 106, 119, 151, 157, 185
Fanon, Frantz 113, 134
Felix, María 2, 97–98, 103, 195*n*19
Fernández, Emilio 44, 122
Fernández, Rosa Marta 167
Fernández Violante, Marcela 6, 17, 18, 19, 22, 23, 167
fetishism 124
FFCC *see* Fondo de Fomento a la Calidad Cinematográfica
Fischer, Lucy 4
Flor Silvestre 7
Fondo de Fomento a la Calidad Cinematográfica 26, 27, 28
Fons, Jorge 25
Foster, David William 174
Un frágil retorno 96, 113–116, 119, 186
Franciscan 50, 72, 183, 195–196*n*23
Freud, Sigmund 11, 99, 108, 121, 138, 142

Galindo, Alejandro 10, 49
García, Sara 9, 11, 37–41, 43, 137–152, **155**, 157, 162, 187
García Tsao, Leonardo 28
Garrido, Consuelo 25
good mother 1, 8, 31, 103, 109, 143, 145–149, 183, 184–186
good wife 8, 103
Grosz, Elisabeth 160
Guadalupe, Virgin of 31–34, 44, 47, 185, 194*n*3
Guerra, Dora 25

Hershfield, Joanne 17, 22, 31, 36, 185, 194*n*3, 195*n*19
heterosexual love 159
Hotel Villa Goerne 96, 115–116, 119, 186, 189*n*2

Ideal of Virgin-Motherhood 9, 10–11, 43–44, 46–47, 49, 72, 97, 100, 107, 122–123, 125–126, 145–150, 183, 186
idealization 10–11, 37, 121–131, 130, 124, 184; definition of 198*n*1, 199*n*10
idealization-at-a-distance 130–131, 185; definition of 199*n*10
Iglesias Prieto, Norma 16, 17, 166
IMCINE *see* Instituto Mexicano de Cinematografía

Inmaculate Conception 35
Instituto Mexicano de Cinematografía (IMCINE) 15, 26, 27, 28, 29, 169
Intimidad 15, 27, 28
Una isla rodeada de agua 96, 103–**104**, 105–106, 108, 118, 184

El Jardín del edén 7
Jesuits 35
Joskowicz, Alfredo 190*n*1, 190*n*2, 192–193*n*35

Kaplan, Ann 189*n*6, 196–197*n*19
Klein, Melanie 197*n*7, 197*n*2, 200*n*10
Kristeva, Julia 9, 35–36, 46–47, 109, 125, 142, 154, 200*n*4, 202*n*17

Lacan 121, 134, 194*n*7, 199*n*10, 200*n*10
Landeta, Matilde 5, 17, 18, 22, 23, 190*n*14, 201*n*8, 201*n*13
Lara, María del Carmen de 16, 164, 167
Leduc, Paul 165–166
Lola 1–2, 11, 16, 27, 29, 126–**127**, 128–132, 151, 153, 160–162, 164–165, 169, 170–**171**, 172–175, 181, 185
Lola Casanova 5, 15
López, Ana 8, 9, 97–98, 102–103, 157, 185, 197*n*1
López-Sánchez, Eva 18, 163
El lugar del corazón 96, 114, 116, 119, 186, 189*n*2
Luna, Ilana 201*n*15
Luna, Marta 178–179
Luz Cruz, Elvira (mother accused of fratricide) 132–135, 176–177

Maciel, David 190*n*6
Macondo (production house) 29
Madre querida 156–157
Marcovich, Carlos 28
María Candelaria (film) 1, 11, 44, 122–126, 147
Martínez de Velasco, Patricia 19, 190*n*4
Mary, Virgin: and crown 41, 146; in feminist films 152; and heart 144; as humble mother 49–50; as mother 9, 11, 34, 36, 41, 125, 142, 145, 154–156, 185, 195*n*19; and mother of the Church 38; and queen 38, 49, 143, 195*n*22; and tears 123
maternal affect 152–154, 156–159, 185
maternal deprivation, theory of 64–65
Mecánica nacional 4, 11, 42, 137, 145–**147**, **148**–149, 151, 158, 185
melancholia 161, 163, 170, 173–174
melodramas 37, 50–52, 58, 66–68, 109, 163
milk 46, 156
Millán, Márgara 1, 22, 167–168, 189*n*1, 189*n*3, 189*n*4, 192*n*25
Miradas de mujer 17, 20, 21
Molina, Alicia 193*n*39

monstrosity and mothers 62–63, 178, 181
Mora, Carl 31, 34, 36, 39, 157, 185, 187
morality 10, 72, 64, 73, 137–149, 185, 201n1
mother, imperfect 127
mother love 137–150, 152, 154, 158–159, 185;
  see also maternal affect
Mothers' Day 39, 41, 157
Los Motivos de Luz 1, 4, 12, 25, 132–135, 161,
  175, 179–183, 187
La mujer del puerto 197n11
Mujeres y cine en América Latina 23
Mulvey, Laura 85–86, 89, 94, 121, 189n6,
  197n2, 198n6

narcissism, primary 99, 142, 199n10
narcissistic idealization 124–125, 183–184
La negra Angustias 5
Negrón-Muntaner, Frances 17
New Latin American Cinema 161, 165–166,
  182–183, 187
NLAC see New Latin American Cinema
Novaro, Beatriz 163
Novaro, María 1, 14, 15, 16, 17, 19, 29, *164*–
  165

oedipal 138, 142–143, 149, 152, 157–158
Old Testament 53–55
Oliver, Kelly 63, 112, 173, 180
O'Reilly, Andrea 5
Ottinger, Ulrike 124–125
Our Lady of Sorrows see Dolores, Virgin of

Partido Revolucionario Institucional 164–
  165, 173–174
Los pasos de Ana 1–2, 4, 10–11, 15, 72, 96,
  110–111, 137, 150–152, 158, 184, 185
Paz, Octavio 31, 75
Pérez Turrent, Tomás 193n49, 196n17,
  196n18
Plant, Rebecca Jo 9, 137–138, 141, 149, 200–
  201n1, 202n23
PRI see Partido Revolucionario Institucional
Primera Muestra de Cine y Video Realizado
  por Mujeres Latinas y Caribeñas 16
prostitutes 31
psychic space 109, 111–119, 186, 202n17
Public Television 24

Ramírez Berg, Charles 8, 31, 36, 44, 157, 185,
  187
Rashkin, Elissa 22, 76, 167, 190n5, 190n6,
  193n46, 201n9
rebellion 55–56
Rich, Ruby 17, 161, 165–168, 187
Río Escondido 2, 195n19
Riptstein, Arturo 197n11
Robles, Oscar 7, 190n16
Rojo, María 21
Rotberg, Dana 1, 4, 12, 14, 15, 18, 25, 27, 28,
  175, 176, 191–192n21

Salinas de Gortari, Carlos 4, 7, 15, 26, 27
Salón México 1–2, 49, 66–69, 73, 163, 186
Schroeder Rodríguez, Paul 201n7
Schumann, Peter 28
Schyfter, Guita 25, 163
second-wave filmmaker 189n1
El Secreto de Romelia 1, 10, 16, 25, 27, 74, **79**–
  82, 151, 203n1
self-actualization, mothers and 68, 73,
  199n11
self-effacement 50–51, 72–73
self-expression 109–110
Señora tentación 10, 89–90, **91–92**, 93–94,
  102–103, 110
separate identity 96, 98–102
Sequeyro, Adela 16
sexenio 15, 26, 27
shame 63, 73
Sherman, Cindy 130–131
Silverman, Kaja 11, 37, 121, 124–126, 130,
  196n9
Sindicato de Trabajadores de la Industria
  Cinematográfica 28
Sindicato de Trabajadores de la Producción
  Cinematográfica (STPC) 18, 25, 191–
  192n21
Sistach, Marisa 1, 14, 15, 17, 25, 26, 28, 137
social melancholy 160, 163–164, 173–174,
  178, 183
Solanas, Fernando 165
Stabat Mater 35, 122, 125, 143–144, 154, 156,
  162
Stella Dallas 189n5, 196–197n19
stereotypes 36
STIC see Sindicato de Trabajadores de la In-
  dustria Cinematográfica
STPC see Sindicato de Trabajadores de la
  Producción Cinematográfica
submission 51

tears 123, 154, 156–158, 162
Televisión Española 29
Tepeyac **32**–34, 47
theological virtues 58
third-wave filmmaker 189n1
third-wave mother 59, 119–120
Torres San Martín, Patricia 8, 23, 191n8
Trotacalles 6
Tuñón, Julia 23, 157–158, 194n12
Turim, Maureen 5

UNAM see Universidad Nacional Autónoma
  de México
Unidad de Televisión Educativa y Cultural
  15, 24, 25, 110
unions 13–16, 25, 27, 29
Universidad Nacional Autónoma de México
  13, 26, 168
UTEC see Unidad de Televisión Educativa y
  Cultural

Vega, Patricia 16–17, 22, 131, 134, 189n1, 193n48, 199nn13–17
violence 111, 116–118

war-hero (mother as) 67, 163, 201n1
Warner, Judith 65, 72–73
Warner, Marina 9, 34–36, 47, 50, 58, 126, 144, 195–196n23, 197n3, 198n3, 199n1, 199–200n3

whore 1, 8
Williams, Linda 189n6

Yamasaki, Tisuka 166

Zafra 26

www.ingramcontent.com/pod-product-compliance
Lightning Source LLC
Chambersburg PA
CBHW032051300426
44116CB00007B/689